Teaching U.S. History

Teaching U.S. History: Dialogues among Social Studies Teachers and Historians offers an innovative approach to social studies teaching by connecting historians to real-world social studies classrooms and social studies teachers. In an unusual, even unprecedented, dialogue between scholars and practitioners, this book weds historical theory and practice with social studies pedagogy.

Seven chapters are organized around key U.S. history eras and events from the time of slavery through the Civil Rights movement, and are complemented by detailed discussions of a particular methodological approach including primary source analysis, oral history, and more. Interviews with historians open each chapter to bring the reader into important conversations about the most cutting-edge issues in U.S. history today and are followed by essays from expert teachers and teacher educators on the rewards and challenges of implementing these topics in the classroom. Each chapter also includes a wealth of practical resources including suggested key documents or artifacts; a lesson plan for middle school and/or high school; and suggested readings and questions for further study.

Teaching U.S. History is a must-read for any aspiring or current teacher who wants to think critically about how to teach U.S. history and make historical discussions come alive in the school classrooms where the nation's students learn.

Diana Turk is an Associate Professor of Social Studies Education in the Department of Teaching and Learning at New York University.

Rachel Mattson is an Assistant Professor at SUNY New Paltz.

Terrie Epstein is a Professor of Education at Hunter College.

Robert Cohen is a Social Studies Professor and chair of the Department of Teaching and Learning and an Affiliated Professor in the History Department at New York University.

Transforming Teaching

Series Editor: James Fraser, NYU Steinhardt School of Education

Teaching U.S. History

Dialogues among Social Studies
Teachers and Historians

EDITED BY
DIANA TURK, RACHEL MATTSON, TERRIE EPSTEIN,
AND ROBERT COHEN

Routledge
Taylor & Francis Group

NEW YORK AND LONDON

First published 2010
by Routledge
270 Madison Avenue, New York, NY 10016

Simultaneously published in the UK
by Routledge
2 Park Square, Milton Park, Abingdon, Oxon OX14 4RN

Routledge is an imprint of the Taylor & Francis Group, an informa business

© 2010 Taylor and Francis

Typeset in MinionPro and Helvetica Neue by Prepress Projects Ltd, Perth, UK
Printed and bound in the United States of America on acid-free paper by Edwards
Brothers, Inc.

Library of Congress Cataloging in Publication Data
Teaching U.S History: dialogues among social studies teachers and historians/edited
by Diana Turk…[et al.].
p. cm.
Includes bibliographical references.
1. United States—History—Study and teaching (Middle school) 2. United States—
History—Study and teaching (Secondary) I. Turk, Diana, B.
LB175.8.T43 2009
973.071–dc22
2009024313

ISBN 10: (hbk) 0–415–95469–X
ISBN 10: (pbk) 0–415–95470–3
ISBN 10: (ebk) 0–203–86369–0

ISBN 13: (hbk) 978–0–415–95469–3
ISBN 13: (pbk) 978–0–415–95470–9
ISBN 13: (ebk) 978–0–203–86369–5

Dedicated in loving memory to

Barbara Turk
(1937–2009)

and

Jhumki Basu
(1977–2008)

Wonderful teachers whose passion for learning and
dedication to others live on in those who knew them

Contents

Series Editor Introduction

It is a pleasure to write an introduction to this volume in the Transforming Teaching series. As an historian the subject matter of this book is near and dear to me. My NYU colleague, Pedro Noguera, has told us that in his research high school students routinely say that "history is their most boring subject." However much we cringe at that report, those of us who are historians have too often seen confirmation of this view when we visit social studies classes at the middle and high school level. We have sat through history lessons in which the information was wrong, or simply made no sense, or in which we ourselves thought "who cares about this material?" I can count too many occasions when I have sat in a high school room listening to a discussion on the ratification of the U.S. Constitution, or the causes of the War of 1812, or the Great Depression and the run-up to World War II, and have thought to myself, "I am bored to death by this discussion, I can only imagine how the kids are feeling." But this need not be the case. Those of us who find the study of history fascinating believe that there can be much better approaches to social studies education at the elementary and secondary level in the schools of the U.S. As this book shows, history can be alive and engaging just as much as it can be static and irrelevant. And those of us who believe that the study of history and other social sciences can be a significant vehicle for creating a cohort of young citizens that is civically aware and engaged believe that it is essential to make it so.

Happily those who want to prepare themselves to be more effective social studies teachers, and those who are already teaching in this field, have a significant new resource to help them in Diana Turk's, Rachel Mattson's, Terrie Epstein's, and Robert Cohen's *Teaching U.S. History: Dialogues among Social Studies Teachers and Historians*.

The authors of this book have delivered exactly what the title promises. Through interviews with some of the leading historians and educators in the United States and equally through careful engagement with social studies teachers in public schools, the authors of this book have created a true dialogue of theory and practice. They help all of us think critically about how to teach U.S.

history so that the discussions will come alive in the school classrooms where the nation's students learn—or don't learn—the nation's story.

The interviews with historians bring the reader into important conversations about some of the cutting-edge issues in U.S. history today—from new debates about teaching the history of slavery and the U.S. Civil War to current research on immigration, the Progressive Era, the New Deal, and the Civil Rights and anti-imperialist movements. They highlight some of the most important current thinking about the major themes that should be taught if U.S. history is to be understood well. (And in the process give social studies teachers significant help in avoiding those dead ends and unimportant lanes that have too often led students to utter boredom with the irrelevant facts, dates, and examples that can clutter the curriculum.)

At the same time the authors of *Teaching U.S. History: Dialogues among Social Studies Teachers and Historians* do more than this. Through their own collaborative work with an extended group of middle and high school teachers, they have also moved from examples of good history to specific curricular plans for presenting that history to real live students in specific classrooms. The fact that we find something fascinating does not mean that our students will agree with us. The fact that using primary documents can make a classroom come alive does not mean that such an approach will always work unless it is planned very carefully. Teachers need specific guidance, and they get it here from expert teachers who have struggled long and hard to find the ways to create social studies classrooms where what is taught is worth learning and where democratic civic engagement is fostered by lively debates that are at the core of the assignments that the classes take on.

For example chapter 6 reports how the fundamental rethinking of the history of the Civil Rights movement that is now happening offers us a valuable glimpse into how contemporary scholarship is looking at a complex story that must include attention to leaders (the traditional focus) but at least equally to organizers (those behind-the-scene players who made sure the taxis ran on time during the Montgomery Bus Boycott and the buses got people to Washington, DC, for the 1968 march). Fascinating though this is, however, the authors also take us on the next step, asking veteran teachers to help us respond to the oft-repeated student phrase "as if I care" with examples that have worked in specific classrooms among real-world young people to engage them in this history and enrich their own education. In this case students were asked to take on the role of organizers themselves. The result was that students remembered the lessons more than a year later (something every teacher knows is most unusual) and also scored far better on statewide tests than others who were given the usual test-prep pabulum of fact after fact.

In a world where the academic study of U.S. history and the hard work of teaching U.S. history to young people are too often separate realms with little or no contact, this volume brings them into a powerful conversation that can have important results.

For anyone who cares about history and who cares about the quality of education in the nation's social studies classrooms of the twenty-first century—and especially for anyone who wants to be an effective social studies teacher—*Teaching U.S. History* is a goldmine of historical information and pedagogical ideas that will serve exceedingly well. I am very pleased to be able to include it in Routledge's Transforming Teaching Series.

James W. Fraser
New York University

Acknowledgements

The authors and editors of the book would like to thank the following individuals, without whom this project would not have come to fruition. First and foremost we wish to pay tribute to the work of Michael Stoll, who, in addition to co-authoring several essays in this volume, provided invaluable research and administrative support. Series editor James Fraser was an enthusiastic supporter of this book from the outset. Our editor at Routledge, Catherine Bernard, was patient with us when personal and professional obligations delayed our progress. We extend special thanks to Patricia Oscategui, Dwight Forquignon, Eric Shed, Vanessa Rodriguez, and Shari Dickstein for providing administrative and creative support and for helping the project take shape. We are also deeply grateful to the many classroom teachers who engaged in this project, and their students too, who both inspired us and made this project possible. We are also grateful to the historians who offered their time and ideas to this project—especially Hasia Diner, Adam Green, Ira Berlin, James Oakes, Kevin Murphy, Laura Briggs, and Marcus Rediker. Laurie Prendergast and Moonmarked Design/Editing/Indexing provided invaluable indexing and other editorial support. Finally, we would like to thank our colleagues, friends, and families for their enduring support over the many years that we worked on this project.

A Note about this Book

This book presents a small subset of the work that a group of public school teachers, teacher educators, and historians conducted over the course of the 2006–2007 and 2007–2008 academic years. Approximately fifty scholars and educators participated in this group, which we have called the New York History Teaching Collaborative (NYHTC). Members of NYHTC taught a wide range of collaboratively developed history lessons in over a dozen classrooms in New York City, Boston, Westchester, and Albany, New York. The chapters that constitute this volume explore only a fraction of the work that NYHTC participants did in these years.

We have changed the names of all schools and classroom teachers in the body of the chapters that follow to preserve the anonymity of these schools and teachers, and of their students.

All statistical information pertaining to school demographics noted in the text was drawn from one of the following sources: Inside Schools (www.insideschools.org), School Matters (www.schoolmatters.com), or the New York State Education Department (www.nystart.gov/publicweb/).

Introduction

Robert Cohen and Michael Stoll

One of the nightmares new history teachers face is ending up an ineffective social studies educator along the lines suggested by the classic Hollywood film, *Ferris Bueller's Day Off* (1986). Droning on about the Great Depression to a class of unresponsive and disengaged students, Ferris' teacher, though in front of a classroom and ostensibly seeking to teach his students, seems to be speaking only to himself when he declares:

> In the 1930s the Republican-controlled House of Representatives in an effort to allevi-
> ate the effects of the . . . Anyone? Anyone? The Great Depression, passed the . . .
> Anyone? Anyone? The tariff bill? The Hawley Smoot Tariff Act? Which, anyone? Raised
> or lowered? Raised tariffs in an effort to collect more revenue for the federal govern-
> ment. Did it work, anyone? Anyone know the effects? It did not work and the country
> sank further into the Great Depression . . .

Though a parody, coming during a movie that mercilessly mocked the American high school, the scene in Ferris's social studies classroom has a sad veracity to it. History teaching in traditional high schools is often ineffective, hampered by antiquated methods, poorly trained teachers, and boring textbooks (Crocco & Thornton, 2002). The history curriculum in these schools centers on standardized tests and survey courses that force a focus on coverage—an exhausting race through thousands of historical names and dates—rather than comprehension. It is not surprising, then, that national studies (e.g. Hess, 2008) consistently show that high school graduates lack a basic understanding of American history.

Even Hollywood, however, knows that social studies teachers can do better than Ferris Bueller's teacher. In the recent feature film *Half Nelson* (2006) we see a talented (though person-ally troubled) teacher making imaginative use of a primary source, '60s Berkeley radical student leader Mario Savio's incendiary speech raging against the machine, to prod his inner city students to think critically about power and oppression in both the past and the present. And John Sayles shows in his film *Lone Star* (1996) how debate can bring history to life in a Texas high school, where in an ethnically diverse setting nobody can agree on whether the Mexicans or the Anglo pioneers were more worthy of valorization or demonization in the social studies curriculum's treatment of early Texas history. Here historical study breeds passionate engagement, critical thinking, and multiple perspectives as both the filmmaker and the school's teachers are, in Sayles's words, concerned with:

> history and what we do with it. Do we use it to hit each other? Is it something that drags us down? Is it something that makes us feel good? You can get six different people to look at the Alamo and they have six different perspectives about what actually happened and what its significance was.
>
> (West & West, 1996)

The difference between the exciting use of history by Sayles and in *Half Nelson* and the tedium of Ferris' social studies class is profound and has important lessons for teachers and educational reformers. Sayles in particular was asking the kinds of difficult and provocative questions about historical meaning that engage professional historians. For historians, history is above all about interpretation, using often conflicting primary sources to make sense of the past, trying to tell a story that is both coherent and meaningful, knowing all the while that that story, like much historical truth, is subject to debate, controversy, and revision (Carr, 1961). This is why the sociologist James Loewen was justified in defining history as "furious debate" about the past "informed by evidence and reason" (1995, p. 16). One of the keys to breaking up the boredom of social studies classes is moving away from the truncated version of history that prevails in this high school and middle school subject area. Such a move will enable teachers to bring to their classrooms the lively controversy, depth of analysis, and powerful inquiry methods of history as a critical discipline. In an historically enriched classroom students are challenged to grapple with real historical evidence, to interrogate primary sources, and to consider questions of bias and temporal context, all the while learning how to draw conclusions and to contrast "lived history" with "textbook history," to see that history is not simply a matter of presidents and generals but includes the experience of ordinary Americans. In such classrooms both teachers and students will realize that names and dates are only tools, not ends in themselves, and that such historical detail has a far better chance of finding its way into long-term memory if connected to history as a way of thinking, one that students find meaningful and engaging.

This book, *Teaching U.S. History: Dialogues among Social Studies Teachers and Historians*, is designed to help promote such a transformation of middle school and secondary history teaching by connecting historians to real-world social studies classrooms and social studies teachers to the historical profession and to history as a critical discipline. These connections are not abstract; they grow out of actual practice, the work of the New York History Teaching Collaborative (NYHTC) under the leadership of editors Diana Turk and Rachel Mattson. The NYHTC brought twenty-five high school and middle school teachers from New York and Boston together with university-based historians and education professors to develop historically rigorous units and lessons—with history curricula driven by debate, inquiry, and primary source document analysis—that could bring the American experience to life for students of diverse ability levels.

This point about diversity in ability is crucial. In the past, the most extensive institutional connection between schools and the historical profession has been in Advanced Placement (AP) classes. There, only the most high-achieving students have gotten to encounter something that supposedly corresponds to introductory college history courses. Such a connection has never been available to the majority of high school students, who do not qualify for AP courses and their college credits. Confined as it is to the secondary schools, the AP program has no impact at all on middle school students. In our view it makes little sense to reserve to an AP high school elite the excitement of historical inquiry, which is why we have sought to democratize access to historians and their work so that we can help enliven history education in a wide range of schools and classrooms.

In saying that we are seeking to enliven history we are not just speaking metaphorically. School history is so often reduced to mere lists of names and dates that middle and high school students see their job in social studies classes as spitting back factoids in response to trivial recall questions at the end of the textbook chapters or in quizzes and exams. For many of them, history seems, as Rachel Mattson puts it, "static, impermeable and essentially dead." It is like a trip to a cemetery, and just as exciting. Only if students are taught in a way that enables them to understand that history is alive, involving them in historical studies that get them to experience history as an unending dialogue between the present and the past—that it is "dynamic, interpretive and relevant"—will we have a chance of engaging their sustained and serious interest in the American past.

A central task we faced in the NYHTC was finding historians who had developed important new insights into American history and who had the potential to illuminate that history in ways that appealed to social studies teachers and their students. Once we selected the historians, Mattson interviewed them with an eye toward making those insights and their applicability to classroom history teaching as explicit as possible. She asked the historians to identify primary sources that they viewed as rich in meaning, relating them and their own work to important historical themes and lively historical debates that would have the potential to interest high school and middle school students. The exception to this was Ira Berlin, whose NYHTC-sponsored presentation on slavery to middle school students and teachers proved so compelling that we did not feel the need to conduct a follow-up interview. We selected historians who represented the broad chronological sweep of American history and whose work addressed the state and national standards in U.S. history, beginning with Ira Berlin on slavery; James Oakes on abolitionists and the Constitution; Hasia Diner on immigration; Kevin Murphy on gender and reform in the Progressive Era; Robert Cohen on Depression-era mass protest and the New Deal; Laura Briggs on expansion and imperialism; and ending with Adam Green on the Civil Rights movement.

In each case, the historian interviews were not merely informative; they were also exciting in the way they offered a new perspective on familiar eras and historical topics. Armed with these interviews, we gathered a group of talented, veteran social studies teachers and brainstormed with them about ways to take the best historical ideas and sources offered by the historians and translate them into engaging historical units and lessons. *Teaching U.S. History: Dialogues among Social Studies Teachers and Historians* narrates the creative processes whereby groups of teachers and educational experts worked to adapt advanced historical scholarship so that it would be both accessible and attractive for high school and middle school students. This process began with teachers reading the interview of the historian who addressed their teaching topic, so each teaching chapter opens with excerpts of those interviews. Next follows a narrative on how each group wrestled with the topic and then how and with what outcomes the teachers ultimately taught their topic. As they read through and analyzed the interviews and decided how to use them in their lessons, the teachers in each group kept their own students, classrooms, and social studies curricula in mind. Which historical sources and themes seemed the most thought-provoking? Which were most likely to interest their students and help them master the historical issues required by their state-mandated history curriculum? What new ideas and unconventional approaches to history seemed most likely to surprise their students and motivate their work in these historical units?

The teachers then began planning units and lessons that were inquiry centered, prodding their students to explore historical questions in depth, becoming historical detectives who interrogate sources much as an historian would. Students studying immigration, for example, as Diana Turk's essay explains (chapter 3), went beyond the usual textbook usage of Jacob Riis's photographs as an unfiltered view of the experience of late nineteenth-century immigrants. Instead, they were taught by their NYHTC teachers to approach these sources critically and three-dimensionally, prodded by the immigration historian Hasia Diner's cautions about how Riis's biases and agenda as a middle-class reformer slanted the way he saw working-class immigrants. Asking questions about the photographs—what they excluded as well as included, why they seemed to make mere victims, and joyless ones at that—of those new immigrants, students began to realize that a critical reading of these photographs showed their limitations as well as their value as historical sources. They were artifacts of middle-class reform, documents with a purpose rather than a simple reporting of historical reality, and tended to show only one side of immigrant life.

From both Diner and the other historians the teachers learned that, when primary sources are studied carefully and in relation to larger historical themes, they can tell the most engaging stories and raise extremely interesting questions. Joan Malczewski shows in her essay (chapter 1) how the historian Ira Berlin could use a single enslaved person to open up a vista not only on the subject of his letter but also on this slave's whole life and the nature of the enslaved community. The letter made it possible for him to raise questions about literacy, family, and culture among enslaved peoples, while at the same time personalizing the slavery story so that its historical drama packed an emotional punch far stronger than any textbook's.

One of the most striking aspects of the historians' interviews is that they show quite explicitly how historians work toward a critical understanding of the past and how carefully they interrogate primary sources to squeeze every bit of historical meaning out of them. This aspect of the interviews was not accidental; it represented interviewer Mattson's attempt at building on the work of the cognitive psychologist Sam Wineburg (2001) in making the thinking of historians visible. In following the historians through a process of posing searching questions followed by hypotheses and conclusions, Mattson was able to elucidate the ways in which historians begin to make sense of the past and see the emergence of creative historical thought. The hope is that middle and high school teachers can themselves get practice in this act of historical discovery and analysis and then be better equipped to involve their students in authentic acts of historical thought.

Teachers took special delight in using the historians' work in social history to jazz up topics that textbooks tend to render lifeless. For example, in Shari Dickstein's essay (chapter 5), we learn that the New Deal reforms come across in many textbooks as little more than a bland alphabet soup of federal agencies, cooked up in Washington by President Franklin Delano Roosevelt (FDR). This presidential framework, the historian Robert Cohen suggested, obscured the most exciting dynamic of the New Deal era, the interaction between grassroots protest movements and the Roosevelt administration. The ideas of, and political pressure exerted by, ordinary citizens in such Depression-era insurgencies as the Townsend, student, and labor movements popularized old age pensions, student aid, and workers' right to unionize—New Deal reforms that are presented in flat, simplistic textbook accounts as coming out of nowhere or inexplicably coming out of FDR's head. The essay by Michael Stoll, Joan Malczewski, and David Montgomery (chapter 4) recounts how the historian Kevin Murphy played a similar role in using race, gender, and sexuality to make the Progressive Era seem larger than the sum of reforms by Presidents Woodrow Wilson and Theodore Roosevelt. This same tendency to challenge the top-down textbook image of history is recounted by Diana Turk in her essay on the Civil Rights era (chapter 6). In his interview, the historian Adam Green complicates the Martin Luther King, Jr.-centered narrative with its focus on heroic leadership, instead highlighting the rank-and-file role of movement activists and less famous community organizers in making possible the epochal changes of the 1950s and 1960s.

The excitement in connecting historians with teachers comes from learning not merely more history, but also cutting-edge approaches to history that challenge older views of America and thus force us to re-examine our assumptions about the past and the present. Traditionally school-taught U.S. history has had a strong nationalistic component, since mandated social studies classes have been seen as a way of breeding patriotism. But for such historians as Laura Briggs the old-fashioned flag-waving ethos seems parochial, and instead she seeks in her work to connect American with global history, freeing historical study from the distortions that arise from a self-centered nation-state view of the American experience (chapter 7). Briggs's work challenges teachers and students to view American history without nationalistic blinders, to see how America looks to those beyond our shores and how the United States connects to historical processes that transcend any single nation-state. She pushes us to ask new questions about the boundaries of American history, to consider how that history encompasses lands the United States has invaded and occupied, such as Cuba and the Philippines, and forces us to confront the problem of how the United States, a nation born in rebellion against empire itself, evolved into a new kind of empire.

The teachers in the NYHTC learned that new historical scholarship can make good teaching even better. For example, a widely used lesson that had seemed to work well pedagogically (one popularized by the American Social History Project) featured a debate over whether President Abraham Lincoln freed the slaves or the slaves freed themselves (Freidham, 1996, pp. 80–81). But James Oakes, through the research for his new book on emancipation, explains in his interview that this debate is historically limiting and, indeed, distorting because it tends to present Lincoln and the slaves in an historical vacuum, leaving out the role of the Confederacy in fighting long and hard to prevent emancipation (chapter 2). For Oakes the central question was not who freed the slaves, but how the process of emancipation functioned, and it was a process far more complex, painful, and protracted—since it went on in the face of violent Confederate resistance—than the old debate over emancipation has implied.

The great pedagogical challenge, of course, is how to make use of primary sources so that they intrigue students but do not overwhelm them. Young students new to the art of historical detection cannot simply be handed sources from distant centuries and be expected to make sense of them with no guidance, the way a professional historian can. So the teachers involved in this project came up with a variety of approaches to building a pedagogical foundation for their history workshops. Some focused on developing framing questions for the sources. Others, concerned about student reading levels, abbreviated the sources and introduced the students to concepts and themes that would equip them to find the meaning within the documents—such as the teacher who focused on power and community as framing concepts for viewing slave sources.

The dominant pedagogical trend reflected in the lessons designed by our groups was to move away from the old reliance on lecturing. The teachers strove to promote as much hands-on learning as possible, since engaging students in problem-solving is a much better way to promote active learning and combat the kind of classroom passivity lampooned in *Ferris Bueller*. The consensus among our groups was that students needed to be more than a bored audience for pontificating teachers. This does not mean, however, that teachers always or exclusively served merely as facilitators. Depending upon the classroom situation, teachers made use of varying levels of direct instruction to prepare students for their work with primary sources. But the overall trend was toward a student-centered pedagogy, and the teachers employed an impressive variety of activities that required students to engage actively in critical historical thinking, including discussions of songs, constructing "community webs," using educational theater and role-playing, conducting historical debates, producing iMovie historical documentaries, engaging in service learning projects, drafting laws, interpreting oral history interviews, and interrogating a vast array of primary sources, ranging from slave testimony to photographs, poetry, and the Constitution.

One of the most fascinating aspects of the teacher dialogues was the way they revealed teachers serving as a bridge between the historical content they were learning and the distinctive worlds of their classrooms in which and students to whom they would be teaching this new material. It is most assuredly not a one-size-fits all approach to pedagogy. Teaching skill was self-evident in all cases, as was how well the teachers know their students and have developed a strong grasp of what pedagogical approaches would work best for them. So there was a tendency within our groups for methods to vary among teachers, even as they were teaching similar materials and historical concepts. It was impressive how hard the teachers involved in the NYHTC labored to vary their own instructional approaches, using such diverse methods as individual inquiry, cooperative learning, and whole-class discussions.

Many of the classes our teachers taught these lessons to were—as is often the case in urban public schools—composed largely of low-income students and students of color. Although social studies textbooks often treat class and race issues as an additive feature, something to be touched on along the way in the name of multiculturalism, our historians tended to see race and class as central to the American experience, as do most leading historians. So, without any special effort, there was a strong correspondence between the historians' scholarship and teacher interest in racial and class inequity, since these are issues many of their students confront and historians study on a daily basis. Our veteran teachers immediately saw that the historians' focus on such issues, though perhaps set in centuries far removed from their students, had great potential to resonate with students—and they came up with creative ways to foster this sense of engagement.

The most important point in all these ventures in educational planning was to design lessons that gave students time, opportunity, and prods to think independently and critically about history and historical evidence. Michael Stoll, David Montgomery, and Candace Villecco show in their essay that this can happen at different levels and in a variety of ways. Whether it was provoked by a teacher offering direct instruction, homework questions, or a classroom debate, it was ultimately left to the students to decide, for example, whether the Constitution was a pro-slavery or anti-slavery document. The students had to think as historians do, probing the relevant historical evidence to consider why the abolitionist leader Frederick Douglass began his political career slamming the Constitution as pro-slavery but later changed his mind and argued forcefully that it was an anti-slavery document. Students pondered whether that change of mind was a sign of political and intellectual brilliance or weakness; they had to account for the change and for the character of the Constitution itself. Whether Douglass's change of mind surprised the students, or angered or pleased them—and all the responses were evident in the classroom—it was the eliciting of such responses, signaling student engagement in history and independent thought about the past, which showed the power of this historically rich pedagogy.

Although the NYHTC historian–teacher collaboration has been enormously valuable—and our project evaluation confirmed the teachers' genuine and overwhelming sense of excitement and intellectual engagement in that collaboration (Stoll, 2008)—it was by no means flawless. The editors of *Teaching U.S. History: Dialogues among Social Studies Teachers and Historians* are committed to discussing this collaboration in a candid, reflective, and self-critical way. The tone of this book will not be akin to that of those televised cooking shows where all the recipes turn out perfectly. In the real world sometimes the best-planned meals run into problems in the kitchen, with some meals burned in the oven. Our view is that teachers can learn much from an honest accounting of mistakes and problems in the classroom, and that accounts of best teaching practices have little credibility if they avoid the fact obvious to veteran teachers: that, at times, even carefully planned lessons can go wrong because of mistakes in conception or implementation. So our failures didn't land on the cutting room floor, but are addressed in each of the topic-centered chapters. They are even featured in the very title of Rachel Mattson's essay, "Pivotal Failures." The lessons, despite their intrinsically motivating subject matter, were not immune to the all-too-familiar challenges of acclimating students to cooperative learning or ensuring high-quality independent research. Yes, there are times when university-level historical scholarship is too complex and theoretical for pre-college students, especially at the middle school level, and if teachers don't recognize when this is the case it can lead to ineffective lessons. But our veteran teachers usually could anticipate such problems, and developed a real eye for zeroing in on the aspects of the historian's scholarship and primary sources that could and actually did work well in their classrooms—after a process of careful adaptation rendered them appropriate to the ages and abilities of their students.

Actually the greatest difficulties in this collaboration were the fault of neither the historians nor the teachers, but instead reflected the obstacles that schools and their social studies curricula inadvertently pose to transformational history teaching. Teachers sometimes found it difficult to spend even a few days helping their students dig into the complexities of historical eras and explore the meaning of rich primary sources when they faced pressure to race from one era to another because the school history curriculum centered on coverage rather than comprehension. As one frustrated teacher reported, "the moments when we wanted to do the *most* critical thinking and the *most* creative work were when we had to stop because it wasn't going to aid in prepping the students for the tests." By that he meant that the need to move to another topic because of the enormous chronological sweep of the history curriculum forced time to run out just as the students were finally equipped to dig the most deeply into their historically enriched topic. This happened with several of our teachers and is a problem with which most of the groups struggled, at some point, in their project engagement.

This is by no means a local problem. As Terrie Epstein's chapter (Concluding Thoughts) reviewing the research on teaching and learning history attests, "the widespread use of standardized high-stakes tests" makes it difficult to teach history as a critical and complex academic discipline in many public schools. Such tests push some history teachers to "'dumb down' their lessons, provide less creative pedagogy . . . and rush through 500+ years of the past in order to cover the curriculum and potential test questions." Committed as our teachers were to resisting such pressures, there were instances in which the role of their classes as purveyors of the mother of all history surveys got in the way of their finishing the units we planned—as they simply ran out of days to complete this work.

Even though the survey course model and test pressures pose obstacles to innovative history teaching, we rarely encountered these as disabling. Our teachers, by and large, managed to design and implement innovative history units and lessons even in their challenging school and curricular environments. The assessments of these historically enriched teaching days revealed that the new lessons taught in them were often viewed by students as "the most interesting activity they had done all year" in their history classes, with many arguing that "we should do it again." Aside from merely being "fun," these lessons also taught students what it meant to think like historians. Most students relished the opportunity to work with primary sources, calling them "most helpful" and "powerful" in developing their understandings of the past. At the same time, however, these sources often provided more questions than answers for students, and required them to "take on a problem at that time in history and try to create a solution for it." In the end, most students found the challenges of these experiences gratifying, because they represented a way for them to "contribute to the conversation" about history that so often does not include them. We suspect that students who feel this way and have a revved up sense of enthusiasm about history can—if that enthusiasm can be sustained—become more motivated and can also improve their performance in these survey courses and on their standardized history exams.

Nor was enthusiasm confined to the students. Our assessment revealed that teachers in the NYHTC found it exhilarating to work with historians and encounter the latest scholarship about the eras and topics they were responsible for teaching. Many reported a great deal of satisfaction about having historians find for them interesting "new teaching ideas and materials," pushing them beyond lessons they had been using, which in some cases seemed stale by comparison. Yet the collaboration was also satisfying because the historians, in turn, recognized the teacher expertise and deferred to them on questions regarding how to adapt historical scholarship to the realities of the middle school and high school educational settings. In fact, it was the teachers, not the historians who, as one teacher put it, "rightfully dominated the conversation when it came to lesson planning." So the teachers came away feeling that the dialogues with historians were more than educational, but were at their best so egalitarian—it was "great to talk about history as equals"—that they affirmed their identity as skilled professionals. Indeed, the teachers' one major complaint about the historians was that in some cases they got to spend too little time with them because busy schedules and logistical problems in some cases limited the amount of contact between the teachers and the historians.

Although our collaborative teaching project focused primarily on historical content and fostering teacher–historian collaboration, we found that it was not just the historian-to-teacher collaborations but also the teacher-to-teacher collaborations that proved beneficial. Most teachers in the collaborative remarked on their post-project surveys how isolated they felt as teachers, and how, prior to the NYHTC experience, they rarely if ever had the opportunity to brainstorm about innovative history teaching with busy colleagues in their schools. So the teachers reported a special sense of satisfaction about spending "a great deal of time together writing and revising lessons," and also that they "built on each other" when it came to planning new approaches to historical teaching. The teacher groups bonded and developed a reformist ethos that led them to become more daring history teachers. These working groups empowered teachers to bring innovative teaching methods into their classrooms. Teachers who were initially timid or skeptical about teaching new kinds of historically enriched and student-centered lessons shed that timidity over the course of this project; they proved willing to lobby their school administrators for the inclusion of these challenging lessons and new approaches by the end of the group work process.

The lessons from the NYHTC's efforts to improve the teaching of history are all here for you to see in *Teaching U.S. History: Dialogues among Social Studies Teachers and Historians*. And those lessons appear in many forms. First there are the actual lessons—including lesson plans and lists of relevant state and national standards—that were taught in the social studies classes of the teachers in the NYHTC, which, in building upon the historians' interviews, offer a wealth of content-rich teaching ideas for classes on slavery, abolitionism, the Constitution, gender, Progressivism, immigration, expansionism and imperialism, the New Deal, and the Civil Rights movement. The accounts on these pages of the designing and teaching of these lessons should give teachers some exciting new ideas about how to approach these important historical topics.

But we see the discussion of these teaching ventures as also offering a different kind of lesson, in this case a lesson for social studies teachers rather than for their students. The lesson concerns a process by which they can strive to improve their teaching of history. Yes, teachers can start—as the NYHTC teachers did—by using the historian interviews (which are included in *Teaching U.S. History: Dialogues among Social Studies Teachers and Historians)* to enhance their understanding of the historical content they are responsible for teaching. But since this book is limited to fewer than a dozen historical topics, teachers will also need to supplement this book with other historical books and articles to upgrade their understanding of the rest of American history. We hope this book will inspire them to do individually what we did collectively, connecting their classrooms to the latest and most exciting developments in historical scholarship, leading them to more thought-provoking historical debates and primary sources. Toward that end we suggest beginning with a regular reading of the major journals that feature such connecting of American historians and social studies teachers, most notably the Organization of American Historians' *Magazine of History*, and *Social Education*, the teaching journal of the National Council for the Social Studies—journals from which members of our group draw regularly and to which they have contributed.

The third lesson is also for teachers, and it concerns organization. Teachers of U.S. history ought not to be isolated. The NYHTC experience attests that it is possible without major funding, but with some creative network building, to forge a supportive community of history teachers that can work as a team to foster new approaches to teaching and enhance historical content knowledge. You can begin in your own school by sharing this book with your colleagues and brainstorming about ways to continue and extend the historical and pedagogical conversations started in *Teaching U.S. History: Dialogues among Social Studies Teachers and Historians*. A second step would be to link up your teacher groups, as we did in the NYHTC, to university-based historians and social studies professors, and in that way enhance your connection to those who do cutting-edge research in history and social studies curriculum and pedagogy. Since Congress continues to fund large-scale school teacher–university historian collaborative educational projects through the Department of Education's Teaching American History grant program (http://www.ed.gov/programs/teachinghistory), there are history educators all over the country engaged in the kinds of collaborative work we did in the NYHTC.

There is also a lesson here for professional historians. *Teaching U.S. History: Dialogues among Social Studies Teachers and Historians* attests that social studies teachers, historians, and the teens in history classes across America stand to benefit when we engage in collaborative educational ventures with high schools and middle schools. Our challenge is to find the time and make the effort to be part of this dialogue with our pre-college colleagues in teaching history. It is time for historians to stop merely complaining about how poorly prepared college freshmen are in history and to work to address this problem by helping to enrich the historical teaching enterprise in the earlier grade levels.

Although this book focuses primarily on dialogues among historians and social studies teachers, the conversation about improving history teaching is richest if it also includes a third partner—educational researchers. As the "Concluding Thoughts" chapter explains, there is a relatively new and important field of educational research that studies the teaching and learning of history. The best of this scholarship looks carefully at the process of historical cognition—how students learn to think historically—and has important classroom implications. For example, Wineburg (2001) finds that historical thinking is a unique cognitive skill that is best developed by involving students in authentic historical reading and questioning through primary source analysis. Such scholarship attests that textbook- and factoid-centered instruction that elevates rote memorization over critical thinking does not prepare students to assess historical issues and sources the way historians do. Unfortunately, as Epstein reveals, national studies find that these archaic teaching methods are still widespread in the world of schools. If more teachers were to become acquainted with the new educational scholarship, such rote methods might disappear more quickly. So it is our hope that every teacher will connect with the recent studies of historical teaching and learning—and a good place to begin making that connection is with Epstein's chapter introducing this scholarship.

Teaching U.S. History: Dialogues among Social Studies Teachers and Historians is at bottom a book that aims to desegregate history teaching by breaking down the walls of status hierarchy and institutional isolationism that have separated schools from universities. In the twenty-first century it is no longer tolerable for historians to be removed from teaching in the lower grades and for middle- and secondary-level teachers to be out of touch with university-based historians—and for both to be disconnected from educational researchers who study what actually works in history classrooms. A rich exchange of historical knowledge and pedagogical practice is possible when these separate educational worlds come together. If motivation for such collaboration is needed, one need only look at the national surveys from the 1940s through the present, which show that a majority of students en route to college learn precious little American history (Hess, 2008; Ravitch, 1989; Ravitch & Finn, 1987). School teachers and historians have been segregated from one another, and the results of this have been disastrous. The story of historical teaching in modern America has been one of persistent failure, a long-term pattern that cannot possibly be broken unless historians and school teachers share their complementary expertise.

Only if school history is better connected to the world of historical scholarship will social studies teachers be equipped to lead their students beyond the boredom of textbooks and factoids, standardized tests, and *Ferris Bueller*-style monologues. We see this book as a step toward that connection and a new school history in which teachers use content-rich lessons that challenge students and let them experience historical study as thought-provoking, controversial, important, interesting, and meaningful. Bringing history to life on the page takes the expertise of a master historian. Doing the same in a classroom requires both that historical skill and the pedagogical savvy of a master teacher—a tall order and one that it will take a working community of teachers and historians to fulfill.

Works Cited

Carr, E. H. (1961). *What is History?* New York: Vintage.

Crocco, M. S. & Thornton, S. J. (2002). Social Studies in the New York City Public Schools: A Descriptive Study. *Journal of Curriculum and Supervision, 17*(3), 206–231.

Freidham, W. (1996). *Freedom's Unfinished Revolution: An Inquiry into the Civil War and Reconstruction.* New York: New Press.

Hess, F. M. (2008). *Still at Risk: What Students Don't Know, Even Now.* Washington, DC: Common Core.

Loewen, J. W. (1995). *Lies My Teacher Told Me: Everything Your American History Textbook Got Wrong.* New York: Touchstone.

Ravitch, D. (1989). The Plight of History in American Schools. In Gagnon, P. (ed.), *Historical Literacy: The Case for History in American Education.* New York: Macmillan, pp. 51–68.

Ravitch, D. & Finn, C. E. (1987). *What Do Our 17-Year-Olds Know? A Report on the First National Assessment of History and Literature.* New York: Harper & Row.

Stoll, M. (2008). The Teaching U.S. History Project: A Pilot Evaluation. Unpublished project evaluation for the Department of Teaching and Learning, New York University.

West, D. & West, J. M. (1996). Borders and Boundaries: An Interview with John Sayles. *Cineaste, 22*(3), 14–17.

Wineburg, S. (2001). *Historical Thinking and Other Unnatural Acts: Charting the Future of Teaching the Past.* Philadelphia: Temple University Press.

One
Slavery

Framing the Questions: A Talk by Ira Berlin, for Middle School Students and Teachers at the Salk School for Science, New York City

Ira Berlin has written extensively on American history and the larger Atlantic world in the eighteenth and nineteenth centuries, particularly the history of slavery. Throughout his long and distinguished career, he has been the recipient of many awards and distinctions. His first book, Slaves Without Masters: The Free Negro in the Antebellum South (1975), won the Best First Book Prize awarded by the National Historical Society. In 1999, his study of African-American life between 1619 and 1819, entitled Many Thousands Gone: The First Two Centuries of Slavery in Mainland North America, was awarded the Bancroft Prize for the best book in American history by Columbia University; the Frederick Douglass Prize by the Gilder-Lehrman Institute; the Owsley Prize by the Southern Historical Association; and the Rudwick Prize by the Organization of American Historians. In 2002, he was inaugurated as president of the Organization of American Historians and in 2004 he was elected a member of the American Academy of Arts and Sciences.

Ira Berlin: For most of the history of this country, this was a society of slavery. Slavery was the central institution of labor, not simply in the South, which we identify with cotton, but in the North as well. Slaves grew those crops, tobacco, rice, sugar, eventually cotton, which brought capital and money into this country, and that money was used then to build a great infrastructure of this country. By 1860 there were 4 million slaves in the United States; those 4 million slaves were probably worth collectively $3 billion. Even today, $3 billion is a lot of money; in 1860 it was really a lot of money. That $3 billion was worth three times the value of the whole manufacturing establishment of the United States—including the railroads—and was seven times more valuable than all the money in all the banks in the United States. Slaves were nearly fifty times more valuable than all of the expenditures of the federal government in the 1860s. So slavery is a big part of the American economy. The people who controlled those slaves, and controlled that great economic power, then, were able to translate that economic power into political power so that when the American government was created after the American revolution all of our earliest presidents were slaveholders. Washington was a slaveholder, Thomas Jefferson was a slaveholder. James Madison was a slaveholder. James Monroe was a slaveholder. Andrew Jackson was a slaveholder. If we looked at the Supreme Court, at all of the Justices in the Supreme Court who served between the establishment of the Republic and the Civil War, we would see that most of them were slaveholders and the two great Chief Justices whom you'll learn about were of course very substantial slaveholders. If you look at the Congress you can see pretty much the same thing, pretty much the same thing was true.

We can't understand our politics without understanding something about slavery. And the same thing is true if we said something about American culture, American nationality. The founding statement of American nationality, the Declaration of Independence, was of course written by a slaveholder, Thomas Jefferson, who wrote those words which became the founding statement of American nationality, "All men are created equal." Why does a slaveholder write "All men are created equal" when slavery is an institution of profound inequality? Part of the reason for that is because slaveholders were very very concerned about questions of freedom and equality and that concern was translated into our founding statement. We can't understand who we are as a people, we can't understand our history without understanding something about the institution of slavery.

What we're going to talk about today is how slavery affected the slaves. I'm going to talk about one historical document where we can hear the voice of a slave, and hear what he had to say about the institution of slavery. That document is a letter from a man by the name of Hawkins Wilson. Let me say about what we know about Hawkins Wilson, which is not very much, and what we know about his letter. First let me say how we found this letter from Hawkins Wilson: That letter was found in the National Archives of the United States, amid the records of an agency called the Bureau for Refugees, Freedmen, and Abandoned Land, which was commonly called the Freedmen's Bureau—an agency of the federal government, which was established that at the end of the Civil War to help former slaves move from slavery to freedom. That agency would become the recipient of a lot of letters from people who thought they needed their help. And Hawkins Wilson thought he needed the help of a Freedmen's Bureau agent. So he wrote to this Freedmen's Bureau's agent about the problem he had. He was trying to find his family. Prior to the Civil War there were no slave families recognized in law. Slaves could not legally get married, slave parents had no legal claim on their children, and because there was no legal basis for a slave family it meant that slaveholders could sell anybody they wanted at any time they wanted and they did that. They sold husbands away from wives, and wives away from husbands, and they sold parents away from children. In fact if you were a slave child, aged 12 or 13, living in Virginia in the nineteenth century, the chances that you'd be sold from your parents were probably one in five. One, two, three, four, five, you. One, two, three, four, five, you. One in five of you would be taken away from your parents and in all possibility you would never ever see them again, they would never ever see you again. There is no possibility of you communicating again. There was no email, there was no regular mail. There would be no connection. That would be it, you'll be on your own at that point. And you would be taken some thousand miles to a plantation in some distant place and that would be pretty much it. And you would then be put to work, working in a cotton field in Alabama or Mississippi or Louisiana, as Hawkins Wilson was. Like him, you would then have to make your own life on a plantation, perhaps with other people precisely your age. Think about what, at age 12, you know about the world, what you bring to that circumstance to enable you to start making your own life apart from your parents. That was Hawkins's problem. Let me read with you from Hawkins Wilson's letter.

It's two years after the Civil War has ended, and he's writing from Texas. Hawkins Wilson is writing to this agent of this newly established bureau.

> Dear Sir, I am anxious to learn about my sisters from whom I have been separated many years—I have never heard from them since I left Virginia twenty four years ago.

So let's presume it's 1867 and subtract 24 and say 1843, and he's 12 years old then, when was Hawkins Wilson born? 1831. He's born in 1831, he was born at the moment just at the height of the cotton boom, just at the point when cotton was most profitable, where cotton was being produced and being shipped out of the South in massive amounts to England, to the North, to be woven into textiles to be made into clothing, driving a new form of production called the Industrial Revolution, and that's when Hawkins will be born, probably beginning of the 1830s in Virginia, then he will be sold.

> I am in hopes that they are still living and I am anxious to hear from them and how they are getting on. I have no other one to apply to but you, and I am persuaded that you will help one who stands in need of your services as I do—I shall be very grateful to you if you oblige me in this matter—One of my sisters belonged to Peter Coleman [. . .] her husband's name was Charles and he belonged to Buck Haskin and lived near John Wright's store in the same county—She had three children, Robert, Charles and Julia, when I left—Sister Martha belonged to Dr Jefferson, who lived two miles above Wright's store—Sister Matilda belonged to Mrs. Botts, in the same county—My dear uncle Jim had a wife at Jack Langley's and his wife was named Adie and his oldest son was named Buck and they all belonged to Jack Langley—These are my only relatives and I wish to correspond with them with a view to visit them as soon as I hear from them. My name is Hawkins Wilson and I am their brother, who was sold at Sheriff's sale and used to belong to Jackson Talley and was bought by M. Wright, Boydtown C.H. You will please send my enclosed letter to my sister, or some of her family, if she is dead—I am, very respectfully your obedient servant, [signed] Hawkins Wilson.

Hawkins Wilson, former slave, sold away from his parents, about the age of 12, sold two thousand miles away to Texas. Now he is trying to find his family, and to help this Freedmen's Bureau agent find his family he has recalled his entire boyhood family. Think about it, you're going to be asked, you're going to be asked in thirty years to remember all your aunts and uncles, and where they lived. Would you be able to do that? And then we have, what is more extraordinary still, Hawkins Wilson encloses the letter that he wants this Freedmen's Bureau agent to give to his sister Jane.

> Your little brother Hawkins is trying to find out where you are and where his poor old mother is—Let me know and I will come to see you—I shall never forget the bag of biscuits you made for me the last night I spent with you—Your advice to me to meet you in Heaven has never passed from my mind and I have endeavored to live as near to my God, that if He saw fit not to suffer us to meet on earth, we might indeed meet in Heaven—I was married in this city on the 10th March 1867 by Rev. Samuel Osborn to Mrs. Martha White, a very intelligent and lady-like woman—You may readily suppose that I was not fool enough to marry a Texas girl—My wife was from Geogia and was raised in that state and will make me very happy—I have learned to read, and write a

little—I teach Sunday School and have a very interesting class—If you do not mind, when I come, I will astonish you in religious affairs…

And then Hawkins Wilson astonishes us by talking about his religious life, his religious affairs just as he has astounded us by his extraordinary ability to seek his family in his mind for over thirty years since he was sent away. Now one of the things that Hawkins said about slavery is that slavery destroyed a slave's family. That the slaves had no legal right to marry, the master could interfere in the slave's life any way he wanted, in terms of rearranging the way parents or sisters disciplined their children, or parents took care of their children. And of course the slaveholders could also sell their slaves away any time they wanted, [. . .] as he clearly did with Hawkins Wilson, selling him away from his whole network of kin that he lived in.

So one of the questions I'd like to start with is to ask you, "Does Hawkins Wilson have a family?" Okay, so he does have a family, he certainly has a family. Emotionally he has a family. He of course has no legal basis for family, but family exists without the law because it is a human relationship. How is Hawkins Wilson and presumably other people who are enslaved able to sustain their family over a long period of time, over a great distance, without the legal structure of family life? How is he able to do this? He thought about it really hard because he misses his parents so much. He was someone who literally rehearsed in his head who all these people were so he would never forget. He literally memorized them. What else do we know about Hawkins Wilson, by the way, just by the fact we have his letter? He knows how to read and write. How does Hawkins Wilson know how to read and write? Does a slaveholder want slaves to learn to read and write? Reading and writing can be subversive, can be revolutionary. So many slaveholders purposely keep knowledge away from their slaves. There may have been a secret school that slaves had. In our secret school, one slave might learn a little bit and, having learned a little bit, he might pass it on to other slaves. Now you're being historians, you're taking little scraps of evidence that we have about Hawkins Wilson from only one letter. We only have one letter from Hawkins Wilson, but we're beginning to reconstruct his life. We are beginning to put his life together. He arrived in Texas as a young boy, aged 12, perhaps, perhaps participates in this secret school and by age 20 he may be thinking to escape, and probably he doesn't go north, he doesn't follow the North Star to the free states, but he actually goes south, south into Mexico, that's probably the closest place if he does it. Does Hawkins Wilson do that? No, he doesn't do that because we know he's still in Texas in 1867.

Let's continue this exercise of being historians and see what else we can learn about the institution of slavery and Hawkins Wilson from his experience in that secret school. The fact that there is that secret school, what else does that tell us about what's going on in Hawkins Wilson's life? What other kind of things is he learning? Who might he meet in that secret school? And is Hawkins Wilson's letter written very well? It's written very very well. Is the only thing that he learnt when he was at school reading and writing and book learning and these kind of things? What other kind of things might Hawkins learn when he's drawn together late at night in his secret school? Maybe learning how to revolt.

Let's talk and think just for a minute about this question of slave revolt. Are there a lot of slave revolts during slavery? Do slaves have a political sense? Do they have a sense of who they are? They have no weapons. And what might happen if they did revolt? They'll probably get shot. In other words, slavery exists because slaveholders have a predominance of political and military power. They have the gun and slaves don't have a gun. In all probability, Hawkins might have thought about revolting. He might have thought about running away, but he doesn't do that and most slaves don't do that because they understand the predominant of political power and military power is against them.

In other words, maybe your teacher sends you on an errand, you go out of your classroom, you're given a pass and you keep going. And the hall monitor stops you and you say, "I have permission to go." Can anyone imagine doing that? Why wouldn't that work? Why can't Hawkins just take off and run away any time he wants? They might have him killed; because slaves are very valuable pieces of property they might not kill them, they might punish them. What kind of punishment would that be? A very severe punishment, or they might do something else that made sure you didn't run away like chop off your toes, or chop off a piece of your leg. That would have been crueler, and you can still use that slave for labor. So there are all kinds of restraint from simply running away or rebelling.

Well, perhaps. I kind of don't think so. I think that if slaves have a chance to run away, they do run away. And we'll see when the Civil War begins and there's a lot of disorganization in the South, slaves do have a chance to run away, and they do. There are many slaves who ran away, but the proportion is very small. That's another way of looking at it. But the point being here, when we talk about resistance and there's a lot of resistance, resisting everything from rebelling, we do have slave rebels running away, burning down the farms, breaking tools. There are whole varieties to systems of resistance but ultimately we know the slaveholders have created a system which is powerful enough to prevent most people from escaping. So Hawkins Wilson is stuck within this system. He is stuck within this system. And his job is to begin to create a life for himself. And we see him partly creating this life for himself through the secret school and perhaps in this secret school he learns how to read, perhaps he learns something about religion, something about God and a sacred world.

What other things would Hawkins have learned in that gathering of slaves at night which we call our secret school? He might have learned songs and where might these songs have come from? They could make up songs: Think about what would happen if you were taken away, brought down two thousand miles away from here, the only thing you knew, those things you made up, might you have carried some things with you? Might you have carried some songs with you in your head? Would there be some melodies, would there be some words that you might take with you? They don't have iPods, that's true, they have many instruments, drums, many string instruments. What would you play on those string instruments? What songs might be particularly important to you? Songs that you learn in church, songs that perhaps your mother sang to you, songs that your father, songs that your aunts and uncle, those might be particularly important to you, just that you remember your family, you might want to remember those songs. In those songs might we see messages? If we think about it, in some of those songs . . . "Sometimes I feel like a motherless child . . ."

It's precisely the experience that Hawkins Wilson had when he was taken away from his parents, so there might be these messages, and if we think about where Hawkins Wilson's father and mother got their songs: Africa. So in other words, handed down from their mothers' mothers' mothers, and in Virginia, in Texas, might become some knowledge of Africa. One of the things that they're sharing is consciously or subconsciously the knowledge of Africa. The point is that slaves are able to begin to reconstruct a life for themselves out of these little pieces that they are able to bring together and as they are able to bring together, they are able to create new understandings of who they are.

Essay: Teaching about Slavery, Learning to Be Historians: A Disciplinary Approach to Teaching History

By Joan Malczewski, with Ryan Mills and Ashley Merriman

In "Dilemmas and Delights of Learning History," David Lowenthal (2000) explains that to believe that "history has nothing to do with me" is a profound error that overlooks the extent to which human consciousness and memory is bound up with the past. Although there is no definitive test of such claims, the role of slavery might epitomize Lowenthal's assertion. Although most students have been exposed to the topic in school and popular culture, few are likely to comprehend its depth and reach. Indeed, the scope of the topic makes it relatively difficult to teach. The institution spanned 250 years and included generations of slaves, in both the South and the North. It defined issues of race, class, and power in the United States both during and long after its disappearance. Racial and ethnic prejudices can complicate classroom discussion in the present. These challenges often lead to a more simplified curriculum that obscures the harsher realities of the institution and its contemporary relevance. It is easier to reduce the topic to a set of facts without substance, providing little opportunity for students to demonstrate connections between the past and the present, and thereby miss an important opportunity for students to recognize that this is a part of history that continues to shape our collective identity.

For this unit, Marion and Daniel, who taught middle school and high school respectively, worked to overcome these challenges with mixed results, given the demands of public school teaching and the difficulty of stepping outside the boundaries of more traditional approaches to teaching history. Although the two classrooms were situated within large urban schools, beyond that they differed in almost every respect. The students shared neither age nor ability, the teachers brought different perspectives to their work, and the curriculum for the semester and year was developed in markedly different contexts. The group, which also included a professor of American history, was challenged to determine how to develop a unit on slavery so that it would be usable at both the middle school and high school level.

The insights of Professor Ira Berlin, a noted historian of slavery, helped to focus the discussion and planning for this unit. Berlin's description of the institution underscored the teachers' perceptions of its complexities. He noted its centrality as an institution of labor to the South as well as to the North. In that regard, he explained that the 4 million slaves in the country were worth approximately $3 billion, which was three times the value of the whole manufacturing establishment of the United States, including the railroads, and seven times more valuable than the money in all of the United States banks. As a central component of the American economy, the people who owned slaves were able to translate economic power into political power. Although the Declaration of Independence was written by a slaveholder and proclaims that "All men are created equal," slavery was an institution of profound inequality. Thus, as Berlin points out, we must understand something about slavery in order to understand American politics and culture. This last point helps to underscore the complexity of the topic and the challenge of teaching it. American history classes often present a shared heritage of democracy and freedom, yet the central role that slavery played in American history is incompatible with this accepted trope. Given this, students might be skeptical about democracy and freedom, and teachers may be uncomfortable with lessons that undermine that shared heritage (Wertsch, 2000).

The Use of Primary Sources: Hawkins Wilson's Letter to the Freedmen's Bureau

Berlin recognized that there was much to be learned from the analysis of primary documents, especially those providing evidence from the perspective of a slave. Rather than describe the institution in "factual" or economic terms, or from the perspective of politicians or masters, slave perspectives can provide a more compelling viewpoint from within the institution itself. Berlin shared a letter from an ex-slave, Hawkins Wilson, which was written two years after the Civil War had ended (Chapter Resources II A). Wilson's letter is located in the National Archives of the United States, as part of the records of the Freedmen's Bureau, which had been established after the Civil War to help former slaves move from slavery to freedom. Wilson had written to the Bureau with a request for help in locating his family, whom slavery had caused to be dispersed throughout the South. His letter included a second attached letter that he hoped the Bureau would forward to his sister Jane. These primary documents are powerful not only because of the obvious historical content, but also because of the disciplinary skills that students might develop through analyzing them.

Although there seem not to be any archival sources that can be used to verify the biographical facts about Hawkins Wilson's life, Berlin spoke about how much there was to be learned from his letter. For example, it is clear from the letter that Wilson was originally a slave in Virginia, but was then sold in 1843 to a slaveowner in Texas. An historian might assume that he was about twelve years old at the time of his sale, give or take a few years, which would put his birth date at around 1831, at a time when cotton was most profitable in the South. Berlin explains how remarkable it is that Wilson's letter recalls so much about his immediate and extended family, given that families were not supported by the institution of slavery, and how helpful it is to be provided with this additional factual information. Beyond these facts, however, students can gather further information by using the letter to develop questions that will inform their historical understanding. For example, since the bonds of family were not legally recognized in the institution of slavery, how did Hawkins Wilson define his own family, and how did others do the same? There were clearly emotional bonds that existed, at least for Hawkins Wilson, in spite of the separation of distance and time between family members.

An analysis of the letter might also lead students to wonder how it is that Hawkins Wilson learned to read and write. Berlin explains that students might consider why slaveholders passed laws making it a crime for slaves to become literate, and then think about how Hawkins Wilson managed to acquire these skills. Might slaves have had secret schools? Did individual slaves learn these skills and pass them on to others? Was it a revolutionary act for Hawkins Wilson to have acquired this skill? What other skills might Hawkins Wilson have learned through this educational process? Beyond reading and writing, the means by which he was educated might also have provided him with connections to other slaves or whites that he might not otherwise have had.

Once students begin to think about how Hawkins Wilson learned to read and write, the door is opened to inquiries about slave communities, the details of slaves' lives within the institution, and resistance. Students might think about what else Hawkins Wilson might have learned, and what they might have hoped to learn if they were in his shoes. Did he learn music? If so, the songs might have been religious or might have included messages about the institution of slavery, or conveyed knowledge about Africa for subsequent generations. Berlin notes that students might think about whether slaves had a political sense, whether they thought about what it meant to be a slave, and the forms of resistance they might have chosen. Once students consider resistance, they would necessarily think about the political and military power that supported the institution of slavery.

Ultimately, as Berlin points out, if students begin to ask these sorts of questions of Hawkins Wilson's letter, in effect, they are doing deeply historical work—"taking little scraps of evidence that we have about Hawkins Wilson from only one letter . . . [and] beginning to reconstruct his life." In reconstructing Wilson's life, students can develop an understanding of the larger institution of slavery. Developing this understanding might lead students—especially if prompted by teachers—to think about the society that sustained the institution of slavery. On a personal level, students might be compelled to think even more about what it might have been like to have been a slave, creating a dynamic that would lead to even more questions. In this process, students would hopefully come to realize that the slaves were individuals who constructed lives for themselves in spite of the parameters in which they had to live.

Berlin's approach to teaching about slavery is interesting in that he does not offer a particular narrative that he believes should be shared with students, nor does he describe detailed historical knowledge that students must acquire, though he is clear about his interest in promoting understanding from the perspective of a slave. Instead, he promotes an approach that allows students to develop the disciplinary skills necessary to create their own historical narrative. He envisions a unit that begins with the reading of Hawkins Wilson's letter as a means of promoting disciplinary knowledge. Utilizing his approach, students would analyze a primary document and consider the perspective of someone who had lived within the institution of slavery. In that process, students could learn how to be historians. This use of Wilson's primary source document is the essence of a disciplinary approach to learning history (Seixas, 2000).[1]

Developing a Unit on Slavery

Marion and Daniel were enthusiastic about how Berlin's presentation on slavery might inform a unit on this subject. However, both teachers were challenged to think about how best to incorporate these ideas into their individual classrooms and into the broader context of their work. They were cognizant of the difficulty involved in teaching the subject matter, and neither was required to teach about it as it was not part of the established or mandated curriculum. This simultaneously meant that the teachers had relatively greater flexibility to develop a creative unit, and a greater challenge in figuring out how to focus the topic in a way that would capture the depth that was possible in Berlin's approach, especially given that both teachers were able to devote only three days of class time. Further, the teachers worked in very different environments, so it would be important to focus the lesson in a way that capitalized on what was most important in each setting.

The middle school was located in an urban area and enrolled about 350 students in grades 6–8. Of these students, almost 75 percent were Hispanic, almost 25 percent were black, and the remaining few were almost evenly divided between Native Americans, Asians and whites. About 15 percent of the students at this school were designated as needing special education, and more than 10 percent were English language learners. Almost 70 percent of students came from families living below the poverty line. Recent progress reports from the school district gave high marks to the principal and to the teaching staff, all of whom were fully licensed and permanently assigned to the school. Of these teachers, almost half had been at the school more than two years and 93 percent had received a masters degree or higher. In spite of some difficult demographics, assessment test scores for this high-needs population had been consistently improving.

The circumstances in the high school were markedly different, with an enrollment of more than 4,000 students in grades 9–12, and a population that was about 30 percent white, 30 percent black, 15 percent Hispanic and 25 percent Asian. Of these students, about 10 percent were English language learners, and 12 percent were in special education. The school did not receive Title I funding, but almost 30 percent of the students were eligible for free or reduced lunch. Although the school had an admissions process designed to ensure that a mix of socio-economic levels were represented, its well-established theater arts program made the admissions process competitive, with more than ten thousand applications annually for one thousand freshmen spots. About 90 percent of the students continued after high school to some post-secondary education. The teaching staff included almost 80 percent of teachers who had been in the school for more than two years and almost 60 percent of teachers who had a masters degree plus 30 hours of post-graduate work or a doctorate.

Marion, the middle school teacher, explained that her seventh-grade students were generally engaged and motivated, but also noted that a majority of these students were reading well below grade level, with many working on fourth-grade-level materials. The structure of the school day included ninety-minute blocks for the teaching of English and social studies together. The slavery unit would be added to the regular seventh-grade curriculum and taught during these ninety-minute humanities blocks. The block format provided opportunities to integrate historical content with reading and creative writing, to provide additional time to scaffold learning, and to develop the literacy skills necessary for a more disciplinary approach to learning history. For example, poetry had become an important medium for the students to work on literacy skills and share their understanding of topics across the humanities curriculum. Marion also noted that students at her school were accustomed to working in collaborative groups in an experiential setting.

Daniel, the high school teacher, would be teaching the slavery unit in a regular history course on Civil Rights that students had chosen as an elective. He estimated that about 70 percent of the students were performing at grade level in reading and noted that only upper-grade–level students were eligible to enroll in the course. Thus, his students had been exposed in previous classes to American and global history. Although this course was not an Advanced Placement course and was more representative of students across the spectrum in general education, it included a self-selected group of students who were interested in history. As such, he expected that the students would be engaged with the topic.

Both schools and classroom environments seemed clean and safe, and the students were generally attentive and engaged. Both teachers explained that visitors were common, and neither felt that the students behaved differently when observed. The walls of Marion's classroom were covered with information, recent assignments submitted by students, teaching aids to support learning, and a number of bookshelves stocked with a wide variety of books. A "poetry basket" was prominently displayed in the room for students to place poems in that they would like to have shared aloud. These poems could be either signed or anonymous and on any topic of interest. Each observed class began with a reading of some of these poems. As a testament to student interest in this pedagogical tool, there were always more poems than time allowed, and Marion had to promise each day to come back to the basket to read additional poems later. The classroom consisted of six tables of about five students each, providing opportunities for the students to work alone or in groups.

Challenges and Opportunities

Marion and Daniel recognized the possibilities of this unit, but also its challenges and limitations. For example, Marion's middle school students had almost no background in the subject of slavery, except for what had been transmitted through popular culture. Difficulties with literacy would make it challenging to use primary documents in the way that a disciplinary study of history might require. However, Marion believed that primary documents and high-level readings and concepts were particularly good for middle school students and that, with appropriate assistance, her students would be able to access the ideas in a significant way. Daniel noted that the reading of primary documents was typical in the high school curriculum, though reading aids were often necessary to facilitate this work. Both Marion and Daniel acknowledged that the increased focus on math and reading assessments in recent years had detracted from the amount of time generally spent exploring historical topics and developing historical skills.

Both teachers felt that the life of Hawkins Wilson would be relevant to students, but for different reasons. Many of Marion's middle school students came from immigrant families where one or both parents, or extended family, were living in other countries, and so had experienced some sense of separation in family and community. In addition, Marion felt that many of her students perceived that they did not have any power in the various communities in which they existed, such as school or family. Given this, she sensed that Hawkins Wilson's life would have particular meaning for these students, and she hoped to capitalize on that meaning to promote interest and understanding in the history of slavery. Daniel felt that many of the high school students who had selected the course did so because of their interest in the political issues surrounding Civil Rights. As such, they would most likely find Hawkins Wilson to be a particularly compelling figure.

Neither instructor was required to teach about slavery to address any of the state standards, so both had flexibility in determining the lesson plans. Given institutional differences, the discussions about how to develop organizing historical questions for the unit within these broad parameters were interesting on multiple levels. Marion believed it was important to focus on family and resistance, given the student population and the particular community in which she worked. She recognized that students would easily grasp those ideas, making the history meaningful and relevant. Thus, an instructional priority would be to make a case for the relevance of Hawkins Wilson's letter early in the unit. Indeed, as Seixas (2000) points out "it is the power of the story of the past to define who we are in the present, our relations with others, relations in civil society—nation and state, right and wrong, good and bad—and broad parameters for action in the future." Marion's belief was that the greater the relevance to student lives, the more likely the students would be to seek or engage in a more disciplinary approach and thus be compelled to seek additional primary sources with alternative perspectives.

Daniel worked within very different parameters. The boundaries of the high school curriculum were more carefully drawn for students, who would need to master particular skills for graduation even if the class was an elective that was not required to meet directly mandated curriculum standards. Students were generally expected to learn in the high school history curriculum about issues of power in the context of the economy and the United States Constitution. Beyond that, Daniel planned to use the topic of slavery as the first unit and foundation of the Civil Rights curriculum that he had developed for the course.

The teachers discussed their instructional goals for the unit and determined that a unifying theme across the two units would be *resistance*. This concept was meaningful for both sets of students and addressed important elements of the required curriculum in the high school. The unit would be defined by two organizing historical questions that might compel students to think about power and resistance. How do we define the value and meaning of an individual life, and how does this relate to the broader context of American culture and its institutions? And, in that context, who "counts" and who can participate in society? The units were unified by the shared theme and questions, which would provide a framework that could guide the development of specific lessons. The lessons that each teacher developed, however, would be very different, tailored to teacher interests and creativity as well as the needs of the particular classrooms.

The organizing historical questions helped to focus the discussions and unit, and indeed were a useful and standard teaching tool. However, this process had implications for how the teachers would incorporate Berlin's advice. In one respect, the use of questions to guide lesson planning was contrary to the strategy Berlin used in his talk. However, albeit potentially more interesting and compelling, starting historical instruction with a primary source document might also be difficult and risky in a public school classroom, where teachers are under enormous pressure to achieve a broad range of instructional goals. It is difficult to leave outcomes to chance, and more creative lesson design might not result in the list of facts and figures that would ultimately be included on standardized tests. Additionally, even though these units were not directly related to student assessment, and the unit was not being offered as part of the regularly planned curriculum in either class, it was important to use class time in the most efficient and useful way possible. Both teachers used the opportunity to emphasize important curriculum themes for middle and high school and, in the process, the lessons that were developed did address a number of state standards.

Daniel had prioritized a set of instructional goals for the unit, including developing understanding of the slave trade, the Constitution, and the institution of slavery. He felt that it would be important to develop lessons that specifically addressed these subtopics. It would have been easier for Marion, in a classroom where there was complete flexibility around what was taught and learned, to follow Berlin's approach exactly as proposed. However, even in that environment literacy issues would require significant preparation and scaffolding in advance of working with Hawkins Wilson's letter. Marion believed that the students would learn a great deal from analyzing the primary documents, but was also concerned that they did not have sufficient knowledge to use it as a basis for the lesson about historical concepts, or the direction she hoped the lessons would take. It would be easier for students to comprehend the document if they had particular goals for reading it. As a result, neither classroom began with a reading of Hawkins Wilson's letter, including it instead as the last lesson of the unit.

Early discussions about a unifying theme also highlighted different conceptions of power and resistance. Would it be best to focus on individual power, or would it be better to connect individual power to civic engagement in explicit ways? Marion explained that civic engagement was her ultimate goal, but believed that was a concept that would develop through adolescence. She felt that her middle school students were not cognizant of the power they had in their various communities. For example, she noted that if middle school students are asked how they might respond if they felt mistreated in school or elsewhere, most would be inclined to tell a parent or guardian who might manage the problem. Especially because slaves did not have that option, she felt that this unit might provide an avenue for helping them to begin to recognize their individual power through their connections as part of a bigger community. Given a spectrum of resistance, ranging from subtle challenge to explicit revolt, she thought it would be important for students to develop some understanding of this continuum and think about how to evaluate different forms of resistance, such as education, as tools of power. Therefore, in the middle school, power would be explored in terms of individual resistance and its relationship to institutions such as the family and community. High school students, however, had a more developed awareness of communities and political action. Thus, the high school curriculum would be more broadly defined. Beyond these general differences, however, both teachers were interested in helping students to explore not just when individuals had an obligation to be civically engaged, but also whether there were situations in which individuals had an obligation to resist.

The Middle School Unit

Marion offered the unit in two of her humanities classes: the first consisting of 50 percent English language learners but with highly motivated students, and the other class consisting of a broader range of levels and more apathy and behavioral problems. In preparation for the slavery unit, she had taught some mini lessons that covered the slave trade and life on a plantation. These mini lessons were not part of the unit that was developed in dialogue with Professor Berlin's work and were not part of the observed teaching. It was clear that the need to focus on the development of literacy skills would make it essential to use a variety of scaffolding exercises before and during the unit, including vocabulary building, the presentation and explanation of essential questions, movement from small to big examples, and graphic organizers. Indeed, as evidence of Marion's commitment to integrating literacy into as much of the curriculum as possible, each of the observed lessons included opportunities for students to work with different forms of texts, including biographies, informational excerpts, pictures, and fictional literature, and all were explored in a way that encouraged discussion and an evolution of ideas. For example, Marion created a simple guide for reading primary documents, in which the text of the primary document was parsed into sections that could be more easily absorbed. Students were asked to record what each section of text meant and their reactions to the text. Students worked in groups with this guide to develop deeper understanding of each text.

Marion designed the first lesson of the observed unit with the goal of helping students think about how an understanding of history is developed and, in that context, whose stories are told. She asked students to match a set of quotes to pictures of historical characters such as Abraham Lincoln, Rosa Parks, Samuel Adams, and Paul Revere, as well as some people who were not well known to the students, including Hawkins Wilson. The students were advised not to guess, but only to match those pictures and quotes when a majority of the students knew it to be a correct match. The students explained that the people that they easily recognized had been designated as "important in history" for a variety of reasons, including that they had sacrificed their lives, or had participated in acts that affect us today. Some students argued that the recognizable figures, such as Abraham Lincoln, were indeed more important than those individuals whose names and images they did not recognize, though other students disagreed. The discussion moved toward a deeper consideration of what it meant to be perceived as "important." Marion asked students to think about the implications for understanding history when only the most well-known people are studied, and explained to students that in history we choose to study the pieces that are available, but then need to think about the pieces that are missing. Students were asked to reflect upon when it was important to think about the "missing pieces," and how studying those missing pieces might enhance understanding. The teacher referred to a lesson earlier in the year in which the students had thought about a puzzle with only the largest pieces available, so that it was impossible to see the whole picture.

In the next lesson, the class explored the meaning of community. Students considered the ways in which power exists in communities and communities facilitate power. Students developed "community webs" in which they delineated the roles that they played in each of their communities, such as school or a sports team, as well as the role that each community played in their life. Marion asked students to reflect on their community web and think about where they might be most important, and whether or not they might be "famous" in particular communities. Students read slave biographies made available from the "Slavery in New York" teaching materials produced by the New-York Historical Society, and used them to develop community webs for these slaves (see Chapter Resources III, p. 32).

The students considered whether the historical figures were important in every community in their own web. This led to a discussion about influence and whether influence in small communities might make one's role in the world more meaningful. Marion asked students to think about the people who had a powerful role in their own world, and what it would mean if history could not recognize all of these contributions. Students discussed how it was possible to understand historical figures who were not associated with communities and considered what would happen if they were taken out of their own communities, or made to live far away from them. Marion asked students to think about how these themes of community and power related to the institution of slavery.

This part of the lesson was particularly challenging. Marion had some concern about whether the lesson would lead students to make unfavorable comparisons with less known historical figures and ultimately feel that their own roles in communities had diminished value. The planning group also considered whether it was pedagogically possible or even appropriate to promote an appreciation for subtle resistance and whether there was a risk of promoting too explicitly political action. Ultimately, Marion felt that it was important for students to recognize that power and value comes from individual choice. This more personal approach to history would hopefully lead to greater interest on the part of the students in carefully considering Hawkins Wilson's life. Both teachers believed that civic engagement was an important part of the curriculum that would not be resolved, or even adequately addressed, in this unit, but had been and would continue to be addressed in other lessons throughout the year.

Marion began the third lesson by reading an excerpt from a fictional story, *Nightjohn*, by Gary Paulsen, about a slave named John who had successfully run away from a plantation only to return by choice for the purpose of teaching reading to the other slaves. Students discussed why John had returned, rather than write his memoirs as a freed man. They worked in small groups to explore why slave literacy was illegal and considered why it was important that John be able to tell or to record his story. They concluded that written records of slaves proved they were real people. In that regard, literacy might prove that slaves were intelligent and, therefore, not appropriately treated as animals.[2] Students recognized that slaves might send letters to people off the plantation or perhaps write their own certificates of freedom.

This turned to a discussion of resistance. Students considered possible forms of slave resistance, from subtle to overt, and worked in small groups to consider activities and biographical information about ten slaves, including Hawkins Wilson. The students discussed where particular actions might lie on a continuum of resistance, an exercise that also challenged students to move beyond more presentist interpretations of history. For example, students were asked to consider whether it was a subtle or obvious form of rebellion when Sojourner Truth sued her owner or publicly spoke against slavery, and most believed both to be "subtle" because of the difficulty in moving outside their present frame of reference, in which lawsuits and free speech are culturally the norm. How would a student classify the case of a slave who pretended successfully to be blind in order to be set free?

These first lessons generated considerable student interest in community structures, resistance, and the relevance of history. They were now ready to read and interpret Hawkins Wilson's letter and were able to analyze it in relationship to other biographies. They were able to think about the implications of the institution of slavery on individual lives and on the lives the slaves led. Students discussed whether there was a collective community of slave resistance, even if much of the resistance took place through individual acts, and considered how they might leave their own mark as individuals or as part of a community. Marion hoped that the relevance of these lessons would lead them to think more substantively about what could be learned from Hawkins Wilson's letter about the institution of slavery. The students might also be compelled to think more about what might be "missing" in their study of history, and how recovering those missing pieces might lead to a more meaningful picture of the past. Marion asked the students not to provide answers, but rather to think about these issues. These were themes that would be repeated in subsequent units throughout the year.

The High School Unit

This unit consisted of four lessons that examined power as it was manifested institutionally in the economy, politics, the family, and community. The specific learning goals included considering the relationship between wealth and power in America, the debate about whether the American Constitution was a pro-slavery or an anti-slavery document, the relationship between the representative and the represented, the means by which citizens exercise power, and the ways in which power is used or abused in society. These themes would not only appeal to this group of self-selected students, but also would provide a useful foundation for the remainder of the Civil Rights course. Daniel believed that these instructional goals would also require lessons aimed at a set of historically specific topics before introducing Hawkins Wilson's letter. The lessons and the discussions were carefully directed by Daniel given the amount of materials that would need to be covered to meet the instructional goals. He distributed a handout at the beginning of the unit that included excerpts from a range of primary documents to inform the lecture and discussion, and teaching aids to facilitate reading and analyzing these documents.

The first lesson focused on the economy and considered wealth and slave labor. The goal was for students to understand the monetary value of a slave and the role of slavery in the political economy of the United States, and by extension American progress. In order to help the students to think about the relationship between the past and the present, Daniel began the lesson with a quote from the current New York City mayor, Michael Bloomberg, about contemporary issues of race and labor. After that, Daniel gave a lesson introducing the economic motivation for the slave trade that captured the brutality of the institution. He combined lecture with class discussion, quoting from secondary sources such as those by the historians Edmund Morgan and John Hope Franklin, as well as from primary sources, including one by a British merchant who spoke of the contributions of African labor to progress. Daniel provided information about the southern slave economy, plantation life, and labor in both the North and the South. This included evidence of slavery in the North in the early republic, again utilizing the "Slavery in New York" teaching materials created by the New-York Historical Society.

For this first lesson, Daniel drew extensively on the themes in Professor Berlin's presentation, and students used primary documents to debate specific questions. For example, was American "progress," or the transformation to a more global world, dependent upon slave labor? As students thought about the economic benefits, Daniel made a compelling case for the harsh realities of the institution. The handouts included an advertisement for a slave auction and the plan and sections of a slave ship. Both documents were accompanied by quotes from slaves about this aspect of the slave trade. The teacher guided the students through each section of the lesson, integrating lecture and discussion, and provided opportunity for students to acquire disciplinary knowledge through the use of sources that were provided as evidence for the points made in the lecture. However, the scope of what the teacher hoped to cover in each lesson limited the amount of time available for discussion and impacted the use of primary documents in the way that Berlin had presented. Whereas Daniel had planned to complete one lesson in each class, for three days, the material included was more than what could be covered in each period. This was a function not only of how much the teacher wanted to accomplish, but also of how little historical context many students had.

The lesson on slavery and political power began with a class reading of the Declaration of Independence. The goal was for students to understand who had power and who was allowed to participate in society. Daniel provided the students with an example of paragraphs that were written but not included in the final document. For example, one passage by Thomas Jefferson that was deleted from the Declaration stated:

[King George] has waged cruel war on human nature itself, violating its most sacred rights of life and liberty in the persons of a distant people who never offended him, captivating and carrying them into slavery in another hemisphere, or to incur miserable death in their transportation thither.

(Kaminski, 1995, p. 7)

The students worked in small groups to read and understand the full text of the document, and to respond in writing to a question in the handout about why the passage had been excluded. As part of this lesson, Daniel discussed the framers of the Constitution, juxtaposing quotes from some with information about their slave holdings. For example, Thomas Jefferson owned slaves but was quoted as saying that slavery was a "hideous blot" on America, and George Mason owned more than three hundred slaves but condemned slavery as evil. In fact, 31 percent of the delegates to the Philadelphia Convention owned approximately 1,400 slaves (Appleby & Schlesinger, 2003; Broadwater 2006). Daniel asked students to think about whether the societal role that the framers of the Constitution had might have influenced the final document that was written and how the exclusion of some groups on the basis of race or gender might also have influenced the final document.

Daniel moved from the Declaration of Independence to a discussion of the tensions that would need to be resolved in order to create the Constitution. For example, northerners and southerners had different views with regard to how slaves would be counted as part of the population for representation purposes. Daniel explained that slave states and free states disagreed about a range of important issues, including the regulation of taxes and its effect on farming exports, the ending of the slave trade, and the rules about how the problem of runaway slaves would be addressed. He distributed excerpts from Articles of the Constitution that dealt with each issue and students discussed how each Article affected slavery and whether the privileged class benefited from the Article or not. Daniel made important connections between politics and the economy and shared basic data to provide evidence of the centrality of slavery in the American economy.

The next lesson focused on slavery and the family. One goal was for students to consider how it is possible for historians to recapture the lives of people who had no power in history. A second goal was to have students consider to what extent power is vested in individuals versus institutions and ask whether individuals have an obligation to exert power in the form of resistance when necessary or possible. Primary sources illustrated for students the harsh realities of the institution of slavery. The focus in the lessons on political power, economic power, and social power had made clear that freedom for slaves would not be as easily attainable in fact as in law. In that context, the use of Hawkins Wilson's letter could be particularly meaningful. Daniel had planned small group discussions in which students would explore the letter and share ideas about the meaning of power and resistance in an individual life. He hoped that his students would consider what resistance meant in an institution so completely defined by power and oppression. Unfortunately, the materials for the first three lessons had taken more time to teach than anticipated. Therefore, this classroom was not able to use the letter from Hawkins Wilson as part of the unit.

Discussion of the Two Units

Although each teacher's approach was fundamentally different, their lessons were guided by a unifying theme and essential questions. Both units provided important information about the historical context, conveyed in a way that went beyond facts and figures, to a more creative and compelling set of lessons. Both Marion and Daniel introduced students to more abstract concepts and asked students to connect the past to the present through primary documents and a more disciplinary-based approach to the study of history. As these units exemplified, both Marion and Daniel were successful teachers who delivered a set of useful and meaningful lessons. However, both had to develop a curriculum that made sense in their particular classroom and make difficult choices about what to include and exclude. Both units incorporated themes from Berlin's presentation, though neither was able to fully incorporate all the ideas that he proposed.

At the beginning of the process, Daniel lamented the lack of depth and breadth in the high school curriculum, yet these ideals often end up being opposing forces in curriculum planning. The teachers faced similar challenges in developing these units. It is hard to go into depth and allow students opportunity to creatively explore when a teacher is concerned about covering a broad range of issues. The reality is that teachers are under enormous pressure to convey as much factual information as possible. On any specific topic, teachers typically must achieve a range of instructional goals, while selecting a set of subtopics in which greater depth might be accomplished and a set that cannot adequately be covered. In the end, the compromise between these two ideals can affect the classroom narrative. As Daniel pointed out, textbooks are often able to provide a relatively "cleaner" narrative because a substantive, in-depth understanding of topics is rarely sought. Berlin had commented on some issues and themes but advocated that students begin with a primary document, prioritizing a goal of teaching them first to be historians. With sufficient time and guidance, they might be compelled to explore the topic in its depth and reach. However, both Daniel and Marion had to make difficult choices about the curriculum.

Daniel utilized a more traditional approach in his lessons, focusing on the use of primary and secondary sources that might lead the students in the direction that would ensure that all of the material was covered. Berlin had influenced the themes, the historical quotes and the primary documents that were included in Daniel's lesson. One result was that the unit presented information that was more in line with recent historical contributions to the literature. However, these lessons did not provide an opportunity for students to use primary documents to construct their own narrative, or similarly to challenge the narrative that was being presented by the teacher. Rather, students likely learned the importance of using primary documents as evidence and of considering different historical perspectives. Ultimately, they developed a potentially more comprehensive understanding about the institution and knowledge about key historiographical debates, as well as greater knowledge of the disciplinary skills necessary to do in-depth historical analysis.

Daniel believed that a significant problem had been one of time, not just in terms of the number of lessons to be included but in all domains of planning. Berlin's framework had been inspirational, but also might represent simultaneously a better way of teaching and a more difficult one, given the parameters of the high school classroom. It is ideal when students can construct historical understanding through disciplinary practice, but the realization of this goal requires that students be given sufficient time to engage in this process. In order to incorporate Berlin's approach in a purer form, Daniel would need to devote more time to research, planning, the preparation of new materials, and a re-evaluation of the curriculum that had been planned for the whole course. With regard to this last point, in order to fit the unit into the curriculum in the most meaningful way, other lessons had to be removed. Daniel was aware of all of these challenges and lamented that there had not been more time for students to engage in historical debate.

Daniel felt that parts of the lesson were particularly successful. In this regard, Berlin's framework had led to a narrative that was compelling for students and useful for the rest of the course. Specifically, he felt that the goal had been for students to comprehend the relationship between the institution of slavery and the economy, political power, and the family. In the end, the students developed an understanding of each of these three areas. So, the unit moved well beyond what would typically be conveyed by a high school history textbook, and utilized a range of primary source documents that might not have otherwise been included. Daniel's approach had been to provide context and hope that students would find the themes relevant and make connections to the present. His obvious self-critique was the feeling of frustration that came from not actually using Hawkins Wilson's letter to explore resistance in greater depth and to help students to make those important connections. Nonetheless, he believed that the unit had achieved the goal of teaching students about the theme of power.

Marion considered the class discussions and inquiry around the ideas of community and resistance largely successful, but also felt the constraints of time. She was pleased with the unit and believed that students ended it with a more well-rounded understanding of slavery and the way that individuals and groups operated within the institution. Students began to recognize different ways that slaves were involved in communities and resistance. It had been challenging for many of the students to grasp the subtleties of resistance, but Marion observed that some of the students demonstrated mastery of these learning objectives. Some easily recognized the extremes, comprehending running away as resistance but with less clarity about the power of education and community. Other students had a harder time grasping the idea that one could have power through subtle acts or that power did not require violence. However, it was more difficult for this understanding to be conveyed in final projects because these concepts were developing. Students indicated that they identified with the sense of impotence that the slaves must have felt and, given this, apparently developed an understanding of the institution from the perspective of a slave. Students also expressed an understanding that slaves resisted in obvious and subtle ways and saw that subtle instances of resistance can be very powerful. Marion felt that students would have more success with these themes the next time the unit was offered if more background lessons were offered to students in advance of the unit. Essentially, a three-day unit was insufficient to cover the scope of the material. For this unit both teachers experienced a problem typical to teaching, in which there are more demands for what should be taught than time to teach it. In the end, both recognized that the goals of the slavery units could be realized fully only if history courses were taught with more time provided for an in-depth examination of historical context and themes.

Marion had promoted a narrative similar to that presented in the high school, albeit in a much more simplified form. She designed the lessons to move from personal relevance to disciplinary knowledge, whereas Daniel had approached it from the other direction. In that regard, she did not present an accepted narrative as much as she asked the students to construct one that was relevant to their own lives, focusing particularly on the theme of resistance. This approach may have developed in the students an interest for greater historical understanding. However, too much focus on developing ideas that are personally relevant might detract from the disciplinary work necessary to engender a deeper understanding of the facts of history. The letter from Hawkins Wilson was intended, in Berlin's discussion, not merely to show an example of resistance, but as a means to ask important questions about slavery. Students did acquire some of this knowledge, but this deeper understanding of the historical context was not the main priority, given the need to narrow the unit to a set of lessons that the teacher felt would be interesting and comprehensible to the students.

One of the more interesting issues from the middle school was the integration of literacy with the curriculum. The lessons systematically integrated historical understanding with the development of literacy skills, an essential part of engaging in a disciplinary study of the past. This process provided further evidence of Marion's conviction that primary source texts and higher-level readings were appropriate with these middle school students, as long as there were opportunities to scaffold ideas and provide additional assistance. The students produced a final project in the form of poetry, captioned drawings, or a diary entry based upon one of the slave biographies, and these writings provided some indication of both student learning and the relevance of poetry to the classroom (see Chapter Resources IV, pp. 33–35).

Daniel used a pre-assessment and post-assessment handout in order to get an indication of what students had learned through the unit. He asked students to list five things that they knew about the slave trade, slavery and the Constitution, the family life of a slave, and slave resistance. For each of these categories the difference between what students knew before and after the unit was significant. Prior to the unit, student descriptions showed some knowledge about slavery, but with less substance, and for some of the four categories there were students who were not able to list any prior knowledge. The assessment after the unit included more depth in understanding. Students were able to include facts such as, "Slaves were not citizens and were 3/5 a person," and that "slavery was the economic basis of the economy." They were also able to list various ways in which slaves might resist. Efforts to assess whether the lesson had been successful provided evidence that students had learned a great deal about the historical context. However, it was not possible to measure how much students had learned about more abstract concepts, nor was it possible to assess how much would be retained because of the topic's meaning and relevance to individual student's development of historical understanding.

Both teachers recognized that the overarching question that guided the unit had been a powerful one. Further, these concepts would be addressed in subsequent lessons. Although understanding of abstract ideas about resistance, civic engagements, and community was an important instructional goal, both Marion and Daniel believed that a priority was to challenge student beliefs. Both of them also noted that where social issues and civic education were integrated into the curriculum, it would be important to integrate issues more pervasively and over longer periods. Ultimately, however, these abstract concepts and themes develop with consistent exposure over time and are difficult to measure. The simplified stories that students are typically offered in textbooks make it very difficult to connect history to personal experience, abstract concepts, and more substantive thinking about social issues. These units on slavery were more creatively designed to make these connections, but this posed particular problems for assessment. While historians, social studies educators, and educational policy experts have debated the use of standardized testing in history and social studies, this study indicates the potential problems of measuring historical knowledge and the relevance of history to the present. It would be easy to develop a standardized test that would measure student knowledge of the historical context of slavery, but the result might be greater reliance on textbook learning and less effort to develop the disciplinary practice that Berlin proposed and that guided the development of these two units.

Works Cited

Appleby, J. O & Schlesinger, A. M. (2003) *Thomas Jefferson: The American President Series: The Third President, 1801–1809*. New York: Times Books.

Broadwater, J. (2006). *George Mason: Forgotten Founder*. Raleigh: University of North Carolina Press.

Kaminski, J. P. (1995). *A Necessary Evil? Slavery and the Debate over the Constitution*. New York: Madison House Publishers, Inc.

Lowenthal, D. (2000) Dilemmas and Delights of Learning History. In Stearns, P. N., Seixas, P., and Wineburg, S. (eds.), *Knowing, Teaching and Learning History*. New York: New York University Press, pp. 63–82.

New-York Historical Society (2005). *Slavery in New York Classroom Materials*. New York: New-York Historical Society.

Seixas, P. (2000) Schweigen! die Kinder! Or, does Postmodern History Have a Place in Schools? In Stearns, P. N., Seixas, P., and Wineburg, S. (eds.), *Knowing, Teaching and Learning History*. New York: New York University Press, pp. 19–37.

Wertsch, J. (2000) Is it Possible to Teach Beliefs, as Well as Knowledge about History? In Stearns, P. N., Seixas, P., and Wineburg, S. (eds.), *Knowing, Teaching and Learning History*. New York: New York University Press, pp. 38–50.

CHAPTER RESOURCES

I. Lesson Framework—Teaching about Slavery

Intended Learning Outcomes (Use NYS SS Standards)

Understandings (Big Ideas):

- Students will understand the importance of recognizing ordinary groups in history and think about what makes them important, valuable, or powerful.
- Students will understand the relationship between resistance and civic engagement.
- Students will understand the important achievements of groups living in the United States.
- Students will understand the role of community in defining and uniting Americans in culture.
- Students will understand the connection between primary documents and historical understanding.

Essential Questions:

- How do we define the value, or meaning, of an individual life within a community?
- How do we define the value, or meaning, of an individual life in history?
- In what ways are the communities that we are a part of important, valuable, and powerful?
- In what ways can resistance be a form of power?
- How did slaves resist?
- How can the disciplinary practice of history help students to capture the lives of individuals in history?

Content Knowledge:

- Students will know what kind of communities slaves could belong to within the institution of slavery.
- Students will know why slaves were denied literacy.
- Students will know what forms of resistance existed for slaves.
- Students will know the difference between subtle and overt forms of resistance.
- Students will have a better understanding of the culture of the slave community.

Skills:

- Students will know how to read primary documents and secondary sources.
- Students will develop an understanding of life in slave communities.

Vocabulary:

- Justice, Resistance, Literacy

Learning Experiences:

- Small-group discussion of life in slave communities.
- Primary source document analysis in groups.
- Exploration of civic engagement and its relationship to resistance.

Resources:

- Hawkins Wilson's letter to the Freedman's Bureau
- Student community webs and slave community webs
- Slave biographies
- *Nightjohn* by Gary Paulsen

II. Primary Document—Two Letters Written by Hawkins Wilson

A. [Galveston, Tex.] May 11th, 1867—

Dear Sir, I am anxious to learn about my sisters, from whom I have been separated many years—I have never heard from them since I left Virginia twenty four years ago—I am in hopes that they are still living and I am anxious to hear how they are getting on—I have no other one to apply to but you and am persuaded that you will help one who stands in need of your services as I do—I shall be very grateful to you, if you oblige me in this matter—One of my sisters belonged to Peter Coleman in Caroline County and her name was Jane—her husband's name was Charles and he belonged to Buck Haskin and lived near John Wright's store in the same county—She had three children, Robert, Charles and Julia, when I left—Sister Martha belonged to Dr Jefferson, who lived two miles above Wright's store—Sister Matilda belonged to Mrs. Botts, in the same county—My dear uncle Jim had a wife at Jack Langley's and his wife was named Adie and his oldest son was named Buck and they all belonged to Jack Langley—These are all my own dearest relatives and I wish to correspond with them with a view to visit them as soon as I can hear from them—My name is Hawkins Wilson and I am their brother, who was sold at Sheriff's sale and used to belong to Jackson Talley and was bought by M. Wright, Boydtown C.H. You will please send the enclosed letter to my sister Jane, or some of her family, if she is dead—I am, very respectfully, your obedient servant,

Hawkins Wilson

B. [Enclosure] [Galveston, Tex. May 11, 1867]

Dear Sister Jane, Your little brother Hawkins is trying to find out where you are and where his poor old mother is—Let me know and I will come to see you—I shall never forget the bag of buiscuits you made for me the last night I spent with you—Your advice to me to meet you in Heaven has never passed from my mind and I have endeavored to live as near to my God, that if He saw fit not to suffer us to meet on earth, we might indeed meet in Heaven—I was married in this city on the 10th march 1867 by Rev. Samuel Osborn to Mrs. Martha White, a very intelligent and lady-like woman—You may readily suppose that I was not fool enough to marry a Texas girl—My wife was from Geogia and was raised in that state and will make me very happy—I have learned to read, and write a little—I teach Sunday School and have a very interesting class—If you do not mind, when I come, I will astonish you in religious affairs—I am sexton of the Methodist Episcopal Church colored—I hope you and all my brothers and sisters in Virginia will stand up to this church; for I expect to live and die in the same—When I meet you, I shall be as much overjoyed as Joseph was when he and his father met after they had been separated so long— Please write me all the news about you all—I am writing tonight all about myself and

I want you to do likewise about your and my relations in the state of Virginia—Please send me some of Julia's hair whom I left a baby in the cradle when I was torn away from you—I know that she is a young lady now, but I hope she will not deny her affectionate uncle this request, seeing she was an infant in the cradle when he saw her last—Tell Mr. Jackson Talley how-do-ye and give my love to all his family, Lucy, Ellen, and Sarah—Also to my old playmate Henry Fitz who used to play with me and also to all the colored boys who, I know, have forgotten me, but I have not forgotten them—I am writing to you tonight, my dear sister, with my Bible in my hand praying Almighty God to bless you and preserve you and me to meet again—Thank God that now we are not sold and torn away from each other as we used to be—we can meet if we see fit and part if we like—Think of this and praise God and the Lamb forever—I will now present you a little prayer which you will say every night before you go to sleep—Our father who art in heaven &c, you will know what the rest is—Dear sister, I have had a rugged road to travel, since I parted with you, but thank God, I am happy now, for King Jesus is my Captain and God is my friend. He goes before me as a pillar of fire by night and a cloud by day to lead me to the New Jerusalem where all is joy, and happiness and peace—Remember that we have got to meet before that great triune God—My reputation is good before white and black. I am chief of all the turnouts of the colored people of Galveston—Last July 1866, I had the chief command of four thousand colored people of Galveston—So you may know that I am much better off, than I used to be when I was a little shaver in Caroline, running about in my shirt tail picking up chips—Now, if you were to see me in my fine suit of broadcloth, white kid gloves and long red sash, you would suppose it was Gen. Schofield marching in parade into Richmond—The 1st day of May, 1867, I had 500 colored people, big and little, again under my command—We had a complete success and were complimented by Gen. Griffin and Mr. Wheelock the superintendent of the colored schools of Texas—We expect to have a picnic for the Sunday School soon—I am now a grown man weighing one hundred and sixty odd pounds—I am wide awake and full of fun, but I never forget my duty to my God—I get eighteen dollars a month for my services as sexton and eighteen dollars a week outside—I am working in a furniture shope and will fix up all your old furniture for you, when I come to Virginia if you have any—I work hard all the week—On Sunday I am the first one in the church and the last to leave at night; being all day long engaged in serving the Lord; teaching Sunday School and helping to worship God—Kind sister, as paper is getting short and the night is growing old and I feel very weak in the eyes and I have a great deal to do before I turn in to bed and tomorrow I shall have to rise early to attend Sunday School, I must come to a conclusion—Best love to yourself and inquiring friends—Write as quickly as you can and direct to Hawkins Wilson care of Methodist Episcopal church, colored, Galveston, Texas—Give me your P. Office and I will write again—I shall drop in upon you some day like a thief in the night.—I bid you a pleasant night's rest with a good appetite for your breakfast and no breakfast to eat—Your loving and affectionate brother—

Hawkins Wilson

III. Example of Student Work—Illustrated Notes on Boston King

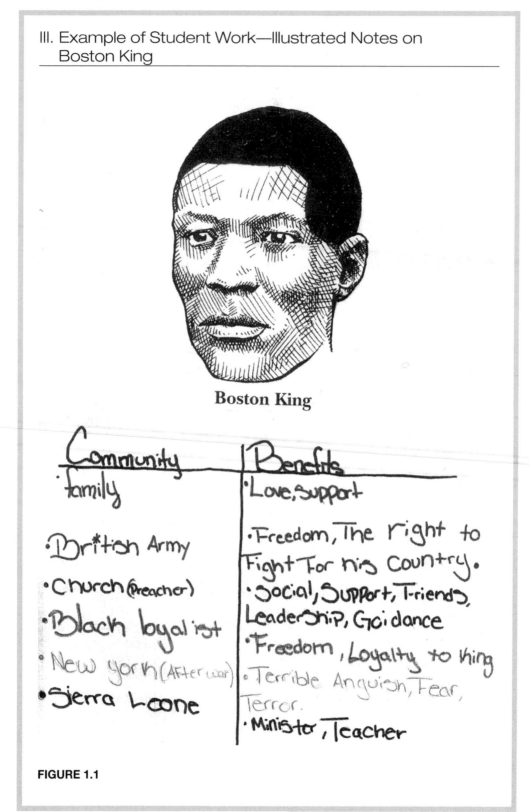

Boston King

Community	Benefits
· family	· Love, support
· British Army	· Freedom, The right to Fight for his Country.
· Church (preacher)	· Social, Support, friends, Leadership, Guidance
· Black loyalist	· Freedom, Loyalty to King
· New york (After war)	· Terrible Anguish, Fear, Terror.
· Sierra Leone	· Minister, Teacher

FIGURE 1.1

IV. Examples of Student Work—Poems

Resistance

by Kimani Jenkins

> Lose the shackles
> and spend the night
> dashing through the woods
> resisting slavery
> and leaving it for good
>
> Master I'm blind
> Master I don't understand
> Maybe I'll act as ignorant
> as they *think* I am
>
> A,B,C
> but shhh!
> Not to [sic] loud
> If Master find out, I'll be dead
> but I'll make my people proud
>
> This is how we resisted
> over years and time,
> this strength and resistance
> will bring us to our prime.

One Day

by Yamilet Marciad

> One day I will learn
> how to read and write
> One day I will escape
> I will run away.
> far away
> where nobody can find me
> cause I am American too
> and all I want
> is to be free
>
> One day I will refuse to work
> and I'll be free,
> free at last
> One day
> I will teach others
> to learn how to read and write

One day
we are all going to be free
cause we're Americans too
and we have the right to be free,
FREE AT LAST!!

How Dare You

by Harold Barreto

How dare YOU!
I'm NOT an animal,
I'm NOT a maid,
Don't take me away from mom,
and call me YOUR slave!

My mom loved me,
I'm sure yours loved you too,
Today is my 14th birthday,
and you expect me to work for YOU!
How Dare YOU!

I could play dumb,
not work, act a fool,
Join the army, suicide,
rather than work for you
How Dare YOU!

If I act dumb he won't expect much,
Eh! What the heck, I'll act blind,
When "Master" turns around,
I'll stab him from behind,
How Dare YOU!

You made me stand in a boat,
chained to hundreds of future slaves,
it was hard for me to breathe,
I thought I was "gonna" die!
I get off the boat to be sold to a white guy!
How Dare YOU!

I went through the horror, pain misery,
I knew once I was sold,
I'll escape and be free,
I ran by got caught and whipped,
I had no one to turn to,
How Dare YOU!

You're havin' a great life,
2 sons, 1 daughter, and a beautiful wife,
I have no family or friends,
I'm lonely here,
so all I can do is pretend,
    How Dare YOU!

I now know what I can do,
Join the British army? That's what dad would do,
I can run again, this time I won't be caught,
I'll have to think it through,
    How Dare YOU . . .

I thought it over, I'll run,
I'm running like the wind!
"Master" looks at me and yells,
"Come back! U'll [sic] pay for this some day!"
I say, "No, you're 'gonna' pay"
He screams
    "How Dare YOU!"

How Dare I? Is he insane?
he hasn't been through all my pain!
I have to run, as fast as I can!
Then! I'll be a free man!
How dare I?
How dare I?
You're a dumb fool.
    How Dare You!

V. Relevant New York State and NAEP Standards: Slavery

New York State Learning Standards, U.S. History

- Students explore the meaning of American culture by identifying the key ideas, beliefs, and patterns of behavior, and traditions that help define it and unite all Americans (MS.1A)
- Students interpret the ideas, values, and beliefs contained in the Declaration of Independence, the U.S. Constitution, Bill of Rights, and other important historical documents (MS.1B)
- Students complete well-documented and historically accurate case studies about individuals and groups who represent different ethnic, national, and religious groups in the United States at different times and in different locations (MS.3A)
- Students gather and organize information about the important achievements and contributions of groups living in the United States (MS.3B)

- Students describe how ordinary people and famous historic figures in the United States have advanced the fundamental democratic values, beliefs, and traditions expressed in the Declaration of Independence, U.S. Constitution, the Bill of Rights, and other important historic documents (MS.3C)
- Students classify major developments into categories such as social, political, economic, geographic, technological, scientific, cultural, or religious (MS.3D)
- Students analyze the development of American culture, explaining how ideas, values, beliefs, and traditions have changed over time and how they unite all Americans (HS.1A)
- Students describe the evolution of American democratic values and beliefs as expressed in the Declaration of Independence, U.S. Constitution, Bill of Rights, and other important documents (HS.1B)
- Students develop and test hypotheses about important events, eras, or issues in U.S. history, setting clear and valid criteria for judging the importance and significance of these events, eras, or issues (HS.2B)
- Students compare and contrast the experiences of different groups in the United States (HS.2C)
- Students compare and contrast the experiences of different ethnic, national, and religious groups, explaining their contributions to American society and culture (HS.3A)
- Students research and analyze major themes and developments in U.S. history (HS.3B)
- Students prepare essays and oral reports about the important social, political, economic, scientific, technological, and cultural developments, issues, and events from U.S. history (HS.3C)

New York State Learning Standards, Historical Thinking

Students:

- Consider the sources of historic documents, narratives, or artifacts and evaluate their reliability (MS.4A)
- Understand how different experiences, beliefs, values, traditions, and motives cause individuals and groups to interpret historic events and issues from different perspectives (MS. 4B)
- Compare and contrast different interpretations of key events and issues in United States history, and explain reasons for these different accounts (MS.4C)
- Describe historic events through the eyes of those who were there (MS.4D)
- Analyze historical narratives about key events in United States history to identify the facts and evaluate the authors' perspectives (HS.4A)
- Consider different historians' analyses of the same event or development in U.S. history to understand how different viewpoints and/or frames of reference influence historical interpretation (HS.4B)
- Evaluate the validity and credibility of historical interpretations of important events or issues in U.S. history, revising these interpretations as new information is learned and other interpretations are developed (HS.4C)

Adapted from *New York State Learning Standards, U.S. History* (1996)

NAEP Learning Standards, U.S. History

Framework 1: Themes in U.S. History

- What individuals and groups have been important in maintaining, testing, and changing America's institutions? (1)
- What are the basic principles and critical assumptions of American constitutional government about the sources of the rights of individuals? What core civic ideas have influenced American society? What individuals and groups have maintained, tested, and influenced these ideas? (1)

Framework 2: Periods of U.S. History

- How did revolutionary rhetoric about equality and civic virtue produce rising expectations for many groups (e.g. slaves and free blacks)? (3.2)
- What actions did African Americans take before the Civil War to secure their freedom and rights as citizens? (5.1)
- How did the social and cultural traditions of the prewar North and South differ? (5.2)
- How did slavery as an economic system affect the economy and social and class systems in the North, the South, and the West? (5.3)

NAEP Historical Thinking Standards

Framework 3: Ways of Knowing and Thinking about U.S. History

1. HISTORICAL KNOWLEDGE AND PERSPECTIVE

Students should be able to:

- Name, recognize, list, identify and give examples of people, places, events, concepts and movements
- Place specifics in a chronological framework and construct and label historical periods
- Define historical themes and give examples of the ways themes relate to specific factual information
- Describe the past from the perspectives of various men and women of the time
- Explain the perspective of an author of a primary source document
- Describe different perspectives related to a historical issue or event
- Summarize the contributions of individuals and groups to U.S. history
- Summarize the meaning of historical sources and link these sources to general themes

2. HISTORICAL ANALYSIS AND INTERPRETATION

Students should be able to:

- Specify and explain cause-and-effect relationships and connect contemporary events to their origins in the past

- Categorize information and develop strategies for organizing a large body of facts
- Examine multiple causes of historical developments
- Explain points of view, biases, and value statements in historical sources
- Determine the significance of people, events, and historical sources
- Weigh and judge different views of the past as advanced by historical figures themselves, historians, and present-day commentators and public figures
- Demonstrate that the interpretation and meaning of the past are open to change as new information and perspectives emerge
- Develop sound generalizations and defend these generalizations with persuasive arguments
- Make comparisons and recognize the limitations of generalizations
- Apply knowledge, draw conclusions, and support those conclusions with convincing evidence

Adapted from National Assessment Governing Board (2006)

Works Cited

National Assessment Governing Board (2006). *U.S. History Framework for the 2006 National Assessment of Educational Progress*.Washington, DC: U.S. Department of Education.
New York State Learning Standards, U.S. History (1996). Albany: New York State Education Department.

Notes

1   Seixas describes three orientations toward historical pedagogy and epistemology. The first is to teach the "best story" in order to "enhance collective memory." The second is to present more than one version so that students can reach conclusions on the basis of documents, historians' assessment, and other materials, an approach that Seixas refers to as disciplinary. The third approach is to present a "best story" but relate it to political uses in the present. For this chapter, I refer to the "disciplinary" study as one in which students are asked to develop a valid historical account on the basis of primary documents and other historical materials.

2   This is the same theme that Frederick Douglass addresses in his autobiography, *Narrative of the Life of Frederick Douglass*. Although the students had not read this text, the book or excerpts from it would be useful to developing a deeper understanding of these ideas.

Two
The Civil War

Framing the Questions: An Interview with James Oakes, conducted by Rachel Mattson

James Oakes received his PhD degree from the University of California at Berkeley, and is currently on the faculty of the City University of New York Graduate Center. He has written extensively about the history of the U.S. South, slavery, anti-slavery and U.S. politics. His books include *The Ruling Race* (1982; second edition 1998), *Slavery and Freedom: An Interpretation of the Old South* (1990), and *The Radical and the Republican: Frederick Douglass, Abraham Lincoln, and the Triumph of Antislavery Politics* (2007), which won the Lincoln Prize for the best Civil War era book.

Rachel Mattson: *Can you talk about what motivates your work?*

James Oakes: My latest book, *The Republican and the Radical*, was motivated by a couple of different things, including my dissatisfaction with how the legacy of the 1960s has affected the way a lot of people of my generation think about politics. Historians of my generation come out of the legacy of the '60s, and were strongly influenced by the assumptions of social and cultural history, which had a kind of anti-political bias to it.

RM: *Anti-political—meaning anti-electoral politics?*

JO: Yeah, or really: politics understood as organized activity aimed at changing state policy— which is a fairly conventional definition, but nevertheless a useful one. And this does not refer strictly to "electoral" politics. It includes women marching in the streets for the vote that they don't have. Or blacks meeting in conventions from the 1830s through the 1850s to insist on their rights, including their right to vote. Social historians of the post-'60s generation often end up saying, "I'm writing about politics," when, in fact, there's nothing the men on the street or the women on the street would recognize as politics. At some point it really does have to connect up to state policy for me. I think the claims have been swung too far. You get into debates, for example, about who freed the slaves. Did the slaves free themselves or did Abraham Lincoln free the slaves? It seemed to me unfortunate but a symptom of the times that that's the way the debate got framed, because a debate should never be framed that way.

RM: *Why? Why is that a bad way to frame a debate?*

JO: Because it's not either/or, and because slaves can't free themselves. And on the other hand Lincoln couldn't free slaves all by himself either. And he knew that. His policy was premised on the assumption that the slaves would do certain things that would make emancipation happen. He presupposed that the slaves would be agents in the process of emancipation. But the slaves couldn't do it without him and Congress and the Union, you know, putting in place and establishing the conditions that would make it possible for that to happen.

In short, framing a debate that way does two things: First, it makes a complicated process too simple. And, second, it removes the struggle from it. And politics for me is about a struggle. If you say the slaves freed themselves, it's as though there were no really major obstacles. If you say Lincoln freed the slaves, it has the same effect. The third party that's missing from that debate over who freed the slaves is the Confederacy. The Confederacy and Southern slaveholders fought back. And it was a huge, difficult, long, violent process, because there weren't just two actors in the process. It was a fight. It was a struggle. It took a long time.

RM: *That's interesting—and yet, I use that debate a lot with public school teachers who have never even been exposed to the idea that it wasn't the Emancipation Proclamation that freed slaves. And, in my experience, just asking that question sometimes opens up an entirely new way to think about the Civil War and emancipation.*

JO: Right, right. And really, you can raise that question that way and then halfway through say, "What's wrong with the way we just raised this question?" And say: "Let's complicate it even further."

But that debate about who freed the slaves is a classic example of the debate between a social historian and a political historian. A social historian might think that if a slave runs away, that in and of itself is politically significant. But I think you have to demonstrate political significance. You have to show how that does, in fact, affect state policy.

RM: *So one of the debates that you're trying to speak to in your work is the debate between social historians and political historians over how to define political action or politics?*

JO: That's part of it. And when I looked at the debate, the dance between Frederick Douglass and Lincoln—and when I put them up side by side to see how their differences of opinion about slavery and politics plays out—I came to the conclusion that buried in the critique that many historians have made of the compromises that go with mainstream politics is a kind of anti-democratic argument. I believe that you can't have democracy without compromise. So to attack the very idea of compromise is to attack the premise of democratic politics.

RM: *Can you explain the nature of the dance that Lincoln and Douglass were doing, the different sides that they were on?*

JO: Sure. Lincoln is a politician as soon as he can stand up on a stump. He was a politician before he was a lawyer. He was a politician before he was an anti-slavery politician. And he comes out of mainstream politics. He is as thoroughly mainstream a political person as you can find in America. And it takes him a while to come to anti-slavery politics.

Douglass, meanwhile, escapes slavery in the late 1830s, becomes an abolitionist around 1840–1841, when he joined the Abolitionist Movement—under the rubric of William Lloyd Garrison and the Garrisonian wing of the Abolitionist Movement. By this time, Garrison had taken an increasingly anti-political position. He wasn't anti-politics in 1831–1832. He took the anti-politics position in 1839–1840. He didn't like the compromises that he saw other anti-slavery activists making. He thought the whole political system was corrupt, and that the Constitution was a pro-slavery document. Thus, he contended that the entire political system that had been erected under the rubric of the Constitution was corrupt. So Douglass starts out anti-slavery. It takes him a while but eventually he comes to the conclusion that being anti-slavery isn't enough. It has to become anti-slavery *politics*. In the late 1840s and the early 1850s he comes to the conclusion that you have to engage in politics. And then he starts wondering how and asking the usual questions like a reformer—or a radical reformer—has to ask about how much compromise are you willing to tolerate in pursuit of anti-slavery politics.

The convergence that I'm playing with in the first chapters of the book (*The Radical and the Republican*, 2007) is Lincoln's move from being a *politician* to being an anti-slavery politician, and Frederick Douglass's move from being *anti-slavery* to being an anti-slavery politician or accepting anti-slavery politics. In the process of coming to anti-slavery politics, they both have to come to terms with the relationship between slavery and the Constitution. Lincoln has to decide what the Constitution allows politicians to do to thwart slavery and what it doesn't allow them to do. And Douglass has to decide that the Constitution is not a pro-slavery document. And although they are converging on anti-slavery politics, they never converge on the Constitution.

This goes back to an historical debate over what the Founders did in the Constitution. On the simplest level, everybody who was sitting in that meeting in Philadelphia understood that they had made a series of compromises on the issue of slavery. The majority of the delegates didn't like slavery. They managed to keep the word *slavery* out of the document. They managed to keep any references that implied that human beings could be property out of the Constitution. But on the other hand, the Southerners, led by South Carolina, made it very clear or explicit that they would not tolerate a Constitution that didn't protect slavery in certain ways. So they insisted on a fugitive slave clause. They got the slaves counted as three-fifths of the population for purposes of representation and taxation. And they got a reprieve on the abolition of the slave trade.

So you get in the South basically the argument for a pro-slavery Constitution that's oddly mimicked by Garrison, who says, "Yes. The U.S. Constitution is a pro-slavery document." And in the North you get a kind of middling position that Abraham Lincoln takes. And then you get the radical position that Frederick Douglass takes.

What Lincoln ends up coming to between 1858 and 1859, as he's struggling with the implications of the decision, and which he articulates in February of 1860 at Cooper Union, is a flat-out assertion that there is no such thing as a Constitutional right to property and slaves. That's a very radical position that nobody has taken. It's not the same position that Douglass took. He basically says states regulate domestic institutions in a way that it's certainly not the business of the government to decide.

RM: *What are some of the best documents that speak to Frederick Douglass's ideas about whether the Constitution was a pro-slavery document?*

JO: After John Brown is arrested and discovered to have some letters from Frederick Douglass in his belongings, Douglass has to run. Douglass runs and leaves the country, because he's going to be arrested. He goes to Great Britain. And while he's in Scotland in late 1859 or early 1860—I'm not sure—he gives a speech. Someone in Scotland gives a Garrisonian speech about how the Constitution is pro-slavery. And in response Douglass gives the fullest, most extended, argument that he ever made for reading the Constitution as an anti-slavery document.

He says, for example, "The slave trade clause allows the federal government to abolish slavery, which the federal government does." Whatever it was up until 1808, from 1808 forward it's an anti-slavery clause. And that's important. The fugitive slave clause, he says, doesn't say slaves. It has no reference to slaves. And for the three-fifths clause, that's tax. To the extent that it refers to slavery, it's punishing the South, because the default position in the Constitution is that every human being counts for purposes of representation. In the North, every man, woman, and child is counted for purposes of representation. In the South, their representation is decreased, because the Southern black population was, under the Constitution's original provisions, not fully counted. And Douglass says that what that means is that the Constitution has built into it a standing incentive for Southern states to increase their representation in Congress by abolishing slavery.

No one else really believed that the three-fifths clause was an anti-slavery clause. Everyone believed it was a pro-slavery clause. Every northerner believed it was a humiliating disgrace. It's one of Lincoln's arguments for why it's not correct to say the North has no business concerning itself with what happens in the territory, because he says that's not true. That three-fifths clause is a humiliating clause for northerners, because it gives us a disadvantage. It creates an advantage for the South. It enhances their representation in both the House of Representatives and the Electoral College. And the result is we have a stake in preventing the South from expanding that humiliating, you know, advantage that's there. So that's the mainstream position. And that is, in fact, how people at the Constitutional Convention understood it, that they were giving the South something, not taking away.

But on the other hand, if you do just read the text, there isn't anything in the text that tells you whether three-fifths means they've been rewarded with three-fifths or punished by taking away two-fifths. So Douglass's argument, if you accept his premises, allows for something that's what I would think is very different from a strict construction.

Lincoln has two places where he works these ideas out. The first is in a major anti-slavery speech in Peoria in October of 1854. That's where he goes through and says, "The Founders intended to restrict slavery. They thought slavery was going to die. They compromised in three places. And one of them is an anti-slavery clause for the slave trade laws. So there are some things we're allowed to do and some things we're not allowed to do. And we're not obliged to let it expand." That's the Constitutional argument he makes starting in 1854. By 1860, at Cooper Union, he's gone further. He's saying Congress should stop the expansion of slavery absolutely everywhere completely. And he's saying there is no such thing as the right to own slaves anywhere in the Constitution.

RM: *That's interesting: The ground upon which he's making that argument is not moral ground at all. It's legal ground.*

JO: Well, you know, the moral premise behind both arguments is that the Founders understood slavery to be a violation of the principle of fundamental human equality. But they had no choice out of necessity if they wanted to create the Union. They had to do this. So they compromised for the sake of the Union, because take away the Union and the principle of fundamental human equality is just a vapor. It only exists in reality if it's embedded in political Constitutional structure. Therefore for Lincoln the Union was the place where the principle of fundamental human equality existed. Destroy the Union and the principle goes away. So arguing for the Union and for the Constitution and the sanctity of the Constitution isn't an alternative to a moral argument for him. The argument for there not being a Constitutional right to property in slaves comes straight out of the premise that black people are human beings. And that's the abolitionist premise that you cannot dehumanize the human being. You cannot deny that these people are human. And once you accept that they're human, then all humans are created equal and are entitled to the fundamental right to freedom, right?

Essay: Personalizing the Lives of Great People in History and Making Historical Documents Come Alive: Frederick Douglass, William Lloyd Garrison, and the Abolitionist Movement

By Michael Stoll, David Montgomery, and Candace Villecco, with Dwight Forquignon and Tiffany Lincoln

Ask anyone why the Civil War happened, and chances are he or she will answer with the word "slavery." While slavery is generally accepted as the chief cause of the Civil War, the connection between the "peculiar institution" and the outbreak of Civil War is quite complex. Many historians over the past few decades have argued that the war was the inevitable result of deep economic, ideological, and cultural differences that divided the antebellum South from the North (see Foner, 1980; Grob & Billias, 1992). Prior generations of "revisionist" historians saw secession as the product of failed leaders and fanatical agitators, igniting a war that could have been avoided had cooler heads prevailed (see Bonner, 1968). These historians argue that it is impossible to comprehend the causes of the Civil War without having a greater understanding of the motivations behind those in power at the time. What unites both of these interpretation is a focus on the larger social and political context of the antebellum period, in which the slavery issue was not only the subject of intense moral debate but ultimately unmanageable within the America political system. Viewed in this way, many of the political debates surrounding slavery can be traced back to the nation's founding, and, in particular, the Constitution itself. Ironically, it was this document and the political system it created, often taught in social studies classes today as the greatest on earth and virtually flawless, that proved unable to prevent one of the bloodiest civil wars in modern history.

Yet teaching the antebellum period is particularly challenging for high school and middle school teachers because there is a tendency to teach the Constitution as a static document and the Civil War as purely a moral crisis over slavery. These interpretations, while easy to understand, tend to flatten the historical experience, leading to confusion about the antebellum period. The group of university educators and public school teachers who came together for this project wanted to add complexity to the teaching of the causes of the Civil War, moving beyond the simplistic explanation of "slavery" by showing how and why the political system and the Constitution upon which it rested proved unable to mediate the escalating conflict over slavery. We wanted to expose students to the long-term trends as well as the ideologies of individual decision-makers. Our challenge was, as a teacher mentioned at one of our meetings, that "you could spend a whole year teaching antebellum politics." Given that most public school teachers have only a few weeks at most to cover the complexities of this time period, we tried to find a way to condense the content while still providing the context needed for students to develop their own interpretations about the Constitution's implications regarding slavery and the crisis of the Union.

The group developed and conducted different lessons on this topic for middle school students, high school students, and undergraduates. Each lesson involved primary and secondary source analyses and a dramatic component to explore the different interpretations within the abolitionist movement during the antebellum period. Students at all levels evaluated the compromises of the Founding Fathers regarding slavery and the ways in which certain clauses in the Constitution were used to argue for its abolition decades later. The central figures students analyzed were not the Founding Fathers themselves, but rather the great abolitionists of the antebellum period, William Lloyd Garrison and Frederick Douglass, whose own work reflected a changing interpretation of the Constitution. Middle school students used the Constitution itself as well as the biography and writings of Douglass to explain how and why historical figures change their mind on important issues, and the extent to which this might reflect weakness. High school students analyzed the Constitution in detail to determine the extent to which the document represented a pro-slavery or anti-slavery position and to understand how debates over this question caused a political crisis prior to the Civil War. Undergraduates explored these issues and more in attempting to reconstruct the events that led to the split between Douglass and Garrison.

To achieve these learning goals, the teachers employed a variety of pedagogical strategies based on current research on the teaching and learning of history, such as journaling, drama, and debate. These lessons were an attempt to apply research on the development of historical thinking using primary source documents (Wineburg, 2001) to the teaching of the causes of Civil War. This analysis of primary sources also required students to question, explain, and otherwise make sense of conflicting interpretations of history, something that is both rare in most history classrooms and developmentally appropriate for adolescents (Lee & Ashby, 2000). At the same time, the group was motivated by the concept of teaching for empathy (see Barton & Levstik, 2004). We hoped that exploring the perspective of people in the past would help students better understand their motivations. Such deeper connections would move students beyond passive historical analysis of events "back then" toward a personal identification with the historical actors they were studying.

The group discovered that implementing the lessons in urban middle school and high school classrooms was difficult given the realities of teaching history in these settings. Indeed, the teachers were torn between the exciting potential of the research of Wineburg and others and everyday concerns such as student attendance and literacy skills. As a result, the group's desire to develop students' historical thinking skills and create opportunities for empathy required a significant amount of improvisation on the part of the teachers. The middle and high school lessons we designed and observed were ones in which students engaged in historical thinking using primary sources and developed sophisticated interpretations of the Constitution's role in the abolitionist movement. Upon reflection, though, the group felt that the lessons, although educationally useful and generally successful, remained too analytical and did not provide enough opportunity for students to engage with the history in a deeply personal way.

Despite these challenges, we remained committed to teaching history for empathy and decided to explore ways in which more personal connections could be made to the study of the abolitionist movement. Ultimately, the group decided to develop another lesson on the same theme and make dramatic elements a more explicit part of the learning process. Group members designed and taught this lesson to undergraduates in a teacher education program, allowing the group to fully explore innovative pedagogies and receive reflective feedback on the value of teaching for empathy in history from future teachers. The experience affirmed for the group the value of personal connections to the learning of history and suggested ways in which teachers at all levels could enhance their pedagogy with the thoughtful combination of historical thinking skills and empathy.

The Constitution and the Abolitionist Movement: Historical Background

In contemplating a new approach to the teaching of antebellum politics, the group turned to the recent scholarship on the Civil War and the antebellum period, especially the work of James Oakes, a professor of American history at the Graduate Center for the City University of New York. Oakes's work includes an analysis of antebellum politics through the perspectives of Douglass and Abraham Lincoln (Oakes, 2007), two figures whose views have been simplified by what he sees as the de-politizing trends of social history. For example, he argues that popular debates about who freed the slaves—Abraham Lincoln or the slaves themselves—are inadequate and tend to reflect more about contemporary times than they reveal about the nineteenth century. Oakes shows that the slaves could not free themselves without Lincoln, and yet, conversely, the Emancipation Proclamation would not have had much force without some agency on the part of slaves. Therefore, a statement such as "Lincoln freed the slaves" is not only inaccurate, but omits the active and passive resistance of the slaves themselves. Such an either/or formulation also ignores the fact that the resistance of the Confederacy made emancipation a long and eventually violent process. In this sense, the emancipation of the slaves was not something that just *happened*, but was also the result of years of work by abolitionists, many of whom did not always agree amongst themselves.

Yet these explanations for emancipation endure. Indeed, the teachers in the group admitted that in previous years they had framed the issue of emancipation as primarily a decision made by Lincoln during the Civil War, because that explanation was easier to present to students. However, Oake's argument against doing so is compelling, and that motivated the group to take a deeper look at the abolitionist movement itself. In most traditional narratives, the embodiment of the ideology is William Lloyd Garrison, a prolific white abolitionist known for publishing *The Liberator*, an anti-slavery newspaper. Adamant that the Consitution was a document that protected slavery, he publicly burned a copy of the Consitution in 1854 and advocated the dissolution of ties between the North and the South (Cohen, 2008). By focusing on these actions, most textbooks portray Garrison as a righteous reformer against an unjust institution and all anti-slavery activists as coming from this same mold.

Yet Oakes discusses the ways in which Garrison's uncompromising and ultimately untenable position became increasingly radical and out of touch with most within the abolitionist movement. In fact, many of the abolitionists were conflicted about the political, legal, and moral justifications for the movement and disagreed about the methods they should be using to end slavery. Oakes demonstrates that two of the movement's major figures, Abraham Lincoln and Frederick Douglass, went through a transformation in their thinking on this issue. Oakes argues that, contrary to most popular narratives, Lincoln emerged as a virulent anti-slavery crusader only late in his career. For most of his career as a politician and lawyer he remained comfortably ambiguous on the issue. Douglass, on the other hand, was a former slave who wrestled with how much compromise he was willing to tolerate in pursuit of anti-slavery politics. Initially a follower of the radical abolitionist and anti-Constitutionalist Garrison, Douglass eventually came to see the Constitution as a document that provided the basis for a legal challenge to slavery and subsequently broke from the Garrisonian position (Cohen, 2008). Oakes (2008) argues that Douglass's change of heart spurred the abolitionist movement in a new direction and led to renewed debates about the Constitution itself. By understanding these debates, students would gain a better understanding of the abolition movement and, ultimately, the political causes of the Civil War.

The Teachers

The group of educators who came together for this project represented a range of historical knowledge and pedagogical approaches. The group consisted of a university historian, a professor of educational theater, a former social studies educator, a humanities coordinator at an urban middle school, and two experienced social studies teachers, Roger and Helen. The size and diversity of the group meant that our discussions included voices from middle school to graduate school. Throughout the project, group members remained cognizant of the differing demands of teaching at each level and allowed the teachers' concerns to guide the planning process.

Both Roger and Helen taught in challenging environments, yet they remained dedicated to improving the quality of their teaching. Roger taught at a large urban magnet high school with a traditional academic curriculum and a fairly diverse student population. The student body, roughly half of whom qualified for free or reduced lunch, was 45 percent Latino, 25 percent black, 15 percent white, and 15 percent Asian. Despite being in a magnet school, Roger's required, regular-level U.S. history class faced many of the challenges endemic to urban schools, including low attendance rates and low student motivation. On a typical day, one-quarter of his afternoon class of roughly thirty students would be absent, meaning that a significant portion of class time was spent on catching up those students who missed previous lessons. A reflective educator and a dedicated intellectual, Roger nevertheless admitted that he felt enormous pressure from school administrators to "teach to the test," and that he spent more time on test prep and rote learning than he would have liked.

Helen was a middle school teacher at a large urban middle school that looked typical both for the neighborhood in which it was located and for the city as a whole. Over 90 percent of the school's roughly five hundred students were black or Latino, and approximately 75 percent qualified for free or reduced lunch. Helen's social studies class of twenty-eight students consisted entirely of black and Latino students in an overcrowded, older-looking school building. Consistently cheerful and demanding of her students, Helen admitted that her two largest daily concerns were classroom management and the low reading skills of some of her students. Although her social studies curriculum was quite traditional, there was considerable pressure for her to incorporate reading practice into daily lessons, meaning that she often had less time for teaching social studies content.

Whereas Oakes's research provided important historical considerations for the project, the group itself came together already having a variety of experiences teaching the antebellum period. Some members of the group had been involved in designing a lesson on the Constitution and slavery and wanted this project to build on that previous work (see Rodriguez, 2008). In that lesson, middle school students read excerpts from the Constitution and from Frederick Douglass and then participated in a debate as to whether or not the Constitution was a pro-slavery document. After the debate, students wrote letters to Frederick Douglass, arguing with him about his changing position. Parts of this lesson were interesting to the group, and we agreed to build them into the current project.

Both Roger and Helen had extensive experience teaching about this time period and the Constitution, and they hoped that this lesson might activate students' prior learning in their classes. Parts of Douglass's autobiography were already included in Helen's curriculum, and she had spent several weeks on the Constitution at the beginning of the school year. Roger made the Constitution a major theme in his class, revisiting the document at various points in his survey of American history. Whereas Helen's middle school students' experience with the Constitution involved reading paraphrased excerpts from their textbook and other curricular materials, Roger's students had actually read and analyzed the entire document earlier in the year. Both Roger and Helen wanted the lesson we developed to provide explicit linkages to what they had already taught.

The Middle and High School Lessons

These experiences and the themes discussed by Oakes provided the basis for the preliminary group discussions and lesson planning. As a group, we decided that we wanted to challenge students to analyze the role the Constitution has played in the great political questions of the past—in this case, the abolitionist movement and emancipation. We felt that exposing students to debate over the Constitution would help them see that it was and still is a product of compromise and political necessity. In short, we wanted students to see that the Constitution is a living document. At the same time, the group agreed with Oakes regarding the simplistic nature of traditional narratives of emancipation and wanted students to understand that emancipation was a long process motivated by more than mere righteousness. Too often, students assume that events in the past happened because historical actors wanted them to happen that way. In other words, students ascribe clarity of purpose and intentionality to people in the past when, in fact, these people were often unsure about their decisions. We wanted students to understand that people of the past, even the great historical figures, often struggled to make decisions and, being human, changed their views on issues from time to time.

The group found the biography of Frederick Douglass and his changing views during the antebellum period to be a particularly compelling and useful way to personalize both the debate within the abolitionist movement and the internal conflicts that historical actors can have. Given the fact that Douglass was such a prolific writer and speaker, we wanted students to see his change of heart in his own words. Yet Douglass was also the spokesman for a larger movement, so it was equally important for students to understand how his changing views brought a new perspective—and controversy—to the abolitionist cause. Indeed, Douglass's change of heart caused a rift with his mentor, Garrison, who saw Douglass's newfound willingness to engage the Constitution as a sign of weakness. The group wanted students to ponder whether changing his mind truly was a sign of weakness, and the ways in which it could be considered a sign of strength. This question seemed particularly salient in the contemporary political context, in which ideological clarity and certainty are often contrasted with indecision and "flip-flopping."

In creating a framework for a lesson on these issues, the group decided on three essential questions: How were interpretations of the Constitution used to defend or refute positions on important historical issues, such as slavery? How and why have historical figures like Frederick Douglass changed their minds? And does the fact that Douglass changed his mind make him weak or strong?

Having decided on these essential questions, the group turned to articulating its goals for the lesson. The group found the research conducted by Oakes to be interesting and useful because he developed his own interpretation from an extensive, yet often contradictory, primary source record. This lesson offered students an opportunity to be historians in the same manner as Oakes. We wanted students to read historical documents and unpack their meanings as well as evaluate the readings of those documents by others. For example, both Garrison and the later Douglass used the same language from the Constitution to make their arguments, but they developed very different interpretations of their meanings. Exposing students to these multiple perspectives would provide some confusion about "who was right," and would require them to piece together an answer for themselves. In doing so, students would be articulating their own historical interpretation of the Constitution as it applied to slavery before the Civil War and defending it using documentary evidence.

When the group turned to the planning of the lesson, it immediately became clear that the differences between Roger's and Helen's teaching situations and student skill levels would require significant modifications to any lesson we developed. Helen's middle school students had less experience working with primary sources, and their lower reading level meant that they needed shorter primary sources. Helen's approach to historical interpretation and debate was therefore more teacher directed and structured. Roger, on the other hand, was able to incorporate more nuanced and complex sources in his high school class. Whereas Roger felt comfortable leading his students in an abstract analysis of the Constitution before discussing Douglass, Helen thought that opening with the biography of Douglass was more appropriate given the age of her students. At the heart of both lessons, however, was a debate as to whether or not the Constitution was designed to legitimate, preserve, and expand the institution of slavery and an exploration of the changing views of Frederick Douglass.

Helen began her one-week lesson by asking her students to write in their journals an answer to the question: Does admitting you are wrong make you weak or strong? She led students through a discussion of examples from the student's own lives in which they had changed their minds. Many students referred to pressure from peers and parents and were quite willing to share the consequences of their own changes of heart. Students then read a short biography of Douglass, noting the events that shaped his life and his major accomplishments, and discussed Douglass's importance to the abolitionist movement. After discussing Douglass, students reviewed paraphrased excerpts from the Constitution with implications for slavery, including the Preamble, the "three-fifths" clause, the "fugitive slave clause," and clauses on domestic insurrections and the slave trade. The class discussed each clause of the Constitution and decided whether each excerpt was an argument for or against slavery. After they reached consensus, Helen taped poster-size versions of the clauses to the wall under signs reading "Pro-Slavery" and "Anti-Slavery." Helen then handed the students excerpts from two works by Douglass, his "Farewell Speech to the British People" from 1847 and an 1860 speech in Glasgow, Scotland. Some of these excerpts argue that the Constitution is pro-slavery, and other, later, ones argue that it supports emancipation. Helen asked students to evaluate the arguments presented in these documents, without revealing that they all came from Douglass. After students had interpreted all the documents, Helen revealed the author to the students and asked them to explain his change of heart, particularly in light of their opening journal entries. The culminating lesson was a town-hall format at which students responded to Garrison's famous burning of the Constitution. Helen asked students to take a stand as to whether or not Garrison was justified, using their own words and the words of Douglass. Following the town hall, students wrote a final journal entry in which they discussed how their experience helped them understand the rift between the Douglass of 1847 and the Douglass of 1860.

Roger's one-week lesson proceeded quite differently. Instead of starting the lesson with a discussion of Douglass, Roger began by analyzing the Constitution with his students. He informed them that the Constitution was a source of disagreement before the Civil War, but also pointed out that the word "slavery" does not appear anywhere in the document. Giving the students a copy of the Constitution as it looked before the Civil War, Roger asked groups of students to find clauses up to and including the 10th Amendment that might relate to slavery or its abolition. After reviewing each group's findings with the whole class, Roger handed out a copy of Douglass's "Farewell Speech to the British People," also hiding the author's name. Two students took turns reading the speech aloud for the class, while the rest of the class played the role of the crowd and reacted in the manner recorded in the document. Students diagrammed the main arguments of the speech and discussed the ways in which they supported or challenged their interpretations of the Constitution. Roger then introduced students to two other Douglass documents, his 1850 "Oath to Support the Constitution" and his 1860 Glasgow speech, although he withheld Douglass's name in both cases. After students made sense of these documents, Roger revealed that Douglass authored all of them. A discussion of Douglass's life and possible motivations for changing his mind followed. The final lesson was to be a debate in which students, acting as Douglass, addressed Garrison upon his burning of the Constitution. This lesson never materialized, however, on account of low student attendance, and Roger opted instead to have students write their own interpretation of the Constitution, making specific references to the document and writing in the same argumentative form as Douglass.

Impressions of the Lessons

In reflecting on the lessons after they were taught, the group agreed that in both cases the lessons deepened students' understandings of the role of the Constitution in the abolitionist movement and of Frederick Douglass. The teachers' choices of entry points for the lesson, however, affected whether students saw this as a lesson about Douglass or about the Constitution. Roger credited the direct engagement with the text of the Constitution for the success of his lesson. He stated that his students developed a much broader understanding of the document and used those understandings to create various arguments about whether or not slavery was constitutional. On the other hand, Helen's students came to understand the abolition movement because of the engaging story of Douglass. Helen noted that the students were drawn to the biography and the intellectual problem of what made him eventually change his mind. Roger was gratified to see students make connections to earlier points in American history, such as the slave trade and the Constitutional Convention, and challenge the wisdom of historical actors, including the Founding Fathers. Helen's effective use of journaling allowed her students to make more personal connections. The question of whether changing one's mind makes him or her weaker or stronger was not merely a useful "hook" to the lesson; it made students more willing to question Douglass and more deliberate in developing their own interpretations.

Observation by group members revealed that, for the most part, the lessons were effective. Both classroom teachers provided the students with the proper background knowledge needed to make the activity successful and employed scaffolding effectively when students worked with the primary sources. Reading aids were especially helpful for Helen's students, who struggled with the reading level of documents at times. Yet the tone of each class and the approach taken by the teacher varied. In Helen's class, there was a lot of purposeful clamor in the room as students engaged in the activity. There were vigorous conversations amongst the students, but there were very few disruptions or off-task behaviors, a remarkable feat for a middle school class. Furthermore, Helen had placed several large sheets of poster paper on the wall where students could write explanations or interpretations as they developed, allowing students to engage each other's written commentary. By the end of the lesson, the walls were covered with student thoughts, reflections, and analyses.

Roger's approach to primary source analysis, on the other hand, combined individual inquiry, cooperative learning, and whole-class discussion. For instance, Roger placed students in groups to engage individual clauses in the Constitution, much as the Founding Fathers did during the drafting of the document. These groups discussed, interpreted, and argued over every word of the text. Then, when reading the speeches of Frederick Douglass, Roger tried to recreate a public meeting as best he could, encouraging audience participation and dramatic readings. Despite their different pedagogical approaches, the teachers in both classes were clearly able to engage their students in the debate over the Constitution.

Student work revealed the value of having students develop their own interpretations on a complex historical issue. Roger stated that, regardless of whether they felt the Constitution was pro-slavery, anti-slavery, or a little of both, his students were able to cite specific instances in the Constitution to bolster their argument. He was quite pleased with the level of sophistication of the results as some students were able to take their argument far beyond the documents they read. For example, one student in particular argued that the Constitution supported slavery because the requirements for citizenship and for holding public office effectively barred slaves from participation. Another student disagreed with Douglass that the slavery question could be resolved by legislation alone by pointing out the depths of the institution's economic and social roots. Helen's students tended to rely more heavily on Douglass, often restating his points rather than developing their own. Yet in doing so, these students were forced to make sense of Douglass's contradictory interpretations and explain why the Douglass they chose to support was the right one. Some students went so far as to explain Douglass's own contradictions as a political necessity: Douglas realized that the Constitution was the abolitionist movement's only hope for a peaceful solution to slavery. By focusing on the Constitution itself or the words of Douglass, it was clear that the students were able to internalize and comprehend the various viewpoints of abolitionists.

Both teachers made the decision to hold back Douglass's name from the documents they gave students until later in their class. Both believed that doing so helped the students understand the complexity of the arguments being made and contradictions within the Constitution itself without distracting students with details of the author. Roger indicated that it helped students explore further the idea of interpretation and promoted the notion that there is rarely one "right" answer on important historical issues. Helen purposefully wanted her students to begin to "take sides" on the issue before returning to Frederick Douglass. Learning that Douglass had written each of the documents then caused students to question their own perspectives and, perhaps, change their minds as Douglass did. Indeed, a few students felt genuine anger toward Douglass for one of his arguments or at his apparent weakness in changing his mind. Both teachers felt that this twist added a useful element of cognitive dissonance.

The culminating lesson for both teachers, the public debate involving Garrison and the burning of the Constitution, did not proceed as smoothly as the rest of the lesson. Helen's town-hall meeting never reached a level of formal debate, as many students simply articulated their positions to the class but did not engage each other. Furthermore, the group hoped that the image of Garrison burning the Constitution would incite strong feelings in students, yet it did not, mainly because the relationship between Garrison and Douglass went largely unexplored. As result, most of the students in Helen's class did not take on the role of Douglass, nor did they address Garrison at all. Attendance issues meant that students in Roger's class were often at different places in the lesson, making conversation between students difficult. Roger was also forced to consistently review and repeat material to get the class on the same page. Roger felt that the debate would have been doomed to failure because the students never had a consistent period of time to explore the issue. Instead, he asked the students to reflect individually on the issue given the sources and their experiences in class. Although he was trying not to punish students for gaps in their knowledge due to absence, he also missed an opportunity to simulate the controversy and compromise that he wanted students to see in the Constitution and the abolitionist movement.

In reflecting on the lessons, the group agreed that the debate activity could have been framed within a dramatic context in which the debate transpired between students playing specific roles. If this had happened, the students could have gone even further, or deeper, into the controversy, combining their developing knowledge of the Constitution with their personal reactions to

Frederick Douglass to create a powerful and memorable drama. Indeed, the classroom teachers never attempted to utilize role work in the lessons. Specifically, the burning of the Constitution and the relationship between Garrison and Douglass, two tremendous opportunities for drama in the classroom, went largely unexplored. Many of Helen's students exhibited an emotional attachment to Douglass after reading his autobiography; these feelings could have been explored as well. Roger and Helen indicated that they would have liked to incorporate more drama into the lesson, especially in terms of role development, yet both had little experience and expressed unease with educational theater pedagogies.

The University Lesson

With these concerns in mind, the group decided to design and implement a new drama-infused lesson around the same themes as the previous lessons. This lesson was taught by two university-level educators and involved twenty-three undergraduate students, all of whom were taking a U.S. history curriculum class designed for those pursuing a major in social studies education. This two-hour lesson included a brief summary discussion on the uses of educational theater in the classroom. Although the lesson still maintained the goals of understanding Frederick Douglass and the role of the Constitution in the abolitionist movement, we wanted the lesson to have an explicit drama focus.

The group discovered that these college students had already read much of the recent scholarship on the Constitution's role in promoting or challenging slavery prior to the Civil War. This allowed the group to avoid re-planning and re-teaching the more successful parts of Roger's and Helen's lessons—the activities involving the analysis of the Constitution itself—and instead enabled the instructors to focus on the meaning of these interpretations of the Constitution to the abolitionist movement. As a result, the group decided that the new objective would be to have students explore the changes in the abolitionist movement through the changing relationship between Douglass and Garrison. The anti-Constitutionalist Garrison began as a mentor to Douglass and convinced Douglass to speak to the general public and contribute to *The Liberator*. Eventually Douglass (1845/1997) wrote an autobiography of his experiences as a runaway slave, for which Garrison wrote a glowing preface. During a time in Europe on speaking tours and promoting his book, Douglass began to reconsider his perception of the Constitution, and soon he changed his views, advocating an interpretation of the Constitution as an anti-slavery document. Although the reasons are not entirely clear, it was at this point that Garrison and Douglass drifted apart, causing a rift in the abolitionist movement (Ripley, 1985). To help students with this background knowledge, they read, in advance of the lesson, short excerpts about Douglass and Garrison (Cohen, 2008; Ripley, 1985) as well as Garrison's preface to the Douglass autobiography (1845/1997).

The way the Douglass–Garrison relationship changed over time is striking and well suited to creating a scene that taps into emotions to which students can relate. An exploration of their relationship undoubtedly must include an exploration of friendship, mentorship, trust, betrayal, mistrust, and anger—all elements that make for good drama. At the same time, this relationship parallels the question of whether or not the Constitution protects slavery, for the debate on this issue was central to their relationship. Although their professional relationship is well documented, there is not much written in the primary source record about their personal relationship (Ripley, 1985). This lack of detail provides a kind of freedom for students to imagine what it could have been like, without feeling obligated to include all the known facts. Thus, the group decided that the core of the lesson would have students creating and writing a dramatic scene between Douglass and Garrison.

The lesson began with several short drama-based activities that required students to physically translate the Preamble of the Constitution into bodily movement. Students paired up, and each couple was instructed to examine the Preamble and decide on three words that had significant meaning for both of them. They circled these words and practiced striking a pose for each word. They were told that movement could be added to this pose if desired and that the word could be represented through literal or more abstract physical expression. One half of the class was asked to observe the other half of the class perform these physical movements, and then the groups switched so that all participants were able to see and perform the movements. The end result was the performance of a movement piece that had purpose and meaning for participants as they were able to express kinesthetically elements of the Preamble that had meaning for them. Another activity explored the words and sound of words in the Preamble. Standing in a circle, students were given a slip a paper with a short excerpt from the Preamble written on it. The instructor stood in the middle and instructed the participants to simply say their line loudly and with clarity when he pointed at them. The instructor proceeded to point randomly to students, sometimes quickly, and at other times slowly and repeatedly. The end result gave the effect of a poetic and choral reading of the Preamble, with the Preamble being "performed" out of order from the way in which it is written, sometimes staggering the phrases and other times repeating a single phrase over and over again.

The physical activity was used by the drama teacher to enhance students' sensory awareness and promote group cohesiveness as they moved into the role work to follow. More importantly, these techniques were intended to serve as physical metaphors for exploring ideas. Dewey (1934) placed art in the realm of experience rather than product and, in this view, learning is emphasized by activities in which young people interact with their environment. It was also important, Dewey believed, to integrate the mind with physical activity in learning. Dewey (1928) said "the question of integration of mind–body in action is the most practical of all questions we can ask of our civilization" and urged: "We need to distinguish between action that is routine and action that is alive with purpose and desire" (p. 36). At the same time, arts-based experiences involve discovery and promote unique, personal responses in learners, as opposed to fixed objectives and right or wrong answers (Eisner, 1998; Gardner, 1973). The intention of these activities was to explore the Preamble in a different way from reading it off the page or hearing someone else recite it. The first activity focused on physicalizing the word, and the emphasis with the choral reading of the Preamble was to explore the sound and meaning of the words. When these activities were finished, the students were ready to proceed more deeply into the lesson content to follow.

Just prior to the start of class, as some students were entering the classroom and others were chatting at their desks, the drama teacher identified two students, approached them, and asked if they would each be willing to read a piece of historical writing aloud and "with feeling." When two students affirmed that they would be willing to read the documents, the drama teacher gave one student a speech by Frederick Douglass. This speech, delivered in Glasgow, Scotland, on March 26, 1860, begins with Douglass quoting the Preamble in order to discuss the ways in which the Constitution is a an anti-slavery document. The second student was given a copy of a letter written by William Lloyd Garrison. This letter, written in January 1850 to Samuel J. May, emphasizes how Garrison felt the Constitution was a pro-slavery document, calling it "a covenant of death and an agreement with hell." After the preamble activity the two students read their speeches aloud as everyone in class appeared to listen closely.

Following a short lecture and discussion on the readings, students were paired up again and told to improvise a scene in which Douglass has decided to publish his own paper and meets with Garrison to tell him. The students were given a time limit of three minutes, and they were instructed to talk the entire time in role, with one of the pair playing Garrison, and the other Douglass. After this short improvisation, the drama intructor told each pair to discuss what each felt was the most interesting or illuminating ten to thirty seconds of the scene they had improvised. The students took a few minutes to make the decision, and soon the sharing of the improvisations began. Each pair performed their scene, and students discussed the themes that emerged in the shared scenes. Most student responses focused on the emotional consequences of Douglass's news, although some discussed the ideological differences between Garrison and Douglass. Student portrayals of Garrison showed him feeling hurt, betrayed, and worried about the future of the movement. Portrayals of Douglass showed him confident in himself and willing to set out on his own.

After hearing and discussing all the scenes and their themes, students were told that they would be working individually to write their own scene. The group thought it a good idea to have all of the students start their scenes at the same place, so the instructors asked students to imagine the point at which Douglass returned from Europe and was confronted by Garrison about his change of views about the Constitution and his decision to start his own newspaper. A first line was provided: "Garrison: Welcome back, Douglass. It's good to see you again. We have a lot to talk about." The students continued writing their scenes from this first line. After spending five to ten minutes composing their dialogues individually, the students paired up again and read each other's scenes, with one student playing Douglass and the other Garrison. Volunteers shared their scenes, acting them out for the others, providing further ideas for the direction of each student's scenes in the sharing. For instance, one pair's scene focused on the personal ambition of Douglass and the resulting jealousy of Garrison. Many students were unhappy with this interpretation, because they felt it was too limiting, and suggested changes to the dialogue. At the same time, however, another pair's portrayal made the relationship of Douglass and Garrison too business-like, and the class reacted by saying they wanted to see more emotion from the characters. The class agreed that the best scene was one in which Garrison was cordial, yet patronizing, toward Douglass, and that Douglass, in turn, was upset by this lack of support. This scene worked best because its emotional aspects lay "below the surface," and students could imagine themselves acting the very same way.

The students' written scenes, although brief, expressed a deep understanding of the relation-ship between Garrison and Douglass and how their split caused emotional and ideological strain on both men. Some students' scenes even mentioned the effect that this split would have on the movement as a whole, with Douglass arguing that his high profile would be beneficial and Garrison worrying about maintaining the ideological clarity of the cause. Although some of the students began to discuss the Constitution as a possible source of conflict, many scenes were cut short before such substantive conversations could flourish. This fact did not go unnoticed by students, who wondered aloud what role the Constitution played in the rift between Garrison and Douglass. Some concluded that perhaps it was not as important as they had previously thought, whereas others believed that its conspicuous absence from the dialogue signaled that it was "the elephant in the room" that neither man wished to discuss. Perhaps most telling of all, though, is the fact that none of the scenes ended in a clear resolution.

Despite their limited experience with drama activities, most students in the class responded enthusiastically and with an appropriate mixture of seriousness and humor. By keeping the scenes very short and pre-rehearsed, a pair who might have been reluctant to perform was not required to do it for very long, and the stakes involved were much lower. While it is undoubtedly scary for many students to act, the teachers wanted to see the students take risks in the drama work, for submitting to the drama experience is "one of the conditions of creativity" (O'Neill, 1995, p. 63).

However, this structure did not require students to be clever at improvisation or act for a long stretch of time, and as students remained sitting in their chairs, it was not necessary to stand up and formally "stage" the scene. Despite the informality of the presentations, students were fully at attention, and encouraged each other to perform. For most students, it was a fun, if a little disconcerting, way to explore the relationship between two prominent figures of the abolitionist movement.

In the reflective discussion that followed the lesson, some students voiced their concern that doing drama might lead to chaos in the classroom as it is often difficult to control young people's excitement with the work. Most agreed, however, that if their students were trained to do drama throughout the year, they would learn to make it part of the class routine and would take it more seriously. For the prospective teachers in the class, using drama involved a certain level of fear of violating what Dorothy Heathcote (in Wagner, 1976) has called a threshold of implicit tolerance. They were concerned not only about the lack of control and the comfort level of their students, but also about their own comfort level using such strategies. Students also remarked that the teacher's leadership and commitment to such activities cannot be understated, and that educational theater activities require sustained effort. Nevertheless, in spite of these challenges, more than half of the students indicated that they would give educational theater strategies a try in their future classrooms. In this case, students felt that they learned a great deal about the abolitionist movement, and that it broke up the monotony of the typical college survey course. They felt that these advantages of using drama were worth the effort it takes to make such lessons successful.

Concluding Thoughts

In the end, these dramatic aspects would have been a great addition to the lessons taught by the middle and high school teachers. Although the scene-writing lesson was by no means perfect, it did give the group an opportunity to explore how character development and dramatic performance can add complexity and depth to historical inquiry. We also saw how educational theater activities could personalize the lives of great people in history and make historical documents come alive for students. Moreover, the lesson with undergraduate students demonstrated to the group that drama activities need not be large productions—in fact, the longest activity conducted lasted for just over ten minutes. That said, the group learned that incorporating drama lessons into history requires a clear purpose and dedication on the part of teachers.

Yet such work would not have been possible without a foundation in the skills of close textual analysis and historical interpretation that Roger and Helen developed in their students. Many teachers claim to incorporate primary sources into their teaching, but few do so with such purpose and sophistication as these two teachers. Helen's students were forced to make sense of conflicting sources to understand how and why Douglass changed his mind on arguably the most important issue of his life. Roger's students went a step further, developing their own interpretations of the sources and the Constitution. In essence, his students were following in the methodological footsteps of Oakes. Furthermore, most teachers cringe at the idea of teaching a lesson involving the Constitution outside its required place in their curriculum. Yet both teachers immediately recognized the opportunities for activating students' prior knowledge and the ways in which a revisiting of the document could help students understand the causes of the Civil War. Their use of the Constitution in such a way provides an effective model for incorporating legal analyses into instruction in any number of political crises, from Supreme Court decisions to Civil Rights disputes.

The gathering of all levels of history teachers dedicated to the same purpose was the most valuable aspect of this project. The historical and educational scholarship was useful to the group in planning the lessons, and having an American historian at every meeting added another intellectual level to our discussions. Teachers were able to see two historians in dialogue, and used this as the model for their students' historical inquiries. Yet the main challenge of the group was for university educators to make their research relevant to the middle and high school teachers. Our work demonstrates that this can be difficult given the constraints placed on those who teach history in middle and secondary schools. The lessons we developed involved significant effort on the part of teachers as well as a willingness to take risks in their teaching. Although the lessons did not turn out as planned, this project created the conditions for such experimentation.

Works Cited

Barton, K. & Levstik, L. (2004). *Teaching History for the Common Good*. Mahwah, NJ: Lawrence Erlbaum Associates.

Bonner, T. N. (1968). Civil War Historians and the "Needless War" Doctrine. In Gatell, F.O. & Weinstein, A. (eds.), *American Themes: Essays in Historiography*. New York: Oxford University Press.

Cohen, R. (2008). Was the Constitution Pro-Slavery? The Changing View of Frederick Douglass. *Social Education, 72*(5), 246–250.

Dewey, J. (1928). Preoccupation with the Disconnected. In Dewey, J. *Body and Mind*. New York: Bulletin of the New York Academy of Medicine. Accessed online at <http:www.alexandercenter.com/jd/johndewey-disconnect.html> on September 12, 2006.

Dewey, J. (1934). *Art as Experience*. New York: Capricorn Books.

Douglass, F. (1845/1997). *Narrative of the Life of Frederick Douglass, An American Slave, Written by Himself*. Andrews, W. & McFeely, W. (eds.). New York: W. W. Norton.

Eisner, E. (1998). Does Experience in the Arts Boost Academic Achievement? *Art Education, 51*(1), pp. 7–15.

Foner, E. (1980). *Politics and Ideology in the Age of the Civil War*. Oxford: Oxford University Press.

Gardner, H. (1973). *Arts and Human Development*. New York: John Wiley.

Grob, G. N. & Billias, G. A. (1992). The Civil War: Repressible or Irrepressible? In Grob, G. N. & Billias, G. A. (eds.), *Interpretations of American History: Patterns and Perspectives*. New York: Free Press.

Lee, P. & Ashby, R. (2000). Progression in Historical Understanding among Students Ages 7–14. In Stearns, P., Seixas, P., & Wineburg, S. (eds.), *Knowing, Teaching and Learning History*. New York: New York University Press.

Oakes, J. (2007). *The Radical and the Republican: Frederick Douglass, Abraham Lincoln, and the Triumph of Antislavery Politics*. New York: W. W. Norton.

Oakes, J. (2008). Frederick Douglass Changed My Mind About the Constitution. *Social Education, 72*(5), 251–252.

O'Neill, C. (1995). *Drama Worlds: A Framework for Process Drama*. Portsmouth, NH: Heinemann.

Ripley, P. (1985). The Autobiographical Writings of Frederick Douglass. *Southern Studies, 24*(1), 5–29.

Rodriguez, V. (2008). Frederick Douglass, the Constitution, and Slavery: A Classroom Debate. *Middle Level Learning, 33*(September), 2–13.

Wagner, B. J. (1976). *Dorothy Heathcote: Drama as a Learning Medium*. Washington, DC: National Education Association.

Wineburg, S. (2001). *Historical Thinking and Other Unnatural Acts: Charting the Future of Teaching the Past*. Philadelphia, PA: Temple University Press.

CHAPTER RESOURCES

I. Lesson Framework: The Constitution and the Abolitionist Movement

Intended Learning Outcomes (Use NYS SS Standards)

Understandings (Big Ideas):

- Students will understand that the Constitution is often ambiguous on major political questions.
- Students will understand that American democracy is an imperfect process of compromise and change.
- Students will understand that the emancipation of slaves involved intense debate and pragmatic compromises, and did not happen simply because of righteousness.

Essential Questions:

- Prior to the Civil War, was the Constitution a pro-slavery or anti-slavery document? How were both interpretations used in the abolitionist movement before and during the antebellum period?
- How could it be possible (and sensible) that Frederick Douglass changed his mind about the Constitution? What was the impact of this decision?

Content Knowledge:

- Students will know the backgrounds and beliefs of two major figures of the abolitionist movement, Douglass and Garrison.
- Students will know the key clauses in the Constitution that caused debate prior to the Civil War.
- Students will know the political and ideological causes of the Civil War.

Skills:

- Students will take on roles and demonstrate multiple perspectives on the issue of slavery.
- Students will read and analyze the meanings of historical documents (i.e. the Constitution) and evaluate the readings of those documents by others (Frederick Douglass, Garrison).
- Students will develop and articulate their own historical interpretation of the Constitution as it applied to slavery to before the Civil War.

Vocabulary/Important Concepts:

- Constitution-specific vocabulary such as Three-fifths clause, Fugitive Slave Act, and Domestic insurrection

Learning Experiences:

- Primary source analysis involving the Constitution. Students in groups find clauses relating to slavery or its abolition, and share their findings with the whole class.
- Historical reenactment of Douglass's "Farewell Speech to the British People," in which students take turns reading the speech aloud for the class.

Resources:

- The Constitution (with clauses dealing with slavery—"fugitive slave" clause, Preamble, three-fifths clause, etc.)
- Frederick Douglass, "Farewell Speech to the British People" (1847)
- Frederick Douglass, "Oath to Support the Constitution" (1850)
- Frederick Douglass, speech delivered in Glasgow, Scotland (1860)

Learning Experiences (continued):

- Students make sense of competing primary sources by diagramming the main arguments of three Douglass speeches and discussing the ways in which they support or challenge their own interpretations of the Constitution.
- Class discussion in which teacher reveals that Douglass authored all of the documents. A discussion of Douglass's life and possible motivations for changing his mind follows.
- Debate in which students, acting as Douglass, address Garrison upon his burning of the Constitution, making specific references to the document and writing in the same argumentative form as Douglass.

Resources (continued):

- Introductory biographical information on Frederick Douglass— excerpts from his autobiography and secondary sources as needed
- Scaffolds and reading guides for reading and interpreting the documents (as needed)

II. Relevant New York State and NAEP Standards

New York State Learning Standards, U.S. History

- Students explore the meaning of American culture by identifying the key ideas, beliefs, and patterns of behavior, and traditions that help define it and unite all Americans (MS.1A)
- Students interpret the ideas, values, and beliefs contained in the Declaration of Independence, the U.S. Constitution, Bill of Rights, and other important historical documents (MS.1B)
- Students describe the reasons for periodizing history in different ways (MS.2A)
- Students investigate key turning points in U.S. history and explain why these events or developments are significant (MS.2B)
- Students describe how ordinary people and famous historic figures in the United States have advanced the fundamental democratic values, beliefs, and traditions expressed in the Declaration of Independence, U.S. Constitution, the Bill of Rights, and other important historic documents (MS.3C)
- Students classify major developments into categories such as social, political, economic, geographic, technological, scientific, cultural, or religious (MS.3D)
- Students analyze the development of American culture, explaining how ideas, values, beliefs, and traditions have changed over time and how they unite all Americans (HS.1A)
- Students describe the evolution of American democratic values and beliefs as expressed in the Declaration of Independence, U.S. Constitution, Bill of Rights, and other important documents (HS.1B)
- Students develop and test hypotheses about important events, eras, or issues in U.S. history, setting clear and valid criteria for judging the importance and significance of these events, eras, or issues (HS.2B)

- Students research and analyze major themes and developments in U.S. history (HS.3B)
- Students prepare essays and oral reports about the important social, political, economic, scientific, technological, and cultural developments, issues, and events from U.S. history (HS.3C)

New York State Learning Standards, Historical Thinking

- Consider the sources of historic documents, narratives, or artifacts and evaluate their reliability (MS.4A)
- Understand how different experiences, beliefs, values, traditions, and motives cause individuals and groups to interpret historic events and issues from different perspectives (MS.4B)
- Compare and contrast different interpretations of key events and issues in United States history, and explain reasons for these different accounts (MS.4C)
- Describe historic events through the eyes of those who were there (MS.4D)
- Analyze historical narratives about key events in United States history to identify the facts and evaluate the authors' perspectives (HS.4A)
- Consider different historians' analyses of the same event or development in U.S. history to understand how different viewpoints and/or frames of reference influence historical interpretation (HS.4B)
- Evaluate the validity and credibility of historical interpretations of important events or issues in U.S. history, revising these interpretations as new information is learned and other interpretations are developed (HS.4C)

Adapted from *New York State Learning Standards, U.S. History* (1996)

NAEP Learning Standards, U.S. History

Framework 2: Periods of U.S. History

- What were the positions of the political parties and their leaders on political participation, individual rights, states' rights, slavery, and social reforms? What primary sources exemplify the key issues of this period? (4.1)
- What was the significance of the Lincoln–Douglass debates? (4.1)
- What role did the process of compromise play in the disputes about slavery, the nature of the Union, individual rights, states' rights, and the power of the federal government? What were Abraham Lincoln's positions on key issues during this period? (5.1)
- What caused the outbreak of Civil War? What were the roles of Webster, Clay, Calhoun, Douglass, Lincoln, and Seward? (5.1)
- How did the Civil War and Reconstruction change conceptions of the Union and the power of the federal government? What were the influences of Lincoln's presidency? (5.1)
- In what ways did the Civil War and Reconstruction challenge earlier ideas about ideas and alter relations between races, classes, and genders? (5.2)

NAEP Framework 3: Ways of Knowing and Thinking about U.S. History

1. HISTORICAL KNOWLEDGE AND PERSPECTIVE

Students should be able to:

- Name, recognize, list, identify, and give examples of people, places, events, concepts, and movements
- Place specifics in a chronological framework and construct and label historical periods
- Define historical themes and give examples of the ways themes relate to specific factual information
- Describe the past from the perspectives of various men and women of the time
- Explain the perspective of an author of a primary source document
- Describe different perspectives related to a historical issue or event
- Summarize the contributions of individuals and groups to U.S. history
- Summarize the meaning of historical sources and link these sources to general themes

2. HISTORICAL ANALYSIS AND INTERPRETATION

Students should be able to:

- Specify and explain cause-and-effect relationships and connect contemporary events to their origins in the past
- Categorize information and develop strategies for organizing a large body of facts
- Examine multiple causes of historical developments
- Explain points of view, biases, and value statements in historical sources
- Determine the significance of people, events, and historical sources
- Weigh and judge different views of the past as advanced by historical figures themselves, historians, and present-day commentators and public figures
- Demonstrate that the interpretation and meaning of the past are open to change as new information and perspectives emerge
- Develop sound generalizations and defend these generalizations with persuasive arguments
- Make comparisons and recognize the limitations of generalizations
- Apply knowledge, draw conclusions, and support those conclusions with convincing evidence

Adapted from National Assessment Governing Board (2006)

Works Cited

National Assessment Governing Board (2006). *U.S. History Framework for the 2006 National Assessment of Educational Progress*. Washington, DC: U.S. Department of Education.

New York State Learning Standards, U.S. History (1996). Albany: New York State Education Department.

Three
Immigration

Framing the Questions: An Interview with Hasia Diner, conducted by Rachel Mattson

Hasia Diner is the Paul and Sylvia Steinberg Professor of American Jewish History at New York University, with a joint appointment in the Department of History and the Skirball Department of Hebrew and Judaic Studies, and is the Director of the Goldstein Goren Center for American Jewish History. She received her PhD in History at the University of Illinois-Chicago, and has been the recipient of many awards and distinctions, including a Fulbright Professorship at the University of Haifa in Israel and a Lilly Fellowship at the Mary I. Bunting Institute at Radcliffe College. A specialist in immigration and ethnic history, American Jewish history, and the history of American women, she is the author of numerous published books, including *In the Almost Promised Land: American Jews and Blacks, 1915–1935* (1977, reissued 1995); *Erin's Daughters in America: Irish Immigrant Women in the Nineteenth Century* (1984); *Hungering for America: Italian, Irish, and Jewish Foodways in the Age of Migration* (Harvard University Press); a new critical edition of the 1890 classic, *How the Other Half Lives,* by the reformer Jacob Riis (W. W. Norton, 2008); and *We Remember with Reverence and Love: American Jews and the Myth of Science after the Holocaust, 1945–1962* (2009).

Hasia Diner: The field that I would say I work in most closely or most intensively is American social history. I'm interested in the relationships between different groups of Americans and how their experiences were specific both to who they were and to where they came from, but at the same time how their experiences touched the experiences of other Americans. I think the idea of calling it social history represents how these different experiences represent the kind of fabric of American society and how, you know, perhaps a little bit tritely, but to say like any fabric, all these strands have to be there together. Each one has an integrity. But the piece of fabric is itself the connectedness of these individual threads.

Rachel Mattson: *What would you say are the parameters of the field of social history? What's it defined by?*

HD: This field is defined firstly by what it isn't. It is not the study of policies and political decisions. It doesn't take as its focus changes in policy, changing legislation, court decisions, although there's obviously a very significant connection between them. It tries as much as possible to look at a group that never existed, called "ordinary people," and how they led their lives. Within the options they had, what did they choose? Where did they choose to live? How did they choose to organize their families? Where they had choice, what choices do they make? So it's about their lived experiences. But it's also how they saw themselves. How did they see themselves in relationship to other Americans? How did they see themselves in relationship to people not in America?

Social history became a force in the field of history in the 1960s. It's not surprising—there was a kind of common arch between the Civil Rights movement, the student struggle, anti-war movement, the women's movement, the rise of those movements and the fact that the academy or the historical profession began to seize on the idea of social history and the idea that ordinary people had agency, that they not only had the ability to change the circumstances of their existence but, when confronted with kind of their fate and their elites, they found multiple ways to resist. And that's when I sort of decided to become a historian. The fact that I grew up in a relatively poor home—I think that probably really affected me also in terms of thinking about the lives of ordinary people as historically significant.

RM: *What kinds of questions—about social history, about U.S. immigration history—do your students find most exciting?*

HD: I think they get particularly interested when you put [immigration history] in broad historic terms, in relationship to the migration the world is experiencing now. Politicians from both the Left and the Right have a stake in saying that our current era of immigration is utterly unlike anything that ever happened before. But in fact, that's not really true. At the turn of the twentieth century, in the 1890s, in 1900, anti-immigration forces also set up a paradigm that there had been an old immigration and new immigration. And, you know, the old was good, the new was bad. They too stood on as flimsy a ground as people now who say, "Oh, the post-1970 immigration, you know, is completely different." I think students really like to see the way in which each generation uses history to derive a political point.

RM: *Is there a primary document that you use to teach about the history of U.S. immigration that speaks to that point?*

HD: Well, I have an extremely enormous document. In 1911 Congress issued a forty-one-volume report—the Dillingham Commission Report [1907–1911] on immigration. The report includes volumes on immigration and crime, immigration and the economy, immigration and schooling, and so on. Forty of the forty-one volumes basically said, "We once had good immigrants. And they came from Northern and Western Europe. They were freedom-loving people who went off to farms and really wanted to become American. And they came with values that were so close American values. And those were the good old days. And we now have these truly inferior stock of people who come purely to make money. And they're going to go back. They can't understand the idea of liberty, individualism, freedom, which are inherent to American values. They're criminals. They don't send their children to school. You know, they congregate in dirty, disgusting cities. And, you know, they are bringing down the quality of American life." I mean, this is in forty of forty-one volumes. And each volume weighs a couple of pounds. The one dissenting volume was written by the anthropologist Franz Boaz, who said, "Actually they're not so different."

But the forty volumes of the Dillingham Commission Report took immigrants to task and imagined a pre-1880s migration, which was really (a) not accurate, but (b) didn't reflect the amount of venom that was spewed on the immigrants in 1850, 1860. [In those decades, native-born Americans] thought, "Oh, my God, these Germans are coming in. And they're drinking all the time. And they cluster in cities," and so on. And certainly the Irish have to be the most despised immigrant group that ever came to the United States, and they came primarily before the 1880s.

RM: *How do you read a document like the Dillingham Commission Report? What kinds of questions are you asking of it as you're reading it?*

HD: First, obviously it's the most simple level: What is it saying? You know, just bare bones, what does this document say? What's the question it's asking? And how is it organized? How does the flow move from page to page, chapter to chapter, page to page, paragraph to paragraph, and so on? What words are being used? What words keep repeating themselves? How does the author—and, by the way, who is the author?—try to make a case? How does the author try to go about the business of answering the question? What's the conclusion?

But at the next level it's: Why did the author ask that question? What assumption has the author brought? What are the value-loaded words? What are the adjectives? Let's get away from the nouns and the verbs. What are the adjectives that are being used here? And who was this person? It's not enough to know that it was a social scientist so-and-so. Let's go to that person's biography. Let's go to their other writings. What was their political position? Why was it that Franz Boaz wrote the dissenting volume, you know, whereas the others, you know, all converged on the same point? What was the author's stake in presenting the material the way he or she did? So from the simple what was in it, the next level is what was the position of the author, the author's motivation?

But then at another level it's: How was this document used? Who read it? Who paid for it? In this case it was the Senate that commissioned this. So what was going on that caused the Senate to commission this? How did they pick their authors? How was it reviewed? How was it received at the time? Was it reviewed in newspapers, magazines? Was it cited as justification for changes in policy or keeping policy in place?

RM: *One of the things we want to do is actually watch historians read primary documents. And I know you couldn't possibly have the forty-one volumes of the Dillingham Commission Report here. But I wonder if you have any document here that you think speaks to these questions we've been talking about that we could read and reflect on together.*

HD: Well, I am actually doing a critical edition right now of Jacob Riis's *How the Other Half Lives*, which was published in 1890. Riis was an immigrant to the United States from Denmark and eventually became a police reporter. And in conjunction with or as a result of his reporting for a number of New York newspapers and as a result of his own, I'd say, very deeply held Christian values, he wrote this book, which was originally serialized in a newspaper and called "How the Other Half Lives: An Exposé of Poverty in New York at the End of the 19th Century." Riis pioneered the use of flash photography to accompany his work.

So when I look at a document like *How the Other Half Lives*, first I want to know: How did Riis see the problem of poverty? For him, I can see, the "other half" are the poor and almost all immigrants—although he does pay some attention to New York's black population. So I want to know what does he mean by "the other half" and where does he locate them? The first thing I do, then, is just go to the table of contents to find out: How is the book organized? How does that give me a sense of what he cares about?

So in the table of contents, I see the very first chapter is "Genesis and the Tenement." That says to me that this is somebody who thinks housing is very important. He says right off the bat, the physical details of something is key to seeing the vicissitudes of poverty. And then he has another chapter called "Downtown Back Alleys." So, again, it's physical place. I say, okay, maybe it's really all about place. Other chapters include "A Raid on the Stale Beer Dives"—so again, place; "Sheep Launching Houses"—place; and "Pauperism in the Tenements." So he is somebody who places housing as really important. And, in fact, the book was used by housing reformers well into the 1960s as evidence about that.

But it's not just housing. Because then I look, and I see he has chapters called "The Italians of New York," "Chinatown," "Jews," "The Sweaters of Jewtown," "The Bohemians," "Tenement House Cigar Making," "The Color Line in New York." So obviously it's housing, but housing as it affected and was affected by the fact that there were millions of immigrants coming into the United States and an enormous percentage were staying in New York.

Then, let me read to you from one of the book's chapters, called "The Mixed Crowd":

> When once I asked the agent of a notorious fourth ward alley how many people might be living in it, I was told, "140 families, 100 Irish, 38 Italian, and 2 that spoke the German tongue." Barring the agent herself, there was not a native born individual in the court. The answer was characteristic of the cosmopolitan character of lower New York, very nearly so of the whole of it whenever it runs to alleys and courts. One may find for the asking an Italian, a German, a French, African, Spanish, Bohemian, Russian, Scandinavian, Jewish, and Chinese colony. Even the Arab who peddles "holy earth" from the Battery as a direct importation from Jerusalem has his exclusive preserves at the lower end of Washington Street. The one thing you shall vainly ask for in the chief city of America is a distinctively American community. There is none; certainly not among the tenements. Where have they gone to, the old inhabitants? I put the question to one who might fairly be presumed to be of the number, since I had found him sighing for the "good old days" when the legend "No Irish need apply" was familiar in the advertising columns in the newspapers. He looked at me with a puzzled air. "I do not know," he' said. "I wish I did. Some went to California in '49, some to the war and never came back. The rest I expect have gone to heaven or somewhere. I don't see them 'round here."
>
> (21)

I read this as first, Riis—who himself was an immigrant—indicating that the nature of American urban life in the nineteenth century was that it was full of change. This one paragraph went back to the days of the Irish migration and then moved forward. What did he call them? "A distinctively American community." He follows up by saying, in fact, the once unwelcome Irishman has been followed in his turn by the Italian, the Russian, Jew, and the Chinaman, and has himself taken a hand at opposition quite as bitter and quite as ineffectual against these later hordes. When the Irish came, they were at the bottom. Now they've moved up. These other successive waves have taken their place. And now the Irishman is as much an opponent of the new immigration as the Americans were of his immigration.

I want to understand what Jacob Riis is trying to get at in this book. And looking at the table of contents and bits of the chapters, I can conclude that he's asking: How do cities work? And what's the relationship between one wave of immigration and the next? And what are the commonalities? What are the differences?

Works Cited

The Dillingham Commission Reports (1907–1911), 61st Cong., 2nd and 3rd Sess.

Diner, H. (ed.) (2008). *How the Other Half Lives*, by Jacob Riis. New York: W. W. Norton & Co.

Essay: Teaching Immigration in a Nation of Immigrants

By Diana Turk, with Dwight Forquignon and Sarah Reiley

> Once I thought to write a history of the immigrants in America. Then I discovered that the immigrants were American history.
>
> (Handlin, 1951, p. 3)

American history is very much a story of immigration. From a time even before this land had the identity of a nation, its history has been characterized by the arrival of newcomers: people who came for many purposes, looking for many different outcomes; some arriving of their own volition, others arriving unwillingly, in chains. The topic of immigration within American history is so vast—so huge, so unwieldy—that often teachers gloss over its nuances. They share with their students the "facts" of immigration: the numbers of immigrants who arrived in the United States at particular points in its history, maybe, or the areas where different groups of arrivals settled. Sometimes they focus on particular immigrant groups: the Irish in the 1840s, for example, or Jewish immigrants from eastern and southern Europe in the 1890s.

Dr. Hasia Diner, like other historians of immigration, has suggested a different way of approaching the study of immigration. In her view, exploring the topic through the lens of social history provides a more useful entry to this vast topic than other approaches. Social history, Diner argues, "is not the study of policies and political decisions, although they're not irrelevant. It doesn't take as its focus changes in policy, changing legislation, court decisions, although there's obviously a very significant connection between them." Instead, social history "tries as much as possible to look at a group that never existed— called *ordinary people*—and . . . how they led their lives." According to Diner, by using this approach, teachers can prompt students to consider how the events outside of people's control framed and shaped the lives they lived. Questions that such an approach might generate, she suggested, include, "Within the options [people] had, what did they choose? How did people choose to live? Where did they choose to live? How did they choose to organize their families? Where they had choice, what choices did they make?" According to Diner, a social history approach to immigration would consider *lived experiences*, and in addition, would look at the sense that people made of those lived experiences. How did they see themselves in relationship to other Americans? How did they see themselves in relationship to people not in America?

As our group began the task of designing lessons on the experiences of late nineteenth- and early twentieth-century immigrants in the United States, Diner's social history approach to immigration proved enormously influential. We wanted a way of thinking about U.S. immigration that would inspire interest and lasting understanding on the part of middle- and secondary-level students. We also wanted an approach that would help students make sense of the sheer numbers of arrivals and enable them to learn their points of origin and where the immigrants ended up settling—but in addition, we wanted students to really see and understand the occupations and daily existences of some of the many millions of immigrants who arrived in America over a particular span of time. Given where all of the teachers were in their year-long curriculums and the vastness of the topic of immigration—which itself could take up an entire year or more of study within

American history—and then considering the emphasis placed on nineteenth-century immigration in most state and federal standards, we decided to focus our attention for these lessons on the late nineteenth century, and to focus largely on European immigration to the United States.

From the outset, our group hoped to create lessons that all members of our collective—which consisted of both middle- and secondary-level teachers as well as an historian and an education professor—could use and feel good about. Our goal was to create lessons that would be deep enough in historical content that they would enable students to pass the impending standardized tests, which would most certainly include questions on immigration. At the same time, we wanted to make our lessons personal in their focus and pedagogically innovative so that the students—attendees of urban middle or secondary public schools—would be inspired to really care about the material and engage with it in a way that might make them more sensitive to contemporary debates surrounding immigration in this country.

The interviews and meetings our group had with Diner provided us with a useful avenue into the topic. She suggested focusing our lessons around the writings and photographs of the reformer Jacob Riis, who wrote *How the Other Half Lives* (1890). Riis was a Danish immigrant to the United States who served as a Sunday school teacher in addition to working as a police reporter and commentator in New York City. Inspired by what Diner termed "deeply held Christian values" that compelled him to want to draw attention to the poverty he saw around him, Riis wrote *How the Other Half Lives*. In the book, which was originally serialized in a newspaper, Riis paired photographs he had taken of New York City tenements—photos that featured the at that time novel use of flash photography, and brought an intimate eye to his subjects—next to text describing his encounters with the inhabitants of these tenement areas. His work proved enormously compelling to many of his contemporaries who read it, and helped open their eyes to the poverty plaguing "the other half" during the later decades of the nineteenth century.

Diner proposed particular strategies for considering Riis's work and suggested that we use his book as an avenue into the wider topic of immigrant histories. She noted:

> So when I look at a document like *How the Other Half Lives*, first I want to know: how did [Riis] see the problem of poverty? For him, I can see, the "other half" are the poor and almost all immigrants—although he does pay some attention to New York's black population. So I want to know what does he mean by the "other half?" and where does he locate them?

Diner noted that the first chapter of Riis's book is entitled "Genesis and the Tenement." This suggests, she argued, "that [Riis was] somebody who thinks housing is very important. Because he says right off the bat, the physical details of something is key to seeing the vicissitudes of poverty." Working through the other chapters, Diner reminded us that physical place and space played an enormous role in Riis's understanding of tenement life. She argued, "So [Riis] is somebody who places housing as really important. And, in fact, the book was used by housing reformers well into the 1960s as evidence [of the need for urban housing reform]."

But, according to Diner, *How the Other Half Lives* addresses questions about not only housing,

> but housing as it affected and was affected by the fact that there were millions of European immigrants coming into the United States and an enormous percentage staying in New York . . . obviously his concern is not just the immigrants and the tenements, but the impact on their children, who will be the next generation of Americans.

Here, Diner pointed us toward questions about who and what was considered "American" during the time Riis was writing, referring us to his statement:

> The one thing you shall vainly ask for in the chief city of America is a distinctively American community. There is none; certainly not among the tenements. Where have they gone to, the old inhabitants? I put the question to one who might fairly be presumed to be of the number, since I had found him sighing for the "good old days" when the legend "no Irish need apply" was familiar in the advertising columns in the newspapers. He looked at me with a puzzled air. "I don't know," he said. "I wish I did. Some went to California in '49, some to the war and never came back. The rest, I expect, have gone to heaven or somewhere. I don't see them 'round here."
>
> (Diner, 2008, p. 21)

Diner reminded us that Jacob Riis was himself an immigrant who believed, in her words, that "the nature of American urban life in the nineteenth century is that it was full of change."

Diner thus pushed us to consider Riis's goals in the book, to see his questions as broader than simply the photographs he took and the individuals or even the groups of immigrants upon whom he focused, as he probed the larger issues of, as Diner framed them: "How do cities work? What is the relationship between one wave of immigration and the next? What are the commonalities? And what are the differences?"

Diner proposed that we use Riis's text and accompanying photographs both as a means of entering the topic of immigration and as a strategy that would help us move from personal stories out to broader questions about nationalization and urbanization. She also insisted on the importance of looking at a wide range of sources and interrogating those sources by asking key questions of them: What is the source saying? What questions is it asking? How is the document organized? How does its prose flow—through chapters, across pages, even within paragraphs? What words does the author use? What words does he or she repeat? What are the arguments? What are the sources? What are the conclusions?

But even beyond these important strategies, Diner advocated asking even more probing questions of primary historical sources and their authors: Who was the author and why did he or she ask the questions the source raises? What assumptions has the author brought to his or her work? What are the value-laden words—the adjectives and adverbs? As Diner argued, "it's not enough to know that [an author] was . . . social scientist so-and-so. Let's go to that person's biography. Let's go to their other writings. What was their political position?"

According to Diner, the really exciting part of doing history entails the "weaving in and out or zigzagging between looking at each group's experience as completely a story into itself . . . versus seeing that in some ways these are also basically variants on the same theme." Using primary sources, such as excerpts from Riis's text and, especially, the photographs he took of tenement residents at the turn of the twentieth century, can provide such a starting point. Then, stepping back and asking questions of the text and accompanying images can help bring students to larger questions and larger issues of context. This approach proved both useful and successful for us in framing the lessons we wrote. Indeed, and perhaps unsurprisingly, our lessons became as much about the process of doing social history as they became avenues for teaching the content of immigration.

The group that came together to work on this chapter consisted of the group leader, a social studies educator who is an historian by training, as well as one middle school humanities teacher and two secondary U.S. history teachers. Hasia Diner, the content expert whose arguments guided our thinking and planning, met with us on multiple occasions as we did our planning and processing and in general was available to us by email and through the liaison of our group leader. Ultimately, as a result of scheduling conflicts, only the secondary teachers, Frank and Megan, taught the lessons we planned. Still, the participating middle school teacher played an important role in the planning and conceptualization of the framing questions and in the choice of topics and themes around which we ended up centering our unit.

Dialogues between Historians and Teachers: Studying Immigration/ Teaching Immigration

Because of the topic's centrality in most U.S. history courses, all of the teachers in our group had a good level of familiarity with the topic, and all had taught about immigration before. We were thus eager to add Diner's materials to our own collection of sources and ideas about teaching immigration. Diner's suggestion to focus on the everyday—on the group she called "ordinary people"—made sense to all of us as a way of starting to frame and narrow the topic. Also, Diner's insistence on interrogating sources, on asking questions of them, and on probing for intention, authorial meaning, and context, gave richness to our lessons and an equal focus on process as on product of history.

In addition to learning a great deal from the transcript of the interview that had been conducted with Diner for this book project, we also benefited enormously from face-to-face discussions with her. In these sessions, we were able to ask follow-up questions and to wrestle with how to "translate" her arguments into planned and then lived curricula. Diner talked to us about the history of *How the Other Half Lives* and why the book received the notice it did at the time: how different it was from other contemporary takes on immigration, in that it took the position that the municipality had a responsibility to improve the lives of the poor. She shared the different ways the book has been received and used by historians and social thinkers throughout the last century: In earlier decades in the twentieth century, reviewers had lavished praise on Riis's arguments and concern about the poor, whereas by the 1970s and into the 1990s, the book was panned as racist, voyeuristic, and focused around staged photos, with a large emphasis on the negative experiences of immigrants, rather than their more complicated lived pasts. In a new edition of the book that she was editing and which she was finalizing for publication at the time of our conversations, Diner chose to view Riis's work as "both" and "all" of these things: in her words, to recognize the (racist) labels Riis used in his text, the staged nature of his photos, and the politics that undergirded his arguments, but at the same time to see the book for the role it played at the time of its publication—as a revolutionary call that galvanized people into action. We as a group determined that we would try to emulate Diner's approach in our lessons, to treat Riis's prose and photographs both as historical "evidence" of past events and experiences and also as pieces of consciously produced propaganda.

The question of who was and is American, which Diner raised in her interview, took on central focus in our discussions and in the lessons as we came to conceptualize them. As Diner noted, Riis's era featured much more constricted notions of what constitutes Americanness than those that are likely to exist today among most urban public school students. So for him, there was a strong need, perhaps, to shock the white middle class into recognizing the humanity of immigrants. This argument prompted deep discussions within our group as to whether the same "shock approach" could work—or was even needed—today: the extent to which on-the-surface multicultural, mixed-class environments of today's urban settings really meant an understanding of "how the other half lives." The teachers in our group were particularly excited about raising this issue with their students and thus eagerly sought ways to raise this question in the lessons.

Planning the Curriculum

As it came time to craft the lessons we would teach, the dual approach Diner advocated—to treat Riis's work both as text and as propaganda—proved a challenge to implement into the curriculum. The participating teachers themselves struggled with how much they wanted to use the topic of immigration and particularly Jacob Riis's work as a straightforward exploration of "experiences of immigrants" to discuss the "who is an American?" question and "how do our views of who is American change over time," as opposed to how much they wanted to access the topic by introducing the idea of propaganda and then bringing the use of photographs as tools of persuasion more to the forefront. Ultimately, we worked to develop lessons that would combine these two approaches—that is, using Riis's photos to discuss immigrants' experiences, but also providing instruction in critical analysis skills to allow students to "read" the photographs as tools created by and for specific purposes, to achieve highly political ends. Indeed, there was a tension at the center of the lessons as the teachers taught them, between reading sources, particularly photographs, as *evidence* of past experiences versus reading them as possible *tools of propaganda*. This tension ended up defining both the explicit teaching and learning that took place in the unit and the implicit messages the students seemed to absorb from the lessons.

Ultimately, the group chose the following as the essential questions for the mini-unit on immigration: "How have immigrants experienced life in this nation of immigrants? What rights does the United States, as a nation of immigrants, grant to its own immigrants?" Additionally, we asked, "What historical information can we draw from photographs and other primary sources? And what are the strengths and limitations of these sources?" Other questions focused around helping students make connections across time periods and groups. The teachers challenged their students to "compare and contrast immigrant experiences over place and time" and to "identify continuities and changes in 'the immigrant experience' across space and time in the United States."

To help students wrestle with these questions and develop deep and meaningful responses, the teachers chose a rich array of source material. In addition to the text and photographs from *How the Other Half Lives*, they selected archival materials from period newspapers about various groups of immigrants in the nineteenth century, as well as transcripts of interviews with immigrants who entered the United States through and were detained at Angel Island. One high school teacher used transcripts of interviews with contemporary immigrants to the United States from the Library of Congress's American Memory Collection, as well as the text of the Immigration Act of 1965. The other high school teacher drew upon excerpts from Upton Sinclair's (1906/2003) *The Jungle*, and timelines and other sources from the Ellis Island website.

To flesh out their lessons, the teachers also introduced secondary materials, in particular textbook chapters addressing nineteenth-century immigration as well as contemporary articles on immigration to the US. Both used Diner's introduction to her (2008) edited edition of Riis's *How the Other Half Lives*; one of the teachers also used the bibliography Diner prepared for the edition.

All members of our group were particularly excited by the notion of exploring physical space in Riis's work and in our study of immigrant experiences. As Diner reminded us, during Riis's era, unlike in later decades of the twentieth century and now in the twenty-first, the physical proximity of different classes was not great; rich and poor did not necessarily interact, which was part of the potency of what Riis did in showing the lives of the downtrodden to those who may not have seen such sights before. Today, especially in the urban neighborhoods where our teachers were teaching, the sense was that there is a greater closeness and familiarity among the classes but also an increasingly jaded and desensitized outlook toward the poor. The teachers in our group thus chose to address physical space explicitly; in addition to the Riis photos, they planned to use virtual tours and images from the New York City Tenement Museum, as well as other sources showing place and space, to press home for students the importance of the physical in their understanding of late nineteenth- and early twentieth-century immigrant experiences.

Translating the Historian's Arguments into Classroom Lessons: What Happened

Midtown High School in New York City serves grades 9 through 12. It is is a magnet school, attracting students from all of New York's five boroughs. Founded in the early 1990s, Midtown currently enrolls about 1,500 students and offers a largely traditional academic curriculum that is bolstered by the possibility of pursuing out-of-school internships. The school graduates roughly 70 percent of its students in four years. Close to 90 percent of its graduates go on to four-year colleges, and another 10 percent to two-year colleges. Still, teachers at the school complain about what we could call typical urban public school challenges: low student motivation, spotty class attendance, and an overemphasis on what they called "Test Prep 101" in some classes.

The ethnic breakdown of Midtown's student population is roughly 45 percent Hispanic, 22 percent black, 17 percent Asian, 15 percent white, and 1 percent unreported. As compared with all city public schools, Midtown has a slightly higher Hispanic and Asian population, and a lower black and white population. Roughly 45 percent of the student body qualifies for free or reduced lunch, which is a number far less than the estimated average of 70 percent for a New York City public school.

On the day that the first high school teacher, Frank, a white man who was in his seventh year of teaching, was scheduled to teach one of his immigration lessons, Midtown was abuzz with springtime energy. As students wound their way to class down hallways, up stairs, and then down another hallway to Frank's classroom, they greeted fellow students and faculty alike with high fives and enthusiastic hellos. An air of informality and collegiality characterized the atmosphere.

Frank's classroom was bright and sunny. Nine round tables arranged in three rows of three dotted the classroom, each table surrounded by clean shiny chairs for the students to sit on. A cart filled with laptop computers awaited the students on one side of the room, and an LCD projector hummed in the middle of the room. Relatively sophisticated student artwork decorated the walls, along with inspirational messages and posters representing historical events.

Of the twenty-five students enrolled in Frank's eleventh-grade U.S. history class, seventeen came to class on the day he introduced immigration, "a good showing," according to Frank, who noted that he generally expects fifteen on a given day. Attendance, both for these lessons and for the class in general, proved a huge challenge for Frank, as he was unable to assume that students today would have heard the lesson from yesterday and therefore could not count on knowledge or skill acquisition from day to day. Of his entire class, only one student attended all lessons of the mini-unit on nineteenth-century immigration. This led him to have to repeat key aspects of lessons, spend extra time playing catch-up, and generally spend half of each class reviewing the lesson from the previous day, in order to ensure that students were on the same page to evaluate new material. Consequently, what was planned as a five-day unit ended up spanning eight 50-minute class periods.

The other high school teacher, Megan, worked at the Downtown School in Manhattan. In her classroom, the lessons moved quicker than expected, and her mini-unit, which covered even more material than Frank attempted to teach, took only three 42-minute classes—a good thing, she noted, since many school-wide events, special meetings, and class trips complicated her curriculum map and left little time for her class to study immigration.

The Downtown School in Manhattan is a "screened" public school, which means that students must apply and be selected for admissions. Student test scores tend to be very high at Downtown, and the school attracts a wealthier and whiter population than most New York City schools. A 6–12 grade school serving just over nine hundred students each year with a 99 percent four-year graduation rate, the Downtown School student population is 57 percent white, 7 percent black, 11 percent Hispanic, and 27 percent Asian. Only 26 percent qualify for free and reduced lunch, compared with the New York City estimated average of 70 percent, and the feeling within the school, including the clothes and accessories of some of the students, belies even this number. Each year, roughly 93 percent of students at Downtown pass the New York Regents Exams in English and a slightly higher percentage pass the exam in math. According to the school's principal, nearly all students go on to four-year colleges, with 86 percent of them earning acceptance to their first-choice institution.

Downtown prides itself on providing an educational environment that combines academic rigor with compassion, diversity, and an emphasis on collaborative work. The teachers plan and offer curriculum in teams, and students demonstrated clear comfort in collaborating with their classmates on group projects and other curricular experiences.

The classrooms at Downtown are bursting with students, as more than the maximum number of students enrolls each year at the school. On the day Megan, a white woman who had been teaching for two years, taught one of her lessons on immigration, thirty-seven students—three more than the legal limit—crowded into her classroom, piling around desks and crammed together in seats behind them when no more desks were available. The classroom was set up in a double U, with an outer and inner row of desks and chairs, and the teacher stood near a computer and projector, which were set up in the center. With only forty minutes for each lesson and thirty-seven students who, almost without exception, had something to say about the topic at hand, the class swept rapidly along, bolstered in speed by Megan's quick speech delivery. Despite the rapid pace of the class, however, few students seemed to get lost—most appeared deeply engaged in the topic and materials presented.

All of the students had had Megan as a teacher the previous year, and as a result, her classroom offered an easy, comfortable environment for student–teacher dialogue. Of all 140 students in the eleventh grade to have taken the high-stakes exam in global history the previous year, all but six had passed; Megan expected the same passing rate for the high-stakes U.S. history exam this year.

To get the class started on the topic at hand, Megan posed the essential questions for the lessons on immigration: "How have immigrants experienced life in this nation of immigrants? What rights does the United States, as a nation of immigrants, grant to its immigrants?" She began by reminding the students of a poll on immigrant rights that they had completed the day before and then immediately launched into a discussion of immigrants' experiences, rights, and living conditions both in the nineteenth century and today. The aims she used for the day were: "How did immigrants at the turn of the century experience daily life in America? What historical information can we draw from photographs and other primary sources? And what are the limitations of these sources?" As Frank did in his classroom, Megan wrote the aims on the board and frequently added additional written questions to the list, as visual prompts for the students as they engaged in student-to-student and student-to-teacher class discussion.

Projecting photographs by Jacob Riis onto a screen from the computer in the middle of the room, Megan led the students through photographic analyses that prompted students to consider what they saw, literally, in the photos; what they knew about the people in the photos from previous discussions on immigration; and what they could infer about immigrants' experiences and what they could extrapolate from the photographs. With few exceptions, the eleventh-grade students were able to get right to work, examining the photos and scribbling answers on individual pieces of paper, responses they later shared aloud and used as springboards for discussion and debate.

When it came time to share responses, Megan's students proved adept at plumbing the photos for meaning, author/photographer's perspective, and larger lessons about immigrant experiences. As Megan moved through several of Riis's more potent photographs, the discussion built from debating what Riis might have wanted to show in each picture to more far-reaching explorations about whether immigrants should be guaranteed basic rights such as housing and sanitation. Without being told explicitly of Riis's larger political and social reform agenda, the students themselves were able to produce arguments, using his photographs as their evidence, for several of the Progressive Era reforms that Riis championed. They made connections between what they observed in the photographs and their own understanding of immigrant issues today, pointing out similarities and differences between what they perceived as larger immigrant-related issues of the nineteenth century and those they considered important today.

After viewing and discussing numerous Riis photographs, the students worked through excerpts from *How the Other Half Lives,* and in addition read transcripts of interviews with immigrants detained on Angel Island as well as excerpts of transcripts from interviews with contemporary immigrants to the United States. Encouraged to think comparatively and to make connections between past and present, the Downtown students at first sought to compare Riis's photographs with contemporary immigrants' written testimonies. They decided that the immigrants in Riis's photos were "hopeless" and mired in "dire" situations, but that contemporary immigrants were more "hopeful," suggesting more positive attitudes and beliefs in their own upward mobility. With Megan's careful guidance, however, the students soon came to see the extent to which the different sources—photographs of people, originally taken to be used as part of a wake-up call by someone with an explicit social agenda, as opposed to self-created accounts presented in poetic and prose form, as well as in the form of written transcripts of oral testimony—might be as much part of the story as the "messages" the sources contained. As Megan noted later, "At first most students quickly made the assumption that immigrants' lives were worse during Riis's time period; however, this led to a fruitful discussion . . . about the difference between information gleaned from photos versus words." In the photos, students projected their own assumptions onto the immigrants' experiences, assuming that the conditions pictured were permanent, that the lives of the immigrants pictured were never changed and that their lives were categorically worse than their lives in their home countries. In the first-hand accounts, many immigrants either spoke in hindsight (after having survived initially terrible conditions) or with hope for improvement despite terrible conditions. Students then began to wonder if perhaps the experiences weren't so drastically different, but rather that the photos, capturing only a moment and, as they had discussed, taken by a photographer to serve as proof of the need to enact specific social reforms, offer a very different picture of the same experience as does an oral or written account that takes a more big-picture look at experience.

Frank's class too, worked closely on analytical readings of the Riis photographs. Without the introduction of more contemporary materials against which to compare and contrast experiences, Frank's students did not encounter the challenges Megan's did, in failing at first to see how the sources they were examining in many ways were shaping their understandings of the subjects' experiences. But Frank's students encountered other issues, most centrally connected to students' lack of background knowledge or exposure to historical events and trends related to immigration. Still, even with his more challenging classroom environment, Frank's students, like Megan's, clearly reaped important concepts from the lesson using the Riis photographs. Their comments in class and in their subsequent homework assignments showed clear understanding of Riis's reform efforts and a nuanced grasp of the complications in trying to understand the experiences of those who were more objects than subjects of the sources under examination. Frank's explicit aim for the lesson, "How did Jacob Riis illustrate the conditions of the new immigrants in New York City?," itself helped guide the students to see the "story" as being as much about perspective and agenda as it was about experience and conditions.

Frank began his series of four lessons on immigration by having his students consider why so many people wanted to come to the United States in the nineteenth and early twentieth centuries. Through close analysis of a political cartoon entitled "U.S. Ark of Refuge," by Joseph Keppler, which depicts different types of immigrants to the United States (Figure 3.1), Frank led the students to list the "push" factors—poverty, lack of jobs and land in home countries, political and religious repression, etc.—as well as "pull" factors—economic opportunities, myths of "roads paved with gold," land, and notions of freedom—that largely drove immigration to the United States during this time period. Rather than starting with the Riis excerpts and photos and then working out into larger questions about immigration, urbanization, and social conditions during the time period, Frank started with the large context of immigration juxtaposed against global social and political conditions, and then led inward, to the city of New York, to the tenements, and then to individuals' experiences as depicted in the Riis photos and text.

Frank had his students examine the difference between "new" (eastern and southern European and Asian) and "old" (northern and western European) immigrants, and to consider the attitudes of those already in the United States toward the newcomers. He had students consider both the "melting pot" theory and the motto, "E Pluribus Unum": Out of Many, One. On their laptops, the students used the application "Google Earth" to view images of Ellis Island and the Statue of Liberty, as a newly arriving immigrant might—from a distance over the water. They then went

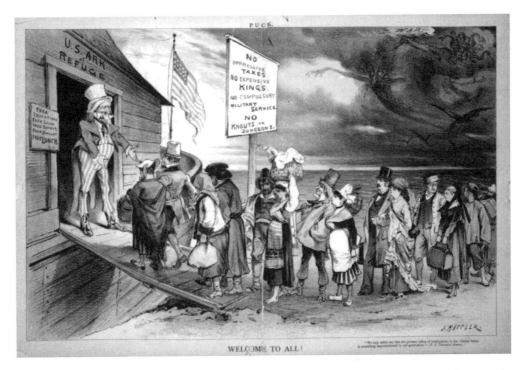

Figure 3.1   *U.S. Ark of Refuge*, by Joseph Keppler (*Puck*, April 28, 1880. Library of Congress)

on a virtual tour of Ellis Island (http://teacher.scholastic.com/activities/immigration/tour) and prepared notes from their "visit" to share with the class.

Once they had a sense of how immigrants might have entered the United States and what they may have gone through as they were processed upon arrival, the students next considered what their experiences may have been like once settled in the United States. As in Megan's class, they viewed selected photographs from Riis's *How the Other Half Lives*, considered what scenes were being depicted in the photos and who was being shown, and then probed what Riis may have been trying to show through his images, especially as the students unpacked them and came to understand that they were not, for the most part, candid photographs. The students had strong reactions to the photos, their comments ranging from, "How much do you think rent was at the time?" to "Those are horrible living conditions" and "I don't know how they did it." Frank then directed them to go on their laptops to the site of the New York City Tenement Museum, where through a virtual tour of the recreated homes of five different families (http://www.tenement. org/Virtual_Tour/index_virtual.html), the students were able to see that the conditions depicted in the Riis photographs, although perhaps staged by Riis for particular reasons and to achieve particular ends, were by no means atypical for immigrants during this time, nor were they wholly exaggerated.

Still, the particular tension between the "immigrants' experiences" during an historical period and what the students came to see as "presentations of experience" in the Riis photos and in the other sources used added both challenge and rich teaching and learning opportunities to Frank's and Megan's lessons. In both cases, the strong reactions the students had to the photographs and the squalor they depicted became complicated by their understanding of Riis as a reformer with an explicit agenda. Does something become "untrue" just because its presentation may have been "managed"? In both classes, the questions that arose from analyses of the Riis photos and text excerpts ended up inviting as much discussion about the attributes of particular kinds of sources as they did discussion about the specific living conditions of nineteenth-century immigrants to the United States. Although this may not have been Hasia Diner's original goal in suggesting that we use Riis's work as a way in to immigration, certainly she foreshadowed it in her insistence on parsing sources and really taking them apart for their tacit as well as explicit meanings. And also, a comparison of the framing questions the teachers used in mapping the topic against the instructional goals they developed for their lessons shows that such an outcome was to be expected:

Framing Questions

- How did immigrants during the Gilded Age experience their arrival to America and what were their lives like once here?
- How did immigration patterns change during the Gilded Age?
- How did Jacob Riis illustrate the conditions of the new immigrants in New York City? What were his goals?
- What impacts did Riis's work have on governmental/social services? How have scholars and the public responded to Riis's work over the years?
- How do immigrants to the United States today experience their arrival and life here and in what ways are their experiences both similar to and different from the experiences of immigrants during the Gilded Age?
- What did it mean to be "an American" in late nineteenth- and early twentieth-century America? What does it mean today?

Central Instructional Goals of the Lessons

- To consider multiple perspectives on issues.
- To recognize that history is not just a collection of dates and names, but rather an argument about the meaning of the past.
- To read primary source documents critically, for their arguments, as well as to interpret statistics and charts.
- To recognize the need to consider competing opinions.
- To see that photographs can and should be read as "texts" with complex meanings, authorial intention, intended audience, etc. and therefore we need to ask of them similar questions to those we ask of written texts.
- To understand that material objects and physical spaces also can and should be read as "texts" with complex meanings, authorial intention, intended audience, etc. and therefore we need to ask of them similar questions to those we ask of written texts.

Assessment of the Lessons

Our group recognized from the start that immigration as a topic can be and often is asked to serve many masters in U.S. history, in that it is often used by teachers to introduce many different ideas and trends over time. Naturally, this means that teachers need to choose their way in to the topic carefully, to ensure that students are able to make sense of the many themes raised in an examination of U.S. immigration and yet still get intimate enough with immigrants' stories to inspire empathy and engagement. As shown in the lessons above, our group found enormous value in presenting many different kinds of sources—photographs, poems, newspaper articles, charts, oral histories, personal reflections, timelines, and virtual tours, to name a few—and exploring the kinds of questions we could ask with each of these, both as a means of engaging student interest and to meet a variety of learning skills and multiple intelligences. As Frank noted:

> All along, we [asked] key questions about authorship and audience, etc., about all the documents. Who were they telling these things to? Who were they trying to impress? Questioning the sources, going back to the Riis photographs, [examining how the] audience of the source really influence[s] how the story is told and what story was told.

Megan concurred, noting that as much as her mini-unit was beneficial in getting her students to learn about immigration, the larger lessons it gave students on questioning sources ended up being an equally important take-away, given the emphasis she had placed in the class on probing the documents and interrogating the photographs. Indeed, one member of the group who observed the lessons, herself an historian and educational scholar, noted in a post-lesson group discussion that:

> It was really amazing how the lessons pushed the students to read the photographs, unpack photographs. I was really wowed in both cases . . . by the in-depth way the students were able to parse apart the photographs and ask questions of the Riis photographs that were really thoughtful and to kind of look at Riis in his complexity.

Yet at the same time as we cheered the successes of the lessons and found that they had by and large accomplished many of the instructional and content-based goals we had set out to fulfill, we all noted some weaknesses inherent within them. In some cases these weaknesses had to do with the time-, coverage-, and school-based pressures facing nearly all teachers whatever their school contexts or disciplines; other weaknesses had to do as much with the contexts of the "lived classrooms" in which the teachers taught as they did with the lessons as our group conceptualized them.

With respect to the time pressures faced by the teachers, one high school teacher found himself without the time he needed to bring his class's discussion of immigration up to the present, as he had planned to do; the other high school teacher found that even though her lessons moved more quickly than expected, outside-of-class assemblies ate away at her time for instruction, to the point that she felt unable to squeeze in an introduction of images from Ellis Island or the Tenement Museum. Most dramatically, the middle school teacher who had helped shape the lessons our group wrote found herself without the time even to teach a single one of them. Although all the teachers recognized the deep importance of immigration, in the end none had the time he or she wanted to do the lessons the justice they deserved—a sad commentary, especially for teachers in a city and a nation very much defined by immigration.

Another weakness we saw in the lessons had to do with the structure of the book project itself and the "mini-unit" format that this book's logic imposed onto the teachers' efforts to teach immigration. In a structural sense, all members of our group found the teaching of immigration—which may very well be used as a way in to an entire course on U.S. history or, indeed, world history at large—in the format of a mini-unit or group of lessons presented together to be an enormous challenge. Further, the scheduling format offered in the two schools, as in many throughout the country, in which courses are offered in forty- or fifty-minute chunks, rather than in larger blocks in which topics can be explored more deeply, added additional stress to the teachers. As Megan noted:

> It's just so much, and how do you do this in a high school classroom when you meet for 40 minutes at a time and you have to cover all these things and how do you possibly do it justice? For me, that was the central challenge of the whole thing.

Diner agreed in our post-teaching debrief session about the challenges posed by the way high school subjects tend to be scheduled, arguing that from her perspective as an academic historian:

> It is just so hard to imagine doing a course on all of U.S. history in an academic year, given the limitations of how much students can read [and] forty-minute classes. It seems to me there is no perfect way to do it, but in a sense, the whole year should be about immigration, is my initial reaction. Of course I understand perfectly why you did it the way you did, but we can in a sense see the whole of U.S. history [as a story of immigration].

In addition, as we reviewed the lessons Frank and Megan taught, we also considered the dangers in encouraging, as Megan did, her students to compare immigrant experiences across time periods, especially using different kinds of sources to get at these experiences. Such an approach can lead to false comparisons: for example, Jacob Riis's photographs of immigrants, which inherently did not contain any immigrant "voices," being compared, perhaps, with testimonies of more contemporary immigrants or with poetry created by them to tell their stories in their own words. Indeed, as Diner noted:

It can really be a red flag, comparing Riis's photos to contemporary poetry and work of immigrants, because in Riis's project, he doesn't give them any voice at all. He was an outsider photographing and writing about them, and on some level was really blind to their self-expression. He didn't recognize and probably couldn't recognize the kinds of social support networks and cultural expressions they had. He considered them hopeless.

Using two different kinds of sources as a way of doing a comparison, therefore, could be a problem. As Diner worried, "I wonder if there's a little unbalance trying to get at similarities or differences if you're not using analogous kinds of material."

Our group shared this worry and considered the extent to which it may have marred the lessons but, ultimately, we decided that because the lessons focused so closely on the sources and on, as one of our members put it:

questioning what kinds of material the different sources could and could not tell and consider[ing] the kinds of information that it's possible to know based on the source, that maybe rather than comparing, maybe it's a case of here are the different pictures we can get given the different sources that we're looking at over a longer stretch of time.

A second potential issue with comparison is the fact that this approach can bring with it the danger of *presentism*, of imposing on the past the standards and expectations of the present, and thereby misunderstanding the deeper contexts of time periods that shape the historical picture. As Diner noted:

There are always pitfalls with comparative [approaches], which is the apple–orange phenomena, in that the two time periods are so different and the American public is so different and the climate of opinion is so different. And while one can certainly think in comparative terms and it's important to do so, I think it is very difficult. And I think there are very few good examples of really comparative scholarship, only because it's so hard to hold something constant to then be able to answer the question, what was similar and what was different?

Not that it's wrong to try, she added, but teachers must approach comparisons carefully and be fully cognizant of the dangers.

Megan in particular recognized these challenges, and so made a strong point of limiting the aspects of immigration that she asked her students to compare across time periods. Rather than asking students to compare day-to-day life across centuries, for example, she focused them instead, as she put it, on

the perception of what America is and that kind of recurring theme, like reasons why people were coming here and how . . . regardless of what was going on politically or socially or economically in this country, there is always this sense from outsiders sort of like the American Dream and upward mobility and those sorts of themes, much broader themes in American history.

Since it is possible to interrogate a variety of sources across time periods for how their subjects may have regarded such notions as the American Dream, how they would have defined it and what their beliefs regarding this myth may have been, this saved Megan's class, she believed, from devolving into presentist assumptions that immigrants of all time periods may have shared and continue to share the same goals and experiences.

Ultimately, our group came to recognize that treating immigration in a single unit or collection of lessons taught together would not be the way we would want to approach the topic again. The lessons themselves we would repeat, but rather than introducing them together, sequentially, we would space them out throughout a semester or year and would include with them lessons about immigration of other groups to the United States and at other points in U.S. history. Doing so would, we hope, enable classes to feed from a buffet of immigration throughout an academic year, returning to fill their plates at different times and in different manners, rather than hoping to get their fill at one single, even if extended, meal. Indeed, addressing immigration throughout a course on U.S. history, rather than segmenting it off in a given unit, we decided, would also help teachers mitigate against potential presentism among their students, by allowing the students to see more clearly the different immigrants' experiences in the contexts of their own time periods and not just in comparison with different groups at different times or with immigration today. Finally, a more continuous approach would help the teachers reinforce the centrality of immigration to the whole of U.S. and even global history, showing in more defined and repeated ways throughout a given course how a nation of immigrants has wrestled throughout its existence with a constant and changing influx of immigrants.

Implications: Lasting Understandings (and Test Scores too)

To critique our collection of lessons approach—a constraint in many ways imposed by the structure of this book—is not to say that the lessons themselves fell short. Indeed, after examining the teachers' lessons and discussing with them what they had taught and why they had chosen to access the topic in the manner they had, our expert historian concluded that the lessons centered on what she considered the important aspects of immigration and noted that the teachers had done an admirable job in their work. Noting the challenges of teaching the entirety of U.S. history in a single year—a commonplace task for most high school teachers but a rarer burden for college- and graduate-level history instructors, Diner stated:

> It seems to me that a great deal was accomplished: students were exposed to important material both in terms of learning that photographs are important historical documents and you have to take time, you can't just take them at face value. It seems to me given the constraints and the difficulties under which you work, you hit on the important themes and important aspects [of the topic].

Indeed, she noted that the teachers had "used the material very well and in ways that [were] totally appropriate for [their] constituencies."

In addition to generating a great deal of student interest in immigration and especially in the experiences of immigrants, Frank and Megan both found many opportunities to weave into their lessons test preparation and explicit instruction in document analysis, in preparation for the Document Based Questions (DBQs) on the state and National Assessment of Educational Progress (NAEP) exams. Both teachers were cognizant throughout the lessons of the competing demands of the curriculum in their schools—"Test Prep 101," as Frank put it, versus using more innovative approaches to instruction. In general, the teachers found that both the lessons as taught fulfilled the requirements of a test-driven curriculum, in that they provided instruction in historical content included in the New York State and NAEP learning standards, but that they also moved well beyond the parameters laid out in mandated standards to encourage students to engage the topic with empathy and also understand the extent to which the sources examined shaped the content shared in the lessons.

Both Frank and Megan found that the primary focus on Jacob Riis, and particularly on his photographs, elicited enough student interest and involvement that they were able to tie in other sources that complicated the historical picture of immigrants during the time period and provided more focused information of use on high-stakes exams, without losing their students' openness to engage the topic. As Frank noted in the wake of teaching:

> I was happy with the outcome [of the lessons]. The kids came away and they knew who Jacob Riis was [and] they were familiar with Riis and Sinclair and Ellis Island. And they could . . . write an essay on how new immigrants experienced life in America based on Riis and Sinclair and the [sources from Ellis Island]. And I thought they put a pretty good thing together at the end, sort of giving a narrative from those sources.

Thanks to the high level of student interest in the lessons generated by the topic of immigration, both teachers reported that their students chose to write about topics related to the unit in their end-of-year exams and on standardized tests that called for students to pick figures in U.S. history upon whom to focus in exam essay questions. Megan found, upon talking with her students about the high-stakes exam they took in the months following their unit, that a "surprising number" of her students had selected Jacob Riis and how he used photography for social reform purposes, in response to a question requiring students to focus on past agents of change who were not U.S. presidents. In Frank's case, too, it is clear that students latched onto the concepts addressed in the lessons: In the academic year following the spring in which they experienced these lessons, Frank's students took a "pre-assessment" of the past year's material, to ascertain what they remembered from the previous year's U.S. history course. Upon evaluating their responses, the teachers found that Jacob Riis and his photographs and agenda were among the few topics that all students recalled, showing not only that they found the unit engaging while experiencing it, but that its lessons stuck with them in subsequent semesters as well.

Of course, providing students with the content to pass high-stakes tests or making sure that they remember potentially surface information about a particular reformer is not the ultimate measure of an immigration unit's success. Of greater importance is the extent to which students came away recognizing both the humanity in the immigrants whose experiences they studied and the powerful sense of how the ceaseless waves of newcomers have so fundamentally shaped and enriched this nation of immigrants. In these respects, written work done by the students provides the best testimony to the lessons' success. The following excerpts from students' essays range in depth and overall sophistication, but all, we believe, suggest nuanced understanding of immigration issues and facility in wrestling with the concepts addressed in the lessons.

Student A (Megan's class)

> While looking through the photos I found myself asking how can people be forced into such horrible living conditions? You look through and you see very small-enclosed spaces packed with too many people. You see dirt and appliances thrown everywhere, as if it was someone's closet used for storage . . . My immediate impression was that people did not enjoy living in the United States due to the lack of housing, opportunities, and sanitation.

Through reading the written portions, I picked up a different perspective. The various narratives introduced immigrants that actually lived through difficulties. I picked up on the reoccurring theme that at first it was difficult to get settled in a place where the natives are not on your side but after overcoming the hardships, many of the immigrants found better living tha[n] what they would have had in their home country . . .

Comparing the photos and the narratives, I got a more depressing impression from the pictures. Because you actually see a visual, rather than hear it through words; I think it is more powerful and real to see an image as an artifact.)

Student B (Megan's class)

In [the Jacob Riis photo] named Men's Lodging Room in the West 47th Street Station, you can see many men sleeping or resting in one small room. There is equipment everywhere such as wood logs and chairs. They are all sleeping either on the floor [or] on wooden boards. All these immigrants are men and none of them are with their wives or children. It may be inferred that they are doing a lot of work, so much that they do not even have the opportunity to see their family. Also, the setting being at a station can illustrate these men's level of desperation to just find a place of shelter. The overpopulation of immigrants made it difficult for everybody to find a place to spend the night and police stations would allow for these immigrants to come in and sleep after a certain hour on a first come, first served basis.

A lot like the poem [from the Angel Island Immigration Station], these people seem powerless and unable to attain what they had come for in the first place. Although conditions may seem bad in America with poor sanitation and malnutrition, their conditions that they were experiencing in their homeland may have been even worse . . . They were hoping to find a better life here, but conditions, however bad they are, may have been the only option they had left in surviving.

Student C (Frank's class)

The immigrant came to America with a hope, a hope for a better life, to earn and live on their own terms. Although they succeeded at many steps, they were often trapped in the disorder of society. They were subjected to the harshest conditions prevalent in America, and had to survive several acts of discrimination and abuse. However, America did provide them with the hope and aspiration to rise to their maximum potential, a feeling profound even today. It is with this belief immigration began and has grown ever since.

Student D (Frank's class)

Immigrants have brought to America positive effects that at the end are being paid back negatively. I believe the American community should realize how high immigrants have put up their economy and the prosperity it has brought as well, appreciating them instead of treating them like animals, insulting them, exploiting them, and even calling them "aliens."

Works Cited

Diner, H. (ed.) (2008). *How the Other Lives,* by Jacob Riis. New York: W. W. Norton & Co.

Handlin, O. (1951). *The Uprooted: The Epic Story of the Great Migrations that Made the American People.* New York: Grosset and Dunlap.

Sinclair, U. (1906/2003). *The Jungle.* New York: Sharp Press.

CHAPTER RESOURCES

I. Unit Framework—Immigration in the Late Nineteenth-Century United States

Intended Learning Outcomes (Use NYS SS Standards)

Understandings (Big Ideas):

- Students will understand that immigration is a constant recurring theme throughout U.S. history.
- Students will understand that most Americans' ancestors are immigrants.
- Students will understand that continuities in immigration include seeking a better life (the "American Dream"), often facing poor working conditions and/or discrimination, the tension between assimilation and integration.
- Students will understand that immigrants have played a major role in the economic, industrial, and urban development of the nation.
- Students will understand that immigrants have historically struggled with issues of rights, nativism, xenophobia, racial profiling, etc.
- Students will understand that changes in immigration include changing policies toward both specific groups and immigrants as a whole, trends in country of origin, public attitudes toward immigrants at various points in time.

Essential Questions:

- How have immigrants experienced life in this nation of immigrants?
- What rights does the United States, as an immigrant nation, grant to its immigrants?
- What story do photographs and other primary sources tell? What do they leave out?

Understandings (Big Ideas) (continued):

- Students will understand that photographs can be read as text like other primary source documents—with meaning, perspective, intended audience, message.
- Students will understand that a primary source offers one perspective—to be read, analyzed, and synthesized with other perspectives for a fuller picture of historical events.

Content Knowledge:

- Students will know about quotas.
- Students will know about "new immigrants" versus old immigrants.
- Students will know major immigration legislation including the Chinese Exclusion Act and the Immigration Act of 1882, 1921, 1924, and 1965.
- Students will know about tenements.
- Students will know about Ellis Island and Angel Island.
- Students will know about nativism, xenophobia.

Skills:

- Interpret primary sources: identify author's perspective, intended audience, bias.
- Identify the untold side of a story from a primary document.

Vocabulary:

Nativism, Xenophobia, Tenement, Quota

Learning Experiences:

- Interpretation and analysis of photographs.
- Interpretation and analysis of oral history accounts.
- Interpretation and analysis of legislation.
- Interpretation and analysis of secondary sources of information.
- Writing prompt.
- Quiz.
- Class discussion.

Resources:

- *Out of Many: The Changing Face of Ethnicity in America* by John Mack Faigher, Mari Jo Buhle, Daniel Czitrom, and Susan Armitage: 1800–1860 (pp. 380–385); 1860–1930 (pp. 708–713); Since 1930 (pp. 986–991)
- Jacob Riis, *How the Other Half Lives*, excerpts
- Chinese Exclusion Act
- Immigration Act of 1965
- National Archives interviews: http://memory.loc.gov/learn/features/immig
- Angel Island primary documents: http://www.aiisf.org/history
- "An Immigrant's Silent Struggle," by Robert Kosi Tette, in *Newsweek*, March 10, 2008
- "The 1965 Immigration Act: Anatomy of a Disaster," by Ben Johnson in FrontPageMagazine.com, December 10, 2002

II. Lesson Framework—Immigration in the Late Nineteenth-Century United States

Intended Learning Outcomes (Use NYS SS Standards)

Understandings (Big ideas):

- Students will understand how photojournalists can help shape public opinion through their work.
- Students will understand how the cramped living quarters on New York's Lower East Side contributed to health issues.

Essential Questions:

- How did new immigrants experience their arrival to Ellis Island?
- How did Jacob Riis illustrate the conditions of New York's working poor?
- How does the Tenement Museum help us understand the living conditions of New York's working poor?

Content Knowledge:

- Students will know the geographic location of Ellis Island and New York's Lower East Side.
- Students will know Jacob Riis and his work.
- Students will know the living conditions of "new immigrants."

Skills:

- Analyzing primary source documents and photographs.
- Using Google Earth to examine geography.
- Using virtual tours of historic sites.

Vocabulary:

Tenement, Incessant, Ramshackle, Abomination, Skulk, Bewilder, Conjecture, Malodorous, Sullen, Swath, Epidemic

Learning Experiences:

- Aerial tours of Ellis Island and New York's Lower East Side.
- Examination of photographs and text from Jacob Riis's *How the Other Half Lives*.
- Virtual tours of the Tenement Museum.

Resources:

- *How the Other Half Lives* (excerpts and photographs)
- Computers with Google Earth software
- Quicktime software to view Tenement Museum

III. Sources Used in Lessons

- Ellis Island website, http://www.ellisisland.org/default.asp, especially a timeline showing the forces behind immigration and their impact on immigrants' experiences upon arrival, http://www.ellisisland.org/immexp/wseix_4_3.asp
- "Immigration Act of 1965," available at http://www.lib.umich.edu/govdocs/fedhis.html
- Johnson, Ben. "The 1965 Immigration Act: Anatomy of a Disaster," in FrontPageMagazine.com, December 10, 2002
- New York City Tenement Museum's virtual tour, http://www.tenement.org/Virtual_Tour/index_virtual.html
- Newspapers-in-Education compilations on immigrants' experiences, drawn from the archives of the Angel Island Immigration Station series: http://static.

acon.org/gems/aiisf/aiisfsfChronrussianfinal.pdf;___http://static.acon.org/gems/aiisf/aiisfsfChronjapane230EC3.pdf; http://static.acon.org/gems/aiisf/aiisfsf-Chronfilipinofinal.pdf; http://static.acon.org/gems/aiisf/aiisfsfChronseAsianfinal.pdf

- Tette, Roberto Kosi. "An Immigrant's Silent Struggle," in *Newsweek*, March 10, 2008
- Transcripts of interviews with immigrants to Angel Island, http://www.aiisf.org/history
- Transcripts of interviews with recent immigrants to the United States, housed in the Library of Congress American Memory Collection, http://memory.loc.gov/learn/features/immig/interv/toc.php
- *U.S Ark of Refuge*, by J. Keppler, *Puck*, April 28, 1880. Library of Congress Prints and Photographs Division, Washington, DC.

IV. Relevant New York State and NAEP Standards

New York State Learning Standards, U.S. History

- Students explore the meaning of American culture by identifying the key ideas, beliefs, and patterns of behavior, and traditions that help define it and unite all Americans (MS.1A)
- Students complete well-documented and historically accurate case studies about individuals and groups who represent different ethnic, national, and religious groups in the United States at different times and in different locations (MS.3A)
- Students classify major developments into categories such as social, political, economic, geographic, technological, scientific, cultural, or religious (MS.3D)
- Students analyze the development of American culture, explaining how ideas, values, beliefs, and traditions have changed over time and how they unite all Americans (HS.1A)
- Students develop and test hypotheses about important events, eras, or issues in U.S. history, setting clear and valid criteria for judging the importance and significance of these events, eras, or issues (HS.2B)
- Students compare and contrast the experiences of different groups in the United States (HS.2C)
- Students examine how the Constitution, United States law, and the rights of citizenship provide a major unifying factor in bringing together Americans from diverse roots and traditions (HS.2D)
- Students compare and contrast the experiences of different ethnic, national, and religious groups, explaining their contributions to American society and culture (HS.3A)
- Students research and analyze major themes and developments in U.S. history (HS.3B)
- Students prepare essays and oral reports about the important social, political, economic, scientific, technological, and cultural developments, issues, and events from U.S.history (HS.3C)

- Students understand the interrelationships between world events and developments in U.S. history (HS.3D)

New York State Learning Standards, Historical Thinking

- Consider the sources of historic documents, narratives, or artifacts and evaluate their reliability (MS.4A)
- Understand how different experiences, beliefs, values, traditions, and motives cause individuals and groups to interpret historic events and issues from different perspectives (MS. 4B)
- Compare and contrast different interpretations of key events and issues in U.S. history, and explain reasons for these different accounts (MS.4C)
- Describe historic events through the eyes of those who were there (MS.4D)
- Analyze historical narratives about key events in U.S. history to identify the facts and evaluate the authors' perspectives (HS.4A)
- Consider different historians' analyses of the same event or development in U.S. history to understand how different viewpoints and/or frames of reference influence historical interpretation (HS.4B)
- Evaluate the validity and credibility of historical interpretations of important events or issues in U.S. history, revising these interpretations as new information is learned and other interpretations are developed (HS.4C)

    Adapted from *New York State Learning Standards, U.S. History* (1996)

NAEP Learning Standards, U.S. History

Framework 1: Themes in U.S. History

- How has the cultural diversity of American society shaped the nation's civic culture, political institutions, and political practices? What major political controversies arose about the issues? Which controversies have remained or reemerged under other circumstances? (1)
- What racial, ethnic, religious, and national groups formed this nation? Why have people immigrated to the United States and why has the country continued to attract so many immigrants? (2)
- What have been the patterns and conditions of immigration? How has the racial, ethnic, and religious composition of the nation changed over time? What racial, ethnic, and religious tensions arose? What issues remain? (2)
- What common and diverse cultural traditions did Americans develop? How did racial, ethnic, religious, and national groups contribute to the creation of American culture? What individuals and defining events contributed to these developments? What primary documents and historical sources reflect the development of American culture? (2)

Framework 2: Periods of U.S. History

- What groups immigrated to the United States in the nineteenth century? Why did they come? Where did they settle? What impact did they have on the national culture and American lifestyle? (4.2)
- What groups came to the United States at the beginning of the twentieth century? Why did they come? (6.1)
- What factors influenced immigration? How did the image of America as a land of opportunity develop? (6.2)
- What was the influence of European immigrants on the United States? (6.2)
- What accounts for the surging growth of the American economy in this era? What were the main features of industrialization, and what were the benefits and costs of this economic development? (6.3)
- Why were restrictive immigration policies enacted after World War I? What groups were restricted and what groups were allowed? Why did large numbers of people continue to seek opportunities to immigrate to the United States? (7.2)
- How has immigration policy changed in the contemporary United States? What groups are immigrating in large numbers? Why?

NAEP Historical Thinking Standards, U.S. History

Framework 3: Ways of Knowing and Thinking about U.S. History

1. HISTORICAL KNOWLEDGE AND PERSPECTIVE

Students should be able to:

- Name, recognize, list, identify and give examples of people, places, events, concepts and movements
- Place specifics in a chronological framework and construct and label historical periods
- Define historical themes and give examples of the ways themes relate to specific factual information
- Describe the past from the perspectives of various men and women of the time
- Explain the perspective of an author of a primary source document
- Describe different perspectives related to a historical issue or event
- Summarize the contributions of individuals and groups to U.S. history
- Summarize the meaning of historical sources and link these sources to general themes

2. HISTORICAL ANALYSIS AND INTERPRETATION

Students should be able to:

- Specify and explain cause-and-effect relationships and connect contemporary events to their origins in the past

- Categorize information and develop strategies for organizing a large body of facts
- Examine multiple causes of historical developments
- Explain points of view, biases, and value statements in historical sources
- Determine the significance of people, events, and historical sources
- Weigh and judge different views of the past as advanced by historical figures themselves, historians, and present-day commentators and public figures
- Demonstrate that the interpretation and meaning of the past are open to change as new information and perspectives emerge
- Develop sound generalizations and defend these generalizations with persuasive arguments
- Make comparisons and recognize the limitations of generalizations
- Apply knowledge, draw conclusions, and support those conclusions with convincing evidence

Adapted from National Assessment Governing Board (2006)

Works Cited

National Assessment Governing Board (2006). *U.S. History Framework for the 2006 National Assessment of Educational Progress*. Washington, DC: U.S. Department of Education.

New York State Learning Standards, U.S. History (1996). Albany: New York State Education Department.

Four
The Progressive Era

Framing the Questions: An Interview with Kevin Murphy, conducted by Rachel Mattson

Kevin Murphy is an Associate Professor of History and American Studies at the University of Minnesota in Minneapolis. He is the author of *Political Manhood: Red Bloods, Mollycoddles, and the Politics of Progressive Era Reform* (2008) and the editor of a special issue of the *Radical History Review* (2008) entitled "Queer Futures." An active public historian, he is also a founding member of the Twin Cities GLBT Oral History Project. He has received many awards for his work, including the 2002 Allan Nevins Prize for the Best Written Dissertation in U.S. History.

Rachel Mattson: *Tell us about your approach to the history of the Progressive Era. What categories or ideas are most important to your understanding of that era in U.S. history?*

Kevin Murphy: Let me take reform—that is a category that's important to me that I use in my work. The basic narrative of U.S. history has privileged this notion that you have this flourishing of a kind of reform that happens toward the end of the nineteenth century, to check the worst kinds of excesses of capitalism. This is the traditional narrative and that happens between 1890 and World War I, up to 1917. I think when I first began doing this work, those kinds of temporal parameters were most important to me. But one of the things I think that's important to the field right now and also important to me is that this idea that Progressive reform might also be better understood to extend beyond those boundaries to see a longer trajectory.

RM: *What is that longer trajectory? What are those extended boundaries?*

KM: One of the things that started me out on the project I'm currently working on was to try to understand why the category of masculinity was so important in American political culture.

I'm interested not necessarily in a social history or a history of individuals or even of particular communities. I'm interested in the ways in which ideas about gender and sexuality and those ideologies are deployed and contested in the realm of politics.

...I think one of the reasons that the Progressive Era itself is understood as so important in this moment is: There's been a looking back to the Progressive Era for a usable past. Lots of change was made in terms of legislation. You can see that things shifted: corporate regulation, woman suffrage—there are these landmark events that suggest a shift especially in the federal government and its intervention in issues of inequality. I think because of that, oftentimes historians and journalists and all kinds of people turn back to the Progressive Era to understand what one might do today: What lessons can be drawn? But it's such a confusing era, it doesn't align with our own understandings of what's liberal and what's conservative. There are lots of ways lots of different people can use it. So you have somebody like George W. Bush claiming Theodore Roosevelt as a model and actually borrowing from a lot of Roosevelt's rhetoric and his performance. At the same time you have people who would identify themselves as really—they even use the term—Progressive to refer to politics that are much more egalitarian.

One of the reasons that a lot of people beyond just academic historians are really interested in the Progressive Era right now is that the division between rich and poor is more pronounced than it has been in a long time, and you also have corporations that are not being regulated as they once were. But there's also a popular philosophy that's gone along with that deregulation, which is that society works best when you don't have these kinds of curbs on economic activity. So those political valences and debates have really animated the work on the Progressive Era. Now sometimes historians aren't as explicit about the political resonance through the present as others—like journalists, for example, who engage in the debate—because historians are trained not to do that. But that is a key reason that it remains such a vital area in U.S. history.

RM: *Who are the major thinkers—the major figures, historical actors—in these areas, in these years that you teach?*

KM: I teach a lot with Theodore Roosevelt, Jacob Riis, Ida B. Wells, Jane Addams. I think the way I teach is similar to the way that I'm doing my research and scholarship, which is to look at where power lies and look at some of the same individuals who've been recognized as powerful but then to ask different kinds of questions about their power—to try to understand how power is deployed and reproduced.

RM: *So what kinds of questions are you asking about those people and their times?*

KM: For Theodore Roosevelt, for example, what's really interesting to me about him is: How did he manage to make his ideas about what American society should look like seem practical, centrist, and pragmatic, and quintessentially American? And that leads you to look a lot at the kinds of speeches he gave and the ways in which he was understood in the press, and I try to think about some of the ways in which he was received—some of his influence that gets translated by other historical actors. So sometimes I'll teach documents where—for example, I have a document where a college student listened to one of Theodore Roosevelt's speeches, then wrote about politics and masculinity in a letter. So that it's not just Theodore Roosevelt, but it's about the way in which others understood him and get at some of the social implications of the kind of discourse he promoted.

RM: *Can you tell us about that document? What does this person say in this letter?*

KM: This is a letter written by an upper-class young man—who I think was at either Harvard or Yale. He hears a speech by Roosevelt where he's arguing that American men had become mollycoddles (and by that he basically was talking to elite white men), that the problem with that was that the United States was losing what had made it a distinct power. What Roosevelt felt was being lost was that kind of energy, that kind of virility. He argued in particular that elite men, men educated at Ivy League schools, should turn their attention to politics and political culture because they needed to be involved. It's a kind of meritocracy argument—our best men are not leading us any more; they're leaving politics to the corrupt, mercenary, and implicitly immigrant, classes—like Tammany Hall. So this student sees Roosevelt's speech as an epiphany. And he understands himself as effeminate for the first time and decides he needs to do something to work against that effeminateness. He decides that the work of politics might be the thing that will cure his weakness. And this civic work is also racial and class work too. So sometimes I'll teach that document.

Then I teach another document, a short travel story by Goldsworthy Lowes Dickinson, who was a British poet and classicist, who is affiliated with Virginia Woolf and part of the Bloomsbury Group, who was in the United States visiting a friend at the time that Roosevelt was going around to colleges making these speeches about mollycoddles and these speeches to young men. And his response was that he felt he was being called not only un-American—he wasn't American—but that his foreignness, through the discourse that was incited by these Roosevelt speeches, was really brought to the forefront at the same time as was his masculinity. He didn't understand himself as conventionally masculine and he also understood himself as a pervert of some kind—or an invert I think is the term that he used—so sort of sexually non-normative too. So he starts to think about what this means—what this kind of strenuous masculinity that Roosevelt was promoting meant. He basically interpreted this as being called homosexual or inverted in some way and then named as dangerous, socially dangerous. So he read that same kind of speech as highly exclusionary—as speaking to his own identity, which was non-normative in gender and sexual terms, but one that might be dangerous, that might be foreign, that might not be accepted in the United States, and was working against a long tradition—and he claimed the mollycoddle figure as his own identity.

I sometimes try to teach both of those documents in connection with each other so that students will see the power that kind of language and that kind of rhetoric has when it's deployed by a figure who's in a position of institutional governmental power, and the ways in which that same kind of move can be identified, both as exclusionary and as a call to action or a call to inclusion. I think in some ways too it was a call to whiteness, when it got extended to men who weren't from elite classes, who were maybe second-generation immigrants, but who were also welcomed into this kind of American masculinity by Roosevelt.

RM: *How do you teach Ida B. Wells?*

KM: Well I teach her in a couple of different ways. I teach her in two ways that I think are really important to this period. When you're talking about race and the contestation of race, especially around African Americans at the turn of the twentieth century—for so long now the conventional approach has been to hold up W. E. B. DuBois and Booker T. Washington as this kind of dyad. So you have Booker T. Washington, the pragmatist, the one who's arguing for ameliorative and gradual reform and accepting of segregation to some extent, and W. E. B. DuBois argues against that. But in recent years historians have begun to complicate these ideas. Washington is understood more now as being strategic, as actually not accepting segregation as a principle—but he had a different approach to how social change was realized. There's more of a recognition now that he was a really strategic and complicated thinker. And W. E. B. DuBois is arguing for a response that is much less accommodating of white racism, but also at the same time promoting a progressive idea about a talented class that could change society—he calls on education as the primary component of social change and uplift and that sort of thing. So even though that dyad has gotten much more complicated, it sort of bothers me in its masculinism and the way that it plays so easily into the barrier of the two sides and "the truth lies in the middle."

So I always say Ida B. Wells-Barnett is a third figure, that I think about her as arguing for something quite different—which is possible armed resistance. She's not just thinking about self-defense as potentially involving violence, or responding to violence with violence, but also, in a way that's really different from DuBois and Washington, understanding the kinds of practices and rhetoric that uphold and extend white supremacy. And I think she really looked in complicated ways—she really understood what underlay these arguments, which were taken as commonplace, for the superiority of white people. She tried to almost dismantle them by unpacking arguments that were understood as commonplace arguments, and one of those ideas was gendered and sexualized—the white supremacist understanding of black male sexuality as especially dangerous, and the racist violence that that engendered.

And so in teaching Ida B. Wells-Barnett, you can get at the questions of gendered power in two ways, which is, first, by disrupting the binary of two great men arguing against each other—by bringing in a third figure—and also by expanding the terrain of the debate. Then I think also that she very much was an observer of the way in which gender and ideas about gender were an integral part of power.

RM: *What kind of documents of hers do you use?*

KM: Well, I teach *The Red Record* and an account that she wrote of when she protested being thrown off a train for sitting in a section that was reserved for white women. That's also a document that's really useful to use because it screws up the Civil Rights historiography too. I have also taught a piece in which she really takes on white feminists and makes some very strong and really compelling claims about the kind of racial underpinning of white feminism at that very moment. That's very useful to teach too because it's hard to teach suffrage in a way that's not a story of progress and to really understand how important race was to feminism and suffrage in that era. So I've used Ida B. Wells-Barnett actually in multiple ways. I've found her useful in so many important debates. And also offering an analysis that's pretty useful and for students, oftentimes really generative. It's both complicated but it's also powerful and clear and it doesn't seem antiquated necessarily in arguments that she's making—they seem very vital still, I guess mainly because so much of the conditions that she was responding to and reacting to are seen to have some kind of continuation to the present or a presence at the moment.

RM: *One of the things that I think is hard to do is to really find a way around teaching through spectacular individuals and heroes. On the one hand I think it's very useful to talk about individuals, but on the other hand I think that how you do it really matters. It sounds like, for one thing, you're talking about Teddy Roosevelt by never actually studying Teddy Roosevelt's life—instead you're talking about how his words were interpreted by regular folks.*

KM: I believe we study individuals who are powerful not because they're more important than anyone else, but because they were in positions that were empowered. And because of that power they had some kinds of influence. And it's thinking about what they were doing with that power that is what's important. It's not the individual him- or herself. For me that's really an important way to teach because there's no pretending that those individuals don't matter or that they're not being addressed, celebrated, interpreted elsewhere. Everywhere else you look this is how history is produced outside of the academy and in lots of places—around individual stories. So to me the more effective way to teach is: Okay, so we have these people, they're getting interpreted and they're getting talked about. Let's think about them in different ways—as agents of power. And let's understand how they were understood at different moments. And in some ways that's asking for a different understanding of an individual—of one who's embedded in a much broader system, rather than an actor who has all kinds of power that lies within him- or herself.

RM: *I would imagine it's harder to do that with Ida B. Wells-Barnett than Teddy Roosevelt. It's harder not to make her a hero.*

KM: Yes, sure. When you do tell individual stories there's a way in which that heroic context is always there—you're either arguing against the hero or you're maybe promoting another one. That's really hard to get around.

RM: *Why do you think it's important to teach about these subjects and what are the stakes of doing so?*

KM: What's important about it to me is not that students come away with a particular interpretation of the Progressive Era, but that they understand the Progressive Era, and any period of history, as contested. It's understanding that period as one filled with struggles over social, political, and economic power that is really, to me, what's so crucial. You don't have to think of the Progressive Era or, for example, Progressive reformers, as really selling out to capitalism or as really pivotal actors in transforming American society from one that celebrated inequality, really, into one that tried to produce democratic participation, etc. Making those kinds of claims, I think, is not so helpful—it doesn't really help one place oneself in really complicated struggles over power, and it also, I think, implies that there are answers and that they are transferable. I think it's important to point out that although there are all of these circumstances that make history useful in the present moment, it's never in a way that's explicit.

Essay: Using Process Drama to Teach Gender, Race, and Reform in the Progressive Era

By Michael Stoll, Joan Malczewski, and David Montgomery, with John Palella and Sarah Reiley

History textbooks typically present Progressivism as the ideological impetus for considerable social, political, and legal reform in the United States between 1880 and 1920. Traditional narratives associate the movement with a popular vision of white middle-class women promoting reform in urban areas and a marked increase in social services through both private initiative and legislative action. Yet Progressivism was, like many movements for social justice, pluralistic. Indeed, historians (e.g. Connolly, 1998; Gilmore, 1996; Link 1992; Montgomery, 2006) have demonstrated that a myriad of religious and ethnic groups participated broadly in reform initiatives and employed progressive rhetoric to their own ends. Additionally, Rodgers (1982) argues that these reformers were not united around a common social or political ideology, but rather shared a common set of practical concerns such as social efficiency, community improvement, health and cleanliness, and education. In this light, the era provides a complexity that lends itself to considerations of identity and, especially, issues of race, class, and gender. However, it is often easier to reduce this topic in the classroom to a more straightforward description of reform without the complicated nuance.

It is difficult in the high school classroom to move creatively beyond the standard accepted historical narrative about any time period, but the Progressive Era is particularly challenging because the term "progressive" has come to have several different meanings. The lesson developed by this group was an attempt to bring nuanced historical notions of Progressivism into the high school classroom. It required significant planning, the development of new materials, additional research, and integration with the mandated curriculum. It also required that educators explicitly confront issues of race, class, and gender in their classrooms. Even when presented in historical context, these issues complicated classroom discussion in the present. The concepts evoked particular feelings from students, and class discussion required that the teachers mediate with skill and sensitivity. At the same time, students learned to set aside emotional reactions and analyze information from an historical rather than a presentist perspective. Thus, the students were able to engage in a sophisticated discussion of progressive reformers and to develop a more mature conception of the disciplinary practice of history.

For this chapter, two high school teachers worked with a cultural historian and scholars of education to create a set of lessons that utilized the methods of historical inquiry and educational theater to teach critical questions about the Progressive Era to high school students. These activities required that students create biographical information, analyze the discourse evident in primary documents, and develop enough of an understanding of the historical context to understand individual discourse as part of a public dialogue. The culminating activity was a dramatic performance in which students played the roles of important Progressive Era figures, giving speeches and challenging each other on the meaning of the term "progressive." Many students came to empathize with the characters they were portraying, resulting in powerful performances from individual students and an intensified learning experience. The dramatic activities deepened students' understandings of the nature of historical debate and provided a means for confronting the difficult topics of race, gender, and class in a high school classroom.

The Progressive Era, an Historical Introduction

Professor Kevin Murphy's comments provided an historical framework for the group's work. Murphy, a cultural historian at the University of Minnesota, has written and taught about the ways in which ideas about gender, sexuality, and race play out in the realm of politics. His research is significant for its ability to capture the depth and the nuance of the Progressive Era, and is particularly useful for reconceptualizing how this time period might be taught. For example, Murphy notes that Theodore Roosevelt managed to make his ideas about American society seem practical, centrist, pragmatic, and quintessentially American. He employed a particular discourse that had broad appeal, promoting a form of masculinity in which men were called upon to quit being "mollycoddles" and instead be more energetic, virile, and engaged with American politics. Although this rhetoric might be interpreted as a progressive call for civic engagement, it was also directed only toward white middle-class men, to the exclusion of other communities, such as those of immigrants or blacks. In that light, Roosevelt's rhetoric is as much about race and class as it is about masculinity. Murphy's approach is to find documents that provide evidence of how listeners interpreted Roosevelt's language so that we can better understand how society was affected by these abstract themes. For example, an educated white man, a second-generation immigrant, and a more effeminate foreigner who was not interested in civic engagement would have very likely experienced and responded to Roosevelt's rhetoric in very different ways. Students might learn a considerable amount about the historical context through an exploration of the use of progressive discourse and the reactions of these different people.

Murphy explains that this approach might add important nuance to other significant discussions of the time period. For example, teachers often frame the debate between Booker T. Washington and W. E. B. Du Bois about the best way to promote equality for the black community as a dichotomous argument of opposite viewpoints. Du Bois called for a "talented tenth," which would be educated to be leaders of the black community, whereas Washington called for a more basic education for all black citizens that would allow for consistent and gradual progress over subsequent generations. However, in considering only these two positions, it is much harder to recognize other perspectives. For example, Ida B. Wells promoted possible armed resistance for the black community, and not just in self-defense. In this call for a more radical approach, Wells provided a more nuanced understanding of white supremacy. She understood the discourse of whites and used it to challenge accepted positions. As Murphy points out, there is a great deal to be learned from Wells' more nuanced and radical discourse. Her work can complicate our understanding by adding gender to a narrative that has been constructed around a binary between two men.

Murphy explains that although there is a tendency to teach about the biographies of individual reformers, or those who had power, there is a great deal to be learned from the discourse itself. He points out that we teach about individuals who are powerful, not necessarily because they are more important than others, but because they were often in positions that were empowered. However, it is helpful to recognize the genesis of their influence and consider how each chose to use the power that came with it. In that regard, a more effective way to teach might be to think about how these individuals are being interpreted and talked about as agents of power. Ultimately, if students can understand individuals and power as part of a larger dynamic system, they can come to realize that any period of history is contested and is often defined in terms of power. The Progressive Era, in particular, is illustrative of struggles over social, political, and economic power. Thus, Murphy suggests it is perhaps not as helpful to think about whether the reformers promoted progressive change or the status quo because these questions cannot be answered definitively, nor can those debates serve to make this period more useful to the present. It might be more helpful to understand multiple perspectives during particular time periods as a means to understand individuals, social structures, and historical context in a deeper and more nuanced way. The intersection between gender, politics, and sexuality provides for a rich context for engaging these questions. These categories add a more cultural or intellectual perspective to political history.

Background on the Teachers and Schools

Because of the complexity of these historical and contemporary issues, our lesson design process was greatly enriched by the inclusion of a variety of viewpoints. The group consisted of a social studies education professor with a research background in American history, a professor in educational theater with experience integrating drama into social studies lessons, a doctoral student and former social studies educator, and two innovative and experienced U.S. history teachers, Rachel and Henry. The group's discussions developed in dialogue with Professor Murphy's research and his suggestions about important topics in this historical time period. The design process itself was collaborative, and leadership of the group remained organic, with Rachel and Henry taking on more dominant roles as the lesson developed.

Although Rachel and Henry both taught eleventh-grade U.S. history classes in schools that mandate traditional curricula, they did so in contexts which differ in several important ways. Additionally, each teacher came to this process with distinct learning goals for their students. Rachel taught at a small, urban magnet school with a selective admissions process, a high level of student achievement—99 percent of its students attended college after graduation—and a reputation for progressive pedagogy. The school's student body consisted of slightly more than five hundred students, roughly half of whom were white and a quarter of whom were Asian. The remaining quarter was equally divided between black and Hispanic. Very few of these students were eligible for free or reduced lunch. Although somewhat diverse, this school was nevertheless quite dissimilar from the typical school in this urban area, in which over two-thirds of students qualified for free or reduced lunch, and almost three-quarters were black or Hispanic. Rachel's school also gave her a significant amount of freedom in her teaching methods and lesson planning, and emphasized cooperative learning as part of its mission. Nonetheless, short class periods (forty-one minutes) and overcrowding made such pedagogy a challenge. Rachel taught her U.S. History class of thirty-seven students in a cramped classroom in a building that her school shared with another school.

Henry, on the other hand, taught at a large, comprehensive high school in a middle-class exurb. The school of approximately two thousand students was more than 85 percent white, with Asians constituting the largest percentage (7 percent) of the remaining students. The median income of the community was higher than the state average, and a low number (around 5 percent) of students were eligible for free or reduced price lunch. In the recent past, the school had received recognition as one of the best in the state. Henry's class consisted of twenty-two students gathered in a spacious classroom for fifty-five minutes a day with access to an array of educational technologies. In his U.S. history class, however, Henry faced extensive oversight from administrators, with the result that his lessons had to be linked explicitly to state standards and assessments.

Given the demands of their teaching situations, Henry and Rachel entered the lesson design process at once excited about the unique opportunity to work with university-level social studies educators, yet at the same time concerned about structural and logistical aspects of the lessons. Both teachers were intent on situating the lesson within their larger units on the Progressive Era and the historical narratives they were helping their students construct throughout the year. As a result, they were adamant that the lesson had to be a "natural fit" with the rest of their curriculum. For instance, Henry mentioned that he normally begins his Progressive Era unit with a class discussion of the term "progress," using images of the 1901 World's Fair, and he wanted the lesson we collaboratively designed to utilize this prior learning. Both teachers, who were used to planning lessons individually, had limited experience with collaborative lesson planning and were worried that the lessons would not be flexible enough for their unique situations. Rachel had significantly more freedom than Henry in terms of lesson *planning,* but her large class size and short class periods meant that she was more focused on aspects of *classroom management.* Navigating the teachers' different teaching situations was a priority from the beginning of the group's work, and their concerns acted as the guiding principles for the lesson development.

A central concern for every member of the group was a lack of time available for meeting together to plan the work ahead. The group spent some time reflecting on the unfortunate fact that teachers very often work in isolation and that school structures often do not budget time for their teachers to plan lessons collaboratively. Both teachers indicated that, in general, it was rare to plan collaboratively; they both noted that they had never been taught, urged, or compelled to do so. Another group member pointed out that collaboration often requires teachers to devote more time to planning than if they were working alone. Nonetheless, the group was uniformly excited to try collaborative lesson design and to proceed despite these challenges.

First Impressions and Introductory Discussions

The group began by listening to each other's lesson ideas and making decisions about how to implement these ideas. This discussion started with a conversation about the Murphy interview, which the group found to be broad and complex, weaving the major questions of the Progressive Era with issues of social reform in twenty-first-century America. Immediately, the group realized that one of its major challenges would be developing guiding questions that would both be faithful to the multifaceted natures of class, gender, and race discussed by Murphy, yet would fit into a traditional, standards-aligned, high school–level "Progressive Era" unit. The group decided to focus on three key arguments that Murphy offered during his interview: (1) that relations of power were essential to understanding social reform; (2) that during the Progressive Era, power relations often could not be separated from race, class, and gender concerns; and (3) that these concerns became not only the driving forces for change during this period, but also a means to block reform. The group wanted students to investigate these abstract concepts in detail and not in the simplified way in which they are often taught in most high school history classes. We also agreed that the lesson should help students see that contemporary debates over the meaning and implication of the term "progressive" are often marked by a set of race, class, and gender conflicts similar to those that existed a century ago. Our hope was to make these issues engaging to eleventh graders who felt far removed from the Progressive Era.

In developing essential questions for the unit, the group had no shortage of good ideas, but we eventually settled on three: How did changing conceptions of race, gender, and class inform social movements in American history? And, what does it mean to be "progressive"? In that regard, how "progressive" was the Progressive Era?

These questions grew directly out of the Murphy interview and offered the teachers an opportunity to connect his central themes to their curricula and to students' lives. Both teachers decided that this unit would take place after a set of introductory lessons that addressed the political context and historical background of the era. Given this, students would already have a contextual frame for the lessons from the beginning of the unit. Rachel and Henry also wanted to teach more about the social issues of the era. Henry indicated that he had introduced his students to notions of gender in modern culture through advertising but that he wanted to build on this prior knowledge and connect it to the history of the feminist movement. Rachel hoped that these lessons would build a stronger disciplinary base for later units such as the Great Depression and the Civil Rights era. What excited the group most, however, were the links that these essential questions had to twenty-first-century issues such as affirmative action, hate crimes, and continuing forms of racism and sexism. For example, both teachers were interested in the stories that regularly appeared in newspapers and on television in early 2008—about the on-going democratic primary campaign between Hillary Clinton and Barack Obama and the scandal involving New York Governor Eliot Spitzer. These were issues that students were already talking about, and we hoped that we could connect these contemporary events to the Progressive Era in a compelling way.

At the same time, the group saw this lesson as chance for students to grapple with what Seixas (2004) calls "historical consciousness"—an awareness of the ways the collective memories of our past can affect our historical interpretations and shape our current identities. The dominant narratives of the Progressive Era, and indeed the major stories that we tell about Progressive Era figures such as Theodore Roosevelt, remain remarkably unquestioned among most students. This was a chance for teachers to add nuance, complexity, and even discomfort to those narratives, and to problematize students' readings of the past. The trouble with such a move, we knew, is that it can feed students' cynicism about America's past, which was certainly not the group's intention. As a result, we set out to find a way to help students move beyond their presentist notions, which can cause them to judge people and events of the past according to today's standards. Students would need to understand the world and the beliefs of people at the time, and be able to explain what "Progressivism" meant to people "back then." In short, students would need to put themselves in the minds of people from the Progressive Era, and develop what researchers of history education (e.g. Barton & Levstik, 2004; Portal, 1987) call empathy towards historical actors in the past. In order to do so, students would need to create their own stories about the past, instead of relying on "someone else's facts" (Holt, 1990).

The Lesson

Having settled on a theoretical framework and essential questions for the lesson, the group then turned to the difficulties of translating Murphy's interview into material useful within high school classrooms. In addition to the structural realities of high school teaching, the largest challenge of the interview was deciding which content to use. Murphy discussed a diverse group of historical characters, such as Theodore Roosevelt, Ida B. Wells-Barnett, W. E. B. Du Bois, and even lesser-known ones such as Goldsworthy Lowes Dickinson. The teachers investigated primary sources that he had suggested, focusing at first on Wells-Barnett's *A Red Record* with the thought of then looking for others, but the group felt that it was too difficult to choose from the compelling range of characters and primary documents that Murphy suggested. Thus, rather than focus on one historical actor's experience or one aspect of the race, class, and gender dynamics at work during this period, the group decided that students should see *as many of these people and issues together as possible*. The lesson would involve students playing the role of a "progressive" figure from the time period and explaining the effects of gender, race, or class issues on their life's work and their notions of social reform. The group brainstormed several possible ideas for lessons, each of which included a dramatic performance. At first, the discussion focused on a talk show or debate format, wherein students who were playing Roosevelt, for instance, would face off against those playing Wells-Barnett. The group also considered inviting the students to use *A Red Record* itself—which included a potential cast of characters—to develop a set of roles that could be portrayed dramatically.

Ultimately, the group decided to develop a theatrical exercise that revolved around a Progressive Era "conference," in which students would take on roles of prominent Progressive Era personalities. In this conference, each personality would argue in front of the class for the passage of their own "progressive" social reform legislation. The group selected, from Murphy's interview as well as other sources, roles that students might play. We chose these personae with an eye toward representing a mix of raced, gendered, and classed perspectives. Among those personas we chose to feature at our "conference" were Francis Willard, Booker T. Washington, W. E. B. Du Bois, Theodore Roosevelt, Emma Goldman, Margaret Sanger, Ida B. Wells-Barnett, and Amanda Berry Smith. Given the large size of Rachel's class, there were additional personalities proposed for her to incorporate, whereas fewer characters were needed for the smaller exurban classroom where Henry taught.

The lesson itself consisted of several parts. Because the key to a dramatic performance is a deep understanding of the character, teachers asked students, after being assigned their roles, to research the life of their chosen personality and create a character sketch. This document included the main events of this person's life and as many personal details as they could discover. In this, we took our cue from Murphy's work—his extensive use of primary sources, we thought, made his discussion of race, class, and gender issues much more powerful. To help participating students approximate the same depth in their portrayals, we also decided to give students an historical document written by each historical personality. For example, those playing Roosevelt read a speech entitled "The Duties of American Citizenship," and those playing Willard read excerpts from *Woman and Temperance* (1883). Although many of these sources were suggested by Murphy, others were already being used by Henry and Rachel. These primary source documents, together with the character sketches, were to be the inspiration for the students' in-class dramatic performances.

The culmination of the week-long lesson was the Progressive Era "conference," at which students gave speeches as the historical characters. Each student was asked to give a speech at this conference, proposing a new law or policy that would make U.S. social, economic, or legal structures more "progressive" in the sense that their character would have understood the word. In preparation for their speech, teachers asked students to review their knowledge of the time, to re-read their character sketches, and to draft a law that proposed a social reform and captured some of the key issues of the time period. Students did this remarkably well. Those playing Margaret Sanger, for instance, drafted a compulsory birth control law for poor and minority mothers; those portraying Frances Willard presented a law that extended rights to women who wanted to file for divorce. After each speech, the other students, while portraying citizens who would have been in attendance at the conference, asked questions of the speaker in an attempt to better understand each proposal. In this way, the students developed a dialogue between the progressive reformer and members of the public, and sought to understand how each person in conversation would have dealt with the issue in historical context. Following this dialogue, students voted on each piece of proposed legislation, in accordance with whether or not the law was "progressive" from their character's point of view. Those proposals that received the most votes were deemed the most progressive.

Impressions of the Lesson

The teachers' decision to employ drama in this lesson was a significant one, especially since neither had extensive experience utilizing such a method beyond the typical student oral presentations and classroom simulations. Yet both teachers immediately realized its potential for helping students to think critically about the legacy of values during the Progressive Era. Through an exploration of the significant questions relevant to their chosen characters, the dramatic process compelled students to reflect deeply on each character. Developing their role required students to synthesize a great deal of material from a variety of primary and secondary sources into their character sketches. As a result, the students were creating their own interpretations of the historical actors they were studying and exploring the dynamic relationship between the values and the behavior of each character toward the public. Prendiville and Toye (2000) argue that, in educational settings involving drama, this development of the role is more important than its dramatic performance. For the group, this was a crucial aspect of the lesson—we did not want students to be mere performers; we wanted them to empathize with the characters' attitudes and viewpoints.

Drama created a structure for students to explore in a meaningful way an historical problem and a source of tension, for which the resolution was unclear—something high school history students rarely have the opportunity to do. Teachers structured roles in such a way that each student's character was forced to argue for a position that many of the other nominally "progressive" characters might oppose. For example, Sanger's quest to make birth control methods available to poor women could be, and was, linked to the eugenics movement of the time; it was not simply an issue of women's rights. The question for each student as an historical character was whether or not he or she could argue well enough to convince other progressives that it was time to vote for their legislation, knowing that the other characters offered distinct and often conflicting social views.

Our use of educational theater methods sparked student interest and enhanced our abilities to simultaneously teach both historical content and historical thinking skills. The "conference" resulted in a greater sense of urgency and fun for students than if the lesson had been delivered in a format that included teacher lecture followed by group discussion, as might typically happen. By and large, the speeches that students wrote and presented in character to the rest of the class were well researched and delivered. In both high schools students were engaged with the unit, developed a relatively deep understanding of the complexity and humanity of the characters, and confronted some of the difficult themes in historical context.

Teacher participation seems to have had some impact on student engagement. In the exurban classroom, Henry developed and played an emcee character that was historically appropriate and different from his usual classroom demeanor. He participated in the conference, introducing each of the characters and moderating the discussion. As a result, students did not merely read speeches directly from their written work; they produced more dramatic deliveries. One of the most memorable moments involved a student playing Theodore Roosevelt arguing passionately and with a straight face for a law akin to eugenics. The student, perhaps the strongest performer of the class, became so wrapped up in her speech that she felt it necessary to pause and temporarily break character and take a few deep breaths so that she could distance herself from the character she was playing. She also felt compelled to apologize to the class for her viewpoints so that she would not be judged in the present for the character she played from the past. A student playing Frances Willard clearly struggled with her character's views as well, at one point apologizing to the class for the sexist language she was using.

Although this behavior was exhibited in both classes, clearly an indication of the success of the lesson, it was more strongly evident in the classroom in which the teacher participated in the drama. In both classes, seeing one of the students fully commit to his or her performance was all that was needed to bring about a marked change in other students' role work that followed. Henry, in his role as emcee for the conference scenario, was especially dedicated in modeling the sort of commitment to role that he wanted to see, exuding energy, empathy, and enthusiasm. His students, following his lead, eventually took over the conference. They engaged in a question-and-answer period with each character, which was guided by historical context and roles, to the point at which conversations had to be cut short for lack of time. Further, because of Henry's involvement, there was little prompting required to keep students in character and keep class discussion focused in historical context. These students became their characters with the opening of the conference and remained as such until the bell rang noting the end of the period.

The key to this lesson, then, was having students talk to each other's characters in a "public" setting. This performance aspect led to greater student engagement and also forced students to be accountable to each other for their learning. Although the students giving the speeches were clearly engaged, it should also be pointed out that the students who were in the audience were actively participating as well, asking critical questions and providing support in their roles as observers of the speeches during the Progressive Era. The most valuable and rich component of the final lesson, in fact, was the back and forth debate that transpired after each presentation finished, when student presenters no longer depended on their written speeches and instead were compelled to answer spontaneously questions from the rest of the class and defend the ideas they had put forth in the speeches. What made this discussion different from an ordinary discussion of ideas was that it transpired within a drama world that was established collectively by the students. This added an element of safety to the discussion, as it was easier for students to confront difficult topics as characters from the past, rather than from their positions in the present. Although there were some challenges with students not fully "owning" roles when the characters' ideas were so foreign to their own, the distance also allowed for class members to criticize the characters who had presented, without fear that the criticism would be taken personally. It was during this section of the lesson that students began to analyze the essential questions—and the changing conceptions of race, class, and gender in social movements—more deeply.

Although the lessons were successful in both classes, there were also some significant differences in the classrooms that affected the presentation of the conference and the discussion that followed. For Henry, the conference took place during one class period, with sufficient time for discussion of each presentation, as well as time for an open question-and-answer period at the close of all of the presentations. Class discussion continued on a second day devoted to the lesson, the added time being on account of student interest rather than because instructional goals had not been attended to. For Rachel, it took three class periods to get to all of the presentations, and discussion had to be carried over to a fourth. Given this, the immediacy of student reaction to the presentation was lost, and it was far more difficult for students to get into and maintain character over multiple class periods. The flow of the discussion was easily lost. Given the large number of students in a small space, it took Rachel about five minutes each day to get students organized and to handle administrative issues. The next few minutes were devoted to reintroducing the lesson, and a few minutes had to be saved at the end of class to close that day's lesson and remind students of assignments. As such, there was only about twenty-five minutes of class time devoted each day to the actual lesson, which left little response time for each presentation and very little open class discussion. Additionally, although Rachel was an excellent teacher with well-developed classroom management skills, the logistics of keeping more than thirty students organized and on-task in a small space, especially given the extent to which the subject matter elicited emotional responses, served to diminish further the amount of time devoted to the specifics of the lesson.

In the days following the conference, both Henry and Rachel conducted debriefing lessons with their students to assess how much they learned and to gauge the students' reactions to the lessons, and they later shared their reactions with the group. Both teachers perceived that the students had sufficiently adopted their characters, enjoyed the process of researching them, and were compelled to learn more about their characters in preparation for the presentation. Indeed, Rachel indicated that many of the students found their characters' lives so fascinating that it was difficult to keep them focused on the more narrow themes of race and gender. At the same time, many students commented that they had never really considered that historical figures might also have been just as conflicted about issues of race, class, and gender as the students themselves. The most surprising aspect of this lesson for the teachers was how much students learned about the characters, including the ones that were portrayed by others. In the end, there were vehement disagreements about which of the characters were truly the most progressive. Henry noted that the textbook mentioned Roosevelt as the most progressive and was pleased to hear his students react with skepticism. Prior to this lesson, he had tried to get his students to challenge statements that were included in their textbook with little effect. Following this lesson, the students were less willing to accept the textbook at face value and more skeptical about the accepted historical narrative.

The written assignments that students submitted in the aftermath of the lesson provided additional indication of what they had learned. Students had prepared a character sketch for each role that included a biographical timeline, a short biography, and at least one primary document that provided information. They used primary documents to describe the character's beliefs with regard to gender and race. The final piece in the character sketch was the conference speech that would propose the piece of progressive legislation. The assignment required that students engage in the disciplinary practice of history through the use of primary documents to understand better the character and the context. The students were guided in their work on primary documents with a learning aid that had been developed by Rachel. This tool included two sets of questions that could be used in the analysis of any primary document. The first set asked students to consider including the intended audience of the document, the main idea of the document, and insights that tell more about the author's beliefs. The second set was more specific to each topic, asking students to consider, for example, how Emma Goldman's strong beliefs about women's liberation could be reconciled with the fact that she opposed woman suffrage.

The dramatic aspects of the lesson proved the most powerful for both the students and their teachers. Worried at first that their image-conscious teenage students might not be willing to get into the roles and perform in front of their peers, Rachel and Henry readily agreed later that they faced little to no resistance on the part of the students. Taylor (1998) writes that teachers are often more concerned with learning that can be recounted or quantified after the lesson ends. However, he adds, "Learning in drama highlights the process of being caught up in events and being challenged to respond to them in the moment they are happening," thus urging teachers not to deny the power of participation in the drama itself (p. 54). Many students, even when they are not speaking in the drama, are still actively engaged in it. Likewise, other students crave performance. Some of the students who were struggling in both classes seemed to love, and succeed at, the performance aspect of this lesson. Henry's strongest performer was a female student who had already failed the course the previous year and who rarely spoke during class. Henry was surprised at her high level of engagement with the lesson, noting that even in this second year in the course, he had struggled to get her to participate in class. Rachel was particularly gratified to see two socially isolated students take on leadership roles during the preparation and performances. Most of all, students enjoyed the opportunity to engage with each other. The conference in Rachel's class could easily have taken longer than three days if she had not cut short the question-and-answer periods. Both teachers said that their students wanted to do lessons like this one again, and for many of students this lesson proved to be the highlight of the course. Henry' supervisor, who was skeptical beforehand about the issues raised in this lesson and the amount of time it was taking from what he considered the "real" curriculum, observed the lesson and was so impressed that he encouraged Henry to share his lesson with other teachers in his department.

Concluding Thoughts

Although Henry and Rachel both admitted to having had limited experience with drama prior to the project, the lessons they delivered were quite successful. Even the students who did not fully own their roles, either because they struggled with acting in front of the class or because they had trouble acting out positions that were so far removed from their own belief systems, learned a great deal about the people they researched. They were successful in their efforts to convey the values of their characters within an appropriate historical context. Infusing drama methodology into the teaching of history allowed historical themes to be put into dramatic action, heightening the importance and raising the stakes of historical exploration for students.

These lessons immediately placed the students into an emotionally charged learning environment in which they did the thinking, talking, decision-making, and problem-solving. It is not surprising, then, that the teachers indicated that students tended to remember more historical content from the Progressive Era than from any other unit they covered in the course. Both teachers commented that they were willing to continue to work with educational theater in the future. The university educators in the group also noted that this process had made them consider using educational theater in their undergraduate courses. Professor Murphy, asked to comment on the lesson after it was completed, was enthusiastic about the unit that was developed, believing it to be innovative and generative. He recognized the extent to which drama would allow students to connect the profile of the famous to a wider network of power relations.

The group did learn some valuable lessons about the uses and implementation of educational theater in the social studies classroom. They concluded that more experience with role-playing would have made the debates better, and that ideally such drama lessons would be incorporated throughout the year. Mini-lessons, in which teachers could work with students on aspects of performing, would have helped to warm up the students for their performances. The group also agreed that future drama lessons would benefit from a debriefing with students on the dramatic process, where they could discuss what made certain performances so memorable and why certain roles were difficult or easy to play. In this way, the teacher could discover what specific ideas from the past challenged students in their portrayals as well as those that connected or resonated with students. The teachers commented that they wished they could have had more time to engage the students in a group discussion on what they had learned about the character and the period of history, and how the dramatic process helped unpack those understandings. Here the role of the teacher cannot be overstated. Whereas it is potentially scary for a student to express the ideas of a character who is not their own, it might also feel safer when exploring large and controversial ideas. In this regard, the role provides the student with a sense of distance from the issues, and with it greater freedom to engage with the ideas. It is up to the teacher to help the class create the safe space for such experimentation and risk.

The lesson involved a great deal of time and effort on the part of all group members, especially the teachers. Developing essential questions and deciding on pedagogical strategies collaboratively were not easy tasks, especially given the fact that the group members did not know each other before this process began. Aside from the group meetings for planning, the lesson development process required time for reflection on the interview and source materials. This was a considerable commitment for a one-week lesson. Research on some of the characters proved challenging because of a lack of accessible details on their lives. Many of the suggested documents from the Murphy interview were not readily available online or in source readers, so teachers had to do considerable historical research on their own to find suitable documents for students. Henry and Rachel put tremendous amounts of effort into this project and allowed others to participate in their lesson development process and to observe their classes. Despite the tremendous time commitment, however, both Henry and Rachel expressed a desire to collaborate with university educators again on other lessons. The experience itself, as well as the opportunity to speak with other practitioners about the teaching of history, proved immensely valuable to all involved.

Works Cited

Barton, K. & Levstik, L. (2004). *Teaching History for the Common Good*. Mahwah, NJ: Lawrence Erlbaum Associates.

Connolly, J. J. (1998). *The Triumph of Ethnic Progressivism: Urban Political Culture in Boston, 1900–1925*. Cambridge, MA: Harvard University Press.

Gilmore, G. (1996). *Gender and Jim Crow: Women and the Politics of White Supremacy in North Carolina, 1896–1920*. Chapel Hill: University of North Carolina Press.

Holt, T. (1990). *Thinking Historically: Narrative, Imagination and Understanding*. New York: College Entrance Examination Board.

Link, W. (1992). *The Paradox of Southern Progressivism*. Chapel Hill: North Carolina University Press.

Montgomery, R. S. (2006). *The Politics of Education in the New South: Women and Reform in Georgia, 1890–1930*. Baton Rouge: University of Louisiana Press.

Portal, C. (1987). Empathy as an Objective for History Teaching. In Portal, C. (ed.), *The History Curriculum for Teachers*. London: Falmer, pp. 83–133.

Prendiville, F. & Toye, N. (2000). *Drama and Traditional Story for Early Years*. London: Routledge.

Rodgers, D. (1982). In Search of Progressivism. *Reviews in American History*, 10(4), 113–182.

Seixas, P. (ed.). (2004). *Theorizing Historical Consciousness*. Toronto: University of Toronto Press.

Taylor, P. (1998). *Redcoats and Patriots: Reflective Practice in Drama and Social Studies*. Portsmouth, NH: Heinemann.

Williard, F. (1883). *Women and Temperance*. Hartford, CT: The Park Publishing Co.

CHAPTER RESOURCES

I. Lesson Framework: Progressive Era

Intended Learning Outcomes (Use NYS SS Standards)

Understandings (Big ideas):

- Students will understand that the social movements of the past (e.g. Progressivism) are connected to the issues of today (race, class, and gender).
- Students will understand that there was significant debate during the Progressive Era as to the definition of the term "progressive," especially in terms of issues involving race, class, and gender.
- Students will understand that the term "progressive" is still used in various ways and can be viewed from different perspectives, and that these historical interpretations cause problems for us today looking back at the Progressive Era.

Essential Questions:

- How have changing conceptions of race, class, and gender informed social movements in U.S. history?
- How was the Progressive Era a time of conflicting views of race, class, and gender?
- What does it mean to be "progressive"? How "progressive" were the major figures of the Progressive Era?

Content Knowledge:

- Students will know the backgrounds and beliefs of the major figures of the Progressive Movement.
- Students will know the major social reforms of the years 1880–1920 and will know the individuals or groups behind these reforms.
- Students will know the causes of the social and cultural movement known as Progressivism.

Skills:

- Students will research, contextualize, and explain the perspectives of different Progressive Era historical actors using primary and secondary sources.
- Students will take on and dramatize a historical role, empathizing with and challenging that person's views on issues related to race, class, or gender.
- Students will write an argumentative essay that defines a concept (Progressivism) and evaluates the actions and ideas of historical actors against that definition.

Vocabulary/Important Concepts:

Progressive (contemporary and historical definitions), character-specific concepts, e.g. "Talented Tenth" (Du Bois) or "Temperance" (Willard)

Learning Experiences:

- Whole-class discussion of race, gender, and sexuality today, as well as student understandings of the term "progressive."
- Primary source document analysis in groups: Students given a source written or spoken by a Progressive Era figure to analyze using primary source reading aid.
- Library research contextualizing their primary source documents and learning about the life experiences of the historical actors.
- Groups create a character sketch of this person, paying specific attention to issues of race, gender, and sexuality, and then propose a law or social change that would have been deemed "progressive" by their character.
- Progressive Era "conference" at which students present these laws (in character) by giving a speech and defending their character's views in front of the class.
- Lesson debrief includes a discussion of what the term "progressive" "really meant", and a vote on which law/reform best exemplified the Progressive Era.

Resources:

- Excerpted documents from Progressive Era individuals focusing directly on race, sexuality, or gender, e.g. Ida B. Wells-Barnett, *A Red Record*, W.E.B. Du Bois, "The Damnation of Women", Theodore Roosevelt, "The Duties of American Citizenship"
- "Official" narrative of Progressivism (from students' textbook)
- Library or computers for character research

II. Relevant New York State and NAEP Standards

New York State Learning Standards, U.S. History

- Students explore the meaning of American culture by identifying the key ideas, beliefs, and patterns of behavior, and traditions that help define it and unite all Americans (MS.1A)
- Students interpret the ideas, values, and beliefs contained in the Declaration of Independence, the U.S. Constitution, Bill of Rights, and other important historical documents (MS.1B)
- Students complete well-documented and historically accurate case studies about individuals and groups who represent different ethnic, national, and religious groups in the United States at different times and in different locations (MS.3A)
- Students describe how ordinary people and famous historic figures in the United States have advanced the fundamental democratic values, beliefs, and traditions expressed in the Declaration of Independence, U.S. Constitution, the Bill of Rights, and other important historic documents (MS.3C)
- Students analyze the development of American culture, explaining how ideas, values, beliefs, and traditions have changed over time and how they unite all Americans (HS.1A)

- Students describe the evolution of American democratic values and beliefs as expressed in the Declaration of Independence, U.S. Constitution, Bill of Rights, and other important documents (HS.1B)
- Students develop and test hypotheses about important events, eras, or issues in U.S. history, setting clear and valid criteria for judging the importance and significance of these events, eras, or issues (HS.2B)
- Students compare and contrast the experiences of different groups in the United States (HS.2C)
- Students compare and contrast the experiences of different ethnic, national, and religious groups, explaining their contributions to American society and culture (HS.3A)
- Students research and analyze major themes and developments in U.S. history (HS.3B)
- Students prepare essays and oral reports about the important social, political, economic, scientific, technological, and cultural developments, issues, and events from U.S. history (HS.3C)

New York State Learning Standards, Historical Thinking

- Understand how different experiences, beliefs, values, traditions, and motives cause individuals and groups to interpret historic events and issues from different perspectives (MS.4B)
- Compare and contrast different interpretations of key events and issues in U.S. history, and explain reasons for these different accounts (MS.4C)
- Describe historic events through the eyes of those who were there (MS.4D)

Adapted from *New York State Learning Standards, U.S. History* (1996)

NAEP Learning Standards, U.S. History

Framework 1: Themes in U.S. History

- What individuals and groups have been important in maintaining, testing, and changing America's institutions? Which democratic institutions and procedures made change possible? (1)
- What are the basic principles and critical assumptions of American constitutional government about the sources of political power and the rights of individuals? What core ideas have influenced American society? What individuals have maintained, tested, and influenced the evolution of these ideas? (1)
- What individuals and groups played important roles in raising and responding to issues about diversity and unity in the American body politic? What major controversies arose about the issues? (1)
- What have been the roles of men and women in American society? How and why have gender roles changed over time? (2)

Framework 2: Periods of U.S. History

- How did Populism and Progressivism lead to changes in basic assumptions about the practice of democracy? Who were the leaders in these reform efforts? How did they affect events? (6.1)
- What gains and losses in individual rights resulted from the Progressive Era? How did these changes relate to other reform efforts? Who was left out of these efforts? (6.1)

NAEP Historical Thinking Standards, U.S. History

Framework 3: Ways of Knowing and Thinking about U.S. History

1. HISTORICAL KNOWLEDGE AND PERSPECTIVE

Students should be able to:

- Define historical themes and give examples of the ways themes relate to specific factual information
- Describe the past from the perspectives of various men and women of the time
- Explain the perspective of an author of a primary source document
- Describe different perspectives related to an historical issue or event
- Summarize the contributions of individuals and groups to U.S. history
- Summarize the meaning of historical sources and link these sources to general themes

2. HISTORICAL ANALYSIS AND INTERPRETATION

Students should be able to:

- Specify and explain cause-and-effect relationships and connect contemporary events to their origins in the past
- Explain points of view, biases, and value statements in historical sources
- Determine the significance of people, events, and historical sources
- Weigh and judge different views of the past as advanced by historical figures themselves, historians, and present-day commentators and public figures
- Demonstrate that the interpretation and meaning of the past are open to change as new information and perspectives emerge
- Develop sound generalizations and defend these generalizations with persuasive arguments
- Make comparisons and recognize the limitations of generalizations
- Apply knowledge, draw conclusions, and support those conclusions with convincing evidence

Adapted from National Assessment Governing Board (2006)

Works Cited

National Assessment Governing Board (2006). *U.S. History Framework for the 2006 National Assessment of Educational Progress*. Washington, DC: U.S. Department of Education.

New York State Learning Standards, U.S. History (1996). Albany: New York State Education Department.

Five
The New Deal

Framing the Questions: An Interview with Robert
Cohen, conducted by Rachel Mattson

Robert Cohen is a social studies professor in the Department of Teaching and Learning and an affiliated professor in the History Department at New York University. He is the author of *When the Old Left Was Young: Student Radicals and America's First Mass Student Movement, 1929–1941* (1993), editor of *Dear Mrs Roosevelt: Letters from Children of the Great Depression* (2002), co-editor of *The Free Speech Movement: Reflections on Berkeley in the 1960s* (2002), and author of *Freedom's Orator: Mario Savio and the Radical Legacy of the 1960s* (2009).

Robert Cohen: The '30s was a time when radicalism entered the mainstream in a way that it never had before and really never has since—because capitalism was really in a state of collapse. There has never been a decade that had as much mass insurgency in American history as the '30s. But when we teach the period, we a lot of times will strain the radicalism out—it's not there. Most textbooks don't talk about socialists or communists or radical intellectuals. Or if they do it's very, very brief and cursory.

Rachel Mattson: *That's true of social movements more generally. Even when folks teach about the black freedom struggles, they tend to speak only of the top three heroes.*

RC: Right, but at least those heroic figures are people who were in that movement, whereas what happened in the '30s is more striking. Most people would not claim that Lyndon Johnson invented the Civil Rights movement, whereas in the '30s, the way that it's presented, the New Deal invented all these things, like the Wagner Act—which Roosevelt initially opposed but he gets credited for—or the Social Security Act. It's like he invented all of these sort of progressive measures, and a lot of them didn't come from him. They came in response to mass movements, and those movements have been kind of erased.

When I teach about the '30s to the young kids, I'll take a bunch of New Deal measures that were associated with FDR and say okay, where did these ideas come from? So okay, the Wagner Act was meant to give workers a chance to decide whether or not to have a union. Roosevelt was initially opposed to it. It was a response to all that ferment—the San Francisco general strike, Minneapolis, Toledo—all of this ferment on the part of the labor movement put this demand on the federal government to do something to stop this violence against labor. It wasn't his idea, but eventually FDR got the credit and became a hero to blue-collar workers. The same thing is true about the student movement. The National Youth Administration essentially created work-study jobs. Where did that come from? That didn't come from Roosevelt's head. That came from communist and socialist and liberal students agitating for something they called the American Youth Act. And if you go down the line—if you think about the AAA [Agricultural Adjustment Act], you can connect that to the Farm Holiday Association, where they were pouring milk out into the streets in the Midwest—these weren't Roosevelt's ideas. It was that there was a mass movement pressing Washington to broaden its vision of reform.

RM: *Can you talk a little bit about the kinds of debates that are happening among people who study radicalism in the '30s, or the Great Depression more generally, and the kinds of historical questions that are most exciting to you about this moment?*

RC: An exciting debate concerns the scope, limits, and impact of radical insurgency. Many social historians highlight the kinds of protest movements that surged in Depression America and which are depicted in this map of mass protest (Chapter Resource II, Figure 5.1, p. 131). Not only were labor and farmers—who have an insurgent tradiion—organizing mass protests, but so were the unemployed, the elderly, and youth—groups with little history of such organizing. So the stress is on the '30s as a great age of mass mobilization in the United States. But, on the other hand, there's the idea put forth by historian Melvyn Dubofsky that the 1930s were actually "Not So Turbulent Years," which is the title of his essay (1986) stressing that even at the peak of labor insurgency it was only a minority of workers who were striking. He implies that social historians (like me) are so excited that masses of protesters were in the motion that their own romantic radicalism leads them to lose their sense of perspective, and so they forget that in the 1930s there were a lot more Americans who weren't protesting than who were. It's an argument that has to be taken seriously. I have problems with it (especially because it is almost always true that history is made by active minorities rather than apathetic minorities)—but if you want to understand the 1930s, you have to think about why we entered the Depression with a capitalist system and came out of it with a capitalist system. So Dubofsky may have a point in cautioning us not to overstate the transformational power of the protest movement of the 1930s.

Equally important is the debate about the New Deal, and that is: How much of a difference did the New Deal make? For a long time—this is before Reagan and the Right got much traction attacking the New Deal in their coded way for being socialistic—the main challenge to the New Deal's reputation came from New Left historians, most notably Barton Bernstein (1969), who deemed the New Deal a failure. He said "the New Deal failed to raise the impoverished. It failed to redistribute income. It failed to extend equality and generally countenanced racial discrimination and segregation" (Sitkoff, 1985, p. 212). He's emphasizing what the New Deal didn't do, and what wasn't transformed because FDR and the New Deal weren't radical and bold enough. This indictment of the New Deal has been challenged by liberal historians who admire FDR, such as William Leuchtenburg, who are much more like "Well wait a second, the New Deal was transformative and it humanized capitalism in way that were almost unimaginable before" What Leuchtenburg says specifically, is:

> If you had walked into an American town in 1932, you would have had a hard time detecting any sign of a federal presence, save perhaps for the post office, and even many of today's post offices date from the 1930's. . . . Washington rarely affected people's lives directly. There was no national old age pension system, no federal unemployment compensation, no Aid to Dependent Children, no federal housing, no regulation of the stock market, no withholding tax, no federal school lunch, no farm subsidy, no national minimum wage, no welfare state. As late as Herbert Hoover's presidency it was regarded as axiomatic that the government activities should be minimal . . . The New Deal sharply challenged these shibboleths. From 1933 to 1938 the government intervened in a myriad of ways from energizing the economy to fostering unionization.
>
> (Leuchtenburg, 1985, p. 213)

So if it wasn't a revolution, it was at least a "halfway revolution" (Leuchtenburg, 1963, p. 347)—where you went from a business state to a broker state. You opened up the system to workers, to immigrants, to blacks, to women. The American political system became much more inclusive than it had ever been. So that's the nature of the debate: How well did Liberalism respond to the Great Depression? People on the Left say, well, not that great. The liberals say basically that Roosevelt saved the American system in a time when other countries were going for extreme solutions, like Europe going fascist. That Roosevelt saved capitalism by humanizing it.

RM: *That is a very complicated thing to try to teach young people, I think.*

RC: I think part of the reason why it's a hard thing to teach and part of the reason why I published the book of letters to Eleanor Roosevelt (*Dear Mrs. Roosevelt*) was that discussion of class has gone out of the American language—basically people don't talk about class. Any politician who talks about class issues is called divisive, and so essentially nobody talks about it. So I think that the challenge is: How do you get students to be able to think about social class issues in a way that they can understand? And the way I do it is—one of the things that I would just say is that you have to use the textbook as a kind of oppositional force. That is, they're already learning about all these indecipherable alphabet agencies that are boring the students to death. It's really just a bland alphabet soup that confuses students. I think you have to, as the teacher, give it meaning—and the meaning is about three different things: recovery, relief, and reform. Of those the most central one for the long term is thinking about reform. That is: How do we understand this response, this great expansion of the federal government in the '30s? What does it mean? I think what it means is for one moment in American history mass movements emerged, challenged the system in some ways, and the system was responsive to it. It didn't adopt exactly what any of these movements asked for, but it was responsive. I think for students to see that protests fermented from below can change policy—that these things that are happening, these alphabet agencies they're reading about did not just come out of Roosevelt's head, but actually were a reflection of mass protests from below—that's really important for them to understand. What protests and ordinary people can do. And not to idolize it. Because there were a lot of problems and a lot of people were left out of these things. One of the things the New Deal did is that it left out migrant workers, and it left out domestic workers—which meant that many African Americans who worked were not covered.

RM: *And still aren't.*

RC: That's right.

RM: *It sounds also like there's a third historical question that you're identifying—about what the '30s can teach us about the effect of social movements on the government and about the historic relationship between popular movements and federal policy.*

RC: Right, that's the other piece of it. What can ordinary people do to effect change in a society that's really not democratic? I think one of the lessons of the '30s is that we can effect change by getting out in the streets and organizing. A lot of these things that happened would just simply not have happened. And I think, by the way, the New Left critique is valid but it also misses something.

RM: *The New Left critique being . . . ?*

RC: Seeing all this failure. There's a question always about what's your yardstick—what's your criteria and how realistic are you being. Are you really expecting an American president to be a socialist? I think it's really problematic to expect that. So the question is: Compared to what came before and what came after, how do you measure the impact of these mass movements? And I have to say they're a stunning success. They didn't overthrow capitalism, but they did move the government in this direction towards social democracy, toward people having a government that's more responsive to their needs. The New Deal didn't end the Depression like World War II did, but it stopped a lot of people from starving. And if you have a humane politics, that matters. I think it's too dismissive to say, well, it didn't end the Depression. One of the things with these letters—the letters that students, the young people, wrote to Eleanor Roosevelt where they were needing more help—is, their parents were already on New Deal dollars. That was stopping them from starving but it wasn't giving them enough to get a graduation dress, or to have an Easter coat, or to have a winter coat in some cases.

RM: *Can you pick one of these questions or debates and then choose a document and literally read it out loud, look at it, and talk about how you think it speaks to those questions and how you would use it with your students?*

RC: When I talk about the New Deal debate I look at the map (Figure 5.1, p. 131), and talk about the degree of insurgency you have going on. Can you imagine, today, what a map of social protest would look like? This map of the 1930s just shows that in almost every region of the country there's one kind of mass insurgency or another; a lot of them are strikes but some of them are like Upton Sinclair's movement in California, which was socialist, the Huey Long movement in the South, the Share-Our-Wealth program, the unemployed strikes in the South, the Bonus Army. Just the degree of ferment that's all over the country throughout the '30s. I think that just to visualize that is to show that it's really important to understand. And this is not a written document, this is a visual, and I think that's better. You can instantly visualize that, no, American politics in the '30s is not really about what's going on in Washington. It's really about all these massive, overlapping, overarching insurgencies that are putting pressure on the people who go to Washington, to make change. In other words, I don't start out with a picture of Hoover or a picture of Roosevelt. I start out with a map of all these mass insurgencies, and from my perspective that's what's defining the '30s, that's what's driving the change. Roosevelt comes into office without an agenda. He didn't come in as a Keynesian saying, yes, I'm going to spend billions of dollars on social welfare. No, he was critical of Hoover for spending much too much money on the federal government.

RM: *Do you have any primary documents pertaining to any of these particular movements that pressured Roosevelt to make some of the federal legislation that he ultimately made?*

RC: Sure. I have here a Declaration of Rights of American Youth in 1936, written by the American Youth Congress—a really interesting organization. It consisted of not just college students but high school students, church youth, labor. When people talk about the labor movement you think about middle-aged guys with pot-bellies and cigars. No, young workers were in those organizations and they were these Civil Rights organizers and farm organizers. So you just can't even imagine what it was like to have that kind of organization as a lobby, as a confederation of youth groups. Nothing like that has ever existed in American history since. It's really an amazing organization, and that was the organization that had this relationship with Eleanor Roosevelt because they were trying to push for legislation to help American youth, and Eleanor was very sympathetic to that goal. She was on the board of the National Youth Administration and was really pushing to expand it.

RM: *What is this document about?*

RC: This document is basically using the Declaration of Independence as a model for saying that we have these rights. I'll read you a part of it: "The Declaration of Rights of American Youth—in Congress July 4, 1936." This is, again, popular—using American imagery to make these social, democratic points.

> On the 4th of July 160 years ago, our forefathers declared their independence from despotic rule in order to realize their inalienable rights to life, liberty, and the pursuit of happiness. Today our lives are threatened by war, our liberties are threatened by reactionary legislation, and our right to happiness remains illusory in a world of insecurity. Therefore this 4th of July, 1936, we the young people of America and Congress assembled announce our own declaration—a declaration of rights of American youth. We declare that our generation is rightfully entitled to a useful, creative, and happy life, the guarantees of which are: formal educational opportunities, steady employment at adequate wages, security in time of needs, civil rights, religious freedom, and peace. We declare that we have a right to life, yet we are threatened by wars.

Then there's a whole segment on wars, which I don't really think we need to read. Then it goes on to say:

> We have a right to liberty. In song and legend America has been exalted as the land of the free, a haven of the oppressed. Yet on every hand we see this freedom limited or destroyed—Progressive forces are persecuted, minority nationalists are exposed to arbitrary deportation, the Negro people are subjected to constant abuse, discrimination and lynch laws, workers who strike for a living wage are met with increasing violence. These we affirm to be the ailments of that modern tyranny . . .

So already they're dealing with racism, they're dealing with the labor movement. It goes on:

> We demand not only the maintenance but the extension of our elementary rights of free speech, press, and assemblage. We oppose company unions and affirm the right of workers to join labor unions of their own choosing in order to advance their economic interests. We consider full academic freedom essential to progress and enlightenment.

> We strongly oppose fascism with its accompanying demagogy as a complete nega-
> tion of our right to liberty. We have a right to happiness. Our country with its natural
> resources and mighty industries can more than provide a life of security and comfort
> for all but today we are not provided with this security, we are not permitted to enjoy
> its comforts. We want to work, to produce, to build, but millions of us are forced to be
> idle. We graduate from schools and colleges equipped for careers and professions but
> there are no jobs . . . We insist upon our right to higher wages and shorter hours. For
> youth on farms the right to work means the right to security in the possession of their
> farms, free from the burden of debts.

So there you have, again—just think about that—it's this incredible coalition that's not just about labor, not just about students, not just Civil Rights, but now they're talking about farmers.

> We stand unalterably opposed to any program which destroys crops and livestock
> while millions remain unfed and undernourished.

Now that refers to the New Deal—they raised the price of crops—and as part of the AAA they destroyed crops.

> We proclaim the right to work for ourselves. We also proclaim the right of freedom from
> the toil of all children for whom labor can only mean physical and mental harm.

That's against child labor.

> Our right to work includes the right of proper preparation for work. Education must be
> available to everyone without discrimination—poor as well as rich, Negroes as well as
> whites—through free scholarships and government aid to needy students. Our edu-
> cational system should provide for vocational training at adequate wages under trade
> union supervision.

And that's again a union issue.

> We declare that workers of hand and brain, the producers of our wealth, the builders
> of our country, are the decisive force with which all true friends of peace, freedom and
> progress must ally themselves.

So that's also interesting and that's a big thing happening in the '30s with students and intel-
lectuals. Instead of looking to above and talking about social immobility, there is this romantic identification with those below—the working class.

> We recognize that we young people do not constitute a separate social group but that
> our problems and aspirations are intimately bound up with those of all people.

In other words, the student movement doesn't stand alone—it's part of a labor movement, which again, is very different from the '60s when the labor movement was seen as pretty corrupt.

> We extend our hand in fraternal brotherhood to the youth of other lands who also
> strive for peace, freedom, and progress. We look at this country of ours. We love it

dearly. We are its flesh and marrow. We have roamed its roads. We have camped in its mountains and forests. We have smelled its rich earth. We have tended its fields and dug its earthly treasures. We have toiled in it. Because we know it so well we know that it could be a haven of peace, security, and abundance for all. Therefore we the young people of America reaffirm our right to life, liberty, and the pursuit of happiness. With confidence we look forward to a better life, a larger liberty and freedom. To those ends we dedicate our lives, our intelligence, and our united strength.

That's the American Youth Congress redefining patriotism so that it is internationalist and egalitarian.

RM: *When you're reading that, what are you reading for? What are you trying to find out when you read a document like that?*

RC: While I read this document I'm asking: Who does this document speak to and who does it speak for? And the answer is, it points to this amazing breadth of concern. It's not just me and my group. If I'm a high school kid from New York City reading this document, I'm not just talking about myself. Say I'm a white middle-class student—I'm talking about African Americans, thinking about how black students are faring. I'm thinking about the people who can't afford to go to high school that are out working—they're in trade unions. I'm thinking about farm youth. Incredible identification with people in unprivileged positions beyond themselves. In other words, what I think of this as representing in a youth version is this idea of social ferment and people organizing to try to challenge the inequities, the suffering, that's come because of the Depression, and the inequities because of capitalism in the '30s.

This runs contrary to the Dubofsky view of "Oh, well, the '30s were not so turbulent." I think in the context of the youth, it was an amazingly turbulent time. It is amazing that you have this many people from all these different walks of life in motion, sitting down together and trying to come up with a platform to use classic American language, discourse like the Declaration of Independence, to talk about an agenda for socially democratic change, which is making new demands and very ambitious demands on the federal government and the New Deal. For me the document is about getting the young people whom we teach to see beyond themselves, to understand that there are groups that are very different from themselves that were in crisis in the '30s that are trying to reach out to each other. I don't want to exaggerate and say they succeeded in getting everything they wanted to. But just the fact that you could have a document—a document like this could not be created today—it's impossible—you just don't have people from these disparate groups talking to each other, let alone sitting down and coming up with a document for social change.

I guess that what's so interesting about the '30s is how much was put into question—even if not in the way that you or I might do it. But the fact that people are having to ask questions about capitalism, about individualism, about inequity, and about power in ways that they don't usually do it—the fact that you could open any college newspaper and find students raising critical questions—seeing socialist ideas being taken seriously—now that's an amazing thing. It's an incredible period where real debate and discourse and serious thinking—even if it wasn't systematic, again, as the way that some theoretician would have it—it's a much more reflective period, introspective period, in a way—even the '60s did not really get into, except for at the very end. I think in a way it belies the term *Depression*. There was a depression economically but politically it's the most un-depressing period—it's the most exciting period—that I've ever studied. Roosevelt gave this speech that no president today would ever dream of giving: He got up and said that we have to do better—there's too many people that don't have clothes, they're not well housed, and they're not well enough fed. The kind of honest confrontation of deprivation and the failures of our economic system is breathtaking. Most politicians today avoid discussing that—it's like they're professionals at avoiding tough economic issues. Under the New Deal it was like, no, no, we're not going to pretend that Depression's about to end, Hoover did that, but we're going to look seriously at these problems and try to address them. I'm not saying that they solved the problems, but just at least they were able to be serious and say look, we have millions of people who are suffering now. We've got to do something about that. I think for students to see that and then the next time there's a presidential election, maybe they'll think about why isn't anybody talking about the fact that there's millions of young people today born into poverty.

New Deal Postscript: Teaching about FDR and Barack Obama, by Robert Cohen

The 2008–2009 academic year has been by far the most exciting in this century for teachers and historians of the Great Depression, the New Deal, and FDR. The parallels between the failed presidencies of George W. Bush and Herbert Hoover—which include stock market crashes, bank failures, the collapse of the housing market, disaster in the American auto industry, surging unemployment, the discrediting of conservative Republican politics and economic doctrines—have sparked new interest in the history of Depression America among journalists, politicians, and the public. With the American economy in its most dire crisis since the Great Depression, key questions about the New Deal have suddenly taken on a new importance and relevance since they are not merely academic but are being pondered as guides to current policy making. Indeed, as Barack Obama ascended to the presidency, he was greeted with dozens of articles by journalists and historians urging him to consider FDR's example of vigorous federal intervention in the economy—massive government jobs programs, reform of the financial industry through new and tighter forms of regulation, and ambitious government stimulus packages to restore economic confidence—as a model for pulling American capitalism out of its crisis.

Time magazine (November 24, 2008) dramatized this new look back at FDR and the 1930s with a cover illustration depicting Barack Obama as Franklin Roosevelt. The cover shows Obama riding in FDR's convertible car, clad in his suit and hat, flashing an FDR style smile, with that distinctive Roosevelt cigarette holder jutting out the President-elect's mouth. This *Time* issue was headlined "The New New Deal: What Barack Obama Can Learn from F.D.R.—and What the Democrats Need to Do." Liberal journalists and historians invoked FDR's famed Hundred Days not merely as a model but also as a yardstick for measuring the launching of the Obama presidency, suggesting that if the new president was to succeed in righting the economy he needed to come into office as FDR did by setting a new tone in Washington, taking "bold action," and seizing opportunity by winning the passage of more than a dozen major economic bills to promote relief, recovery, and reform in his first three months in the White House (*Nation*, January 26, 2009).

This attention to FDR and the New Deal creates vast opportunities for teachers, who can use the Obama–FDR comparisons as a novel way of exploring perennial questions about the New Deal's meaning and impact, showing students that debates about the lessons of the Great Depression are important not only to historians but also to American society today.

The key questions about the New Deal concern not its start but its long-term impact. And here is where the Obama–FDR comparative framework is most useful for motivating discussion of the New Deal legacy. Should FDR and the New Deal be held up as models for President Obama to emulate, as the press has done recently? The answer depends, of course, on how one addresses the New Deal's impact and the question of whether or not FDR's recovery, reform, and relief programs succeeded. None of these questions is simple. With regard to recovery, how one answers depends on how we define success. If the bar for success is set at the highest possible point, complete economic recovery, it may seem tempting to argue that the New Deal failed since it was not the New Deal but the massive government spending in the mobilization for World War II that returned the American economy to major growth and full recovery from the Depression. Yet this all-or-nothing framework ignores significant areas where the New Deal achieved notable progress toward recovery, including the restoration and reform of the banking system, rescuing the agricultural economy from collapse, restoring growth to the educational system, and reducing unemployment massively from about 25 percent when FDR took office to close to 10 percent in 1937.

It is worth considering the ideological and political constraints that both FDR and Obama face as they consider modifications in the economic system. Critics on the Left took aim at FDR for missing the opportunity to radically revamp the collapsed American banking system. Had he wanted to, FDR might well have nationalized the banks. The same was true of President Obama. Yet in both cases the presidents, though supporting an expanded federal role and new regulation, drew back from challenging the basic private enterprise model and never seriously considered nationalizing the banks. Students ought to debate the pros and cons of this Obama–FDR reverence for capitalist structures, and consider whether or not it is fortunate that experimentation with new economic forms is bounded by the traditional American reverence for capitalism.

Works Cited

American Youth Congress (July 4, 1936). *The Declaration of the Rights of American Youth.* New York: Robert Cohen Personal Collection. Downloaded November 1, 2007 from http://www.newdeal.feri.org/texts/757.htm.

Bernstein, B. (1969). "The New Deal: The Conservative Achievements of Liberal Reform," in Bernstein, B. (ed.), *Towards a New Past: Dissenting Essays in American History.* New York: Vintage Books.

Cohen, R. (ed.) (2002). *Dear Mrs. Roosevelt: Letters from Children of the Great Depression.* Chapel Hill: University of North Carolina Press.

Dubofsky, M. (1986). "The Not-So-Turbulent Years: A New Look at the American 1930s," in Stephenson, C. and Asher, R., (eds.), *Life and Labor: Dimensions of American Working Class History.* Albany: State University of New York Press.

Leuchtenburg, W. (1963). *FDR and the New Deal, 1932–1940.* New York: Harper and Row.

Leuchtenburg, W. (1985). "The Achievement of the New Deal," in Sitkoff, H., *Fifty Years Later: The New Deal Evaluated.* New York: Alfred A Knopf.

Sitkoff, H. (1985). *Fifty Years Later: The New Deal Evaluated.* New York: Temple University Press.

Time magazine, November 24, 2008.

Essay: Teaching the New Deal in Multi-Ethnic Urban Public Schools

By Shari Dickstein, with Cara Fenner and Benjamin Geballe

The New Deal is a very rich topic of study that history and social studies classrooms can approach through a variety of avenues of inquiry. The "canonic" knowledge of the New Deal (assuming state and national standards define a canon) usually involves student understandings of the economic reasons for the crash of 1929; a familiarity with Hoover's volunteerism and hands-off approach to solving the economic crisis; and characterizing the presidency of Franklin Delano Roosevelt (FDR) as a testament to the merits of executive leadership, while recognizing that such an extension of executive power may have violated separation of powers and checks and balances.

Essentially, most state and national standards about the era elicit a political and economic history of the 1920s and 1930s.

It is often difficult not to conceive of the New Deal without conflating the social, political, and economic accomplishments of the era with FDR's public persona as the propelling force for change. The more interesting and engaging story, however, is the social history of the Great Depression. This chapter chronicles how a teacher educator, a social historian, and two urban secondary school teachers worked collectively to develop a unit on the New Deal that did not allow FDR to monopolize center-stage and opened up the possibility of engaging students in meaningful questions about effective social mobilization. In this collaboration, Dr. Robert Cohen, New Deal historian and Chair of the Department of Teaching and Learning at New York University's Steinhardt School of Culture, Education, and Human Development, encouraged our group to re-think instructional goals in teaching the New Deal, and conveyed that the era was as much a story of social activism and the will of a people to be heard as it was a story of economic crisis and lasting political and economic change.

According to Cohen, when teaching the New Deal in secondary history and social studies classrooms, teachers oversimplify the political and economic history of the era by making the Roosevelt administration seem the only major source of reform. As he noted in the interview excerpted above,

> The '30s was a time when radicalism entered the mainstream in a way that it never had before and really never has since—because capitalism was truly in a state of collapse. There has never been a decade with as much mass insurgency in American history as the '30s. But when we teach the period, we a lot of times will strain the radicalism out—it's not there. Most textbooks don't talk about socialists or communists or radical intellectuals . . . It's like [FDR] invented all of these sort of progressive measures, [but most of them] came in response to mass movements, and those movements have been kind of erased.

Cohen's comments challenge the tendency of history teachers to center New Deal era instruction on the political and social heroism of the Roosevelt administration, and instead call upon educators to re-frame traditionally accepted understandings of the period's historical message. His comments revolutionized *our* thinking, compelling us to frame for and with our students a portrait of a nation in dire straits, a newly elected administration faced with a poor, hungry, weak, and disenfranchised people, explore what needed to be done in order to remedy these ills in our democracy, and examine the *true* processes through which these remedies occurred, for they were the result of actions taken not only by the government but *by the people*. Armed with this new framing of an historical era, we engaged in a collaborative planning process.

Framing the New Deal

The task facing our group of teachers and scholars was a difficult one: How might we frame the era with social activism at the center while upholding the integrity of the rich political and economic history of the time period? The 1920s and 1930s were fraught with political upheaval; economic triumphs and deep economic strife; world peace and world war. Emphasizing the social aspects could not occur without a focus on the economic and political implications of the era, both in their own right *and* in tandem with the unit's social message. Emily, the tenth-grade Boston history teacher collaborating on the unit, noted, "I believe that one important lesson of the Great Depression and New Deal is economic in nature." She continued:

> In the absence of an economics requirement for our city (Boston) and state (Massachusetts), the New Deal might be the only place where a Boston Public School (BPS) student might be exposed to ideas having to do with the economic cycle and the stock market, investment, speculation, inflation, deflation, overproduction, unemployment, and even public assistance as a landscape of specific programs. Because there is no meaningful treatment of economics anywhere in a BPS student's scope and sequence, I feel that it's incumbent on history teachers to teach economics within the content in a very explicit manner and tie those understandings to current economic realities, and the New Deal is the place in the curriculum for those goals.

Tom, an eighth-grade collaborating teacher on Manhattan's Lower East Side, shared Emily's sentiments:

> Middle school students do not really get economics or have any kind of understanding of how the markets work. Teaching students the causes of the Great Depression in more depth than getting them to say that the stock market crash caused it (which is a gross oversimplification) is tough given their limited knowledge of the inner workings of the market.

Clearly, comprehensive coverage of the economic and political upheaval that characterized the era *through* the lens of social history would be critical to a nuanced student understanding of the time period. We needed, then, to determine how this might be done in the most relevant and meaningful way for students. The students in this project consisted of more than one hundred New York City eighth-graders and close to one hundred Boston tenth-graders. The New York City students included some who struggled with special needs and many for whom English was a second language. The Boston students, one-third of whom had special needs, lacked common experience learning about history because of Boston's school choice system and the lack of a standardized test requirement for history and social studies in the early and middle grades, causing them to enter high school with different levels of knowledge about particular historical time periods. For these reasons, it was necessary that we consider the diverse needs of the students involved in this project, the characteristics of their schools and their communities, and the perspectives of our collaborating teachers, in order to develop our unit.

A Tale of Two Cities

The complexity of our task was compounded by our distance and grade-specific contexts. Half of our team was based in Boston and the other half in New York City, in both middle and high school classrooms. Beyond that, the knowledge, skills, and experiences of our students varied greatly. One commonality that facilitated our efforts, however, was the capacity, experience, and commitment to equity and social justice that each team member brought to the project.

Tom and Tower Middle School, New York City

Tom, an eighth-grade teacher at Tower Middle School, was in his seventh year teaching social studies. He began his career in Oakland, California, teaching seventh- and eighth-grade history at a low-performing school. He later moved to New York, where he taught tenth-grade social studies at a small high school, before moving to Tower Middle School, where he teaches eighth grade and also works as the social studies coach. In his current capacity as coach, he works with the social studies teachers on their pedagogy and organizes departmental activities, professional development activities, and curricular planning.

Tower Middle School is located in the heart of New York's Chinatown, and serves a largely immigrant population. With a student body of just over seven hundred, divided into three smaller academies within the school, the faculty is able to collaborate regularly and develop close personal relationships with the students. Tom works closely with his fellow eighth-grade teachers through weekly department meetings largely used to plan by grade level, and in individual curricular planning meetings with his two colleagues who also teach eighth-grade social studies. Tower has in the past few years won grants that enable every student in school to have a personal laptop throughout the day. As a result, the teachers regularly use technology in the classroom and for all kinds of activities. Blogging, video projects, PowerPoint presentations and all manner of digital production are regular features of a student's experience in the school—both in day-to-day learning as well as in unit and exit projects. Such a prevalence of technology in the classroom is important in Tower's community because many of the students do not have access to computers at home. The student body is mostly Chinese-American, and is a mix of both first- and second-generation immigrants. The 20 percent of the school that is not from a Chinese background is made up of African-American, Dominican, and Puerto Rican students. The Tower students participating in our project were either native English speakers who grew up in the United States or students who tested out of transitional language classes. Although the students at the school are divided into honors and general education classes, there is still a wide academic gap within each class.

Tom planned to teach the curriculum to three classes at Tower. One was a "Special Programs" class, essentially a tracked class with students who had scored threes (illustrating that the student is "at the standard," or has "met grade level") and fours (meaning student performance "exceeds grade level") on their state tests for Math and/or English Language Arts (ELA). The other two classes were more heterogeneous; one had five students with an Individualized Education Plan (IEP), and the other had seven. These twelve students received extra time on tests and were entitled to simple accommodations, such as being allowed to sit in the front of the room. Most of them tested at either the two (indicating that student performance is "below grade level") or three level on their standardized Math and ELA tests. One IEP student with severe emotional issues had an aide in the classroom with him at all times.

Ethnically, Tom describes his eighth-graders as Asian (60 percent); Dominican or Puerto Rican (30 percent); or African-American (10 percent). Tom notes, "most come from poor or working-class families, with many parents working long hours and not at home, with jobs such as restaurant workers, cab drivers, and police officers." Adding to the complexity of teaching to a socio-economically, ethnically, and academically diverse group of students, Tom faces an additional challenge in that he teaches in English, which is not the native language of many of his students. He notes that although a number of his students "are bi- or trilingual, many of them do not speak English at home."

The instructional challenges Tom faces are quite common to the urban context. The demographic breakdown of New York City's schools writ large is as diverse as the student composition in Tom's eighth-grade classrooms. The challenge of finding ways to teach history in a relevant and meaningful manner to such a diverse student body, entering the classroom with different skill sets and language capacities, necessitates constant reflection. We checked ourselves throughout our collaborative process, asking questions such as: "How might this document be perceived by students in a mixed-ability middle school class?" or "Might we need to change the wording of this question to make it more relevant and understandable for non-native English speakers?"

Emily and Success High School, Boston

Emily, a tenth-grade teacher at Success High School, was in her sixth year of teaching social studies. After training at Teachers College in New York City and teaching in a bilingual school in Queens, Emily moved to a suburban New York community, where she taught AP U.S. history and global studies in high school. For the past three years, Emily has been teaching at Success High School, a small public school in Boston, where she is head of the History Department.

Similar to Tower, Success also provides instructional challenges and a characteristically diverse urban student population. The student body totals 392 students, 37 percent of whom are African-American, 27 percent Asian, 19 percent Hispanic, and 17 percent white; about 21 percent of all of Success's students are classified as special education, and 20 percent identify as English language learners and are taught in sheltered English instruction classrooms.

For almost a decade, Success has been part of a larger education complex, which was originally one large school erected in the early twentieth century. Initially, Success's mission was a focus on information technology; although the school's students still enjoy two computer classrooms and three mobile MacBook Labs, Success's mission has shifted to college preparation. Known throughout the city for academic rigor, Success receives students through Boston's School Choice Program, and is among the most highly requested non-exam high schools in the district. Success is a very high-achieving school that has been awarded prizes for academic achievement and strong performance indicators. Its performance stems largely from being a small and cooperative environment, having a strong student population, many of whom have chosen the school, and having a dedicated faculty.

Initial Conversations

Initially, two members of our team met in Boston to brainstorm the major themes (e.g., activism) the unit might include, and to draft an essential question. Robert Cohen had identified three primary source documents that he felt illuminated the era's rich social history: a map of the United States entitled "Popular Protest in the Great Depression, 1933–1939," detailing the various strikes, demonstrations, and acts of protest taken by Americans in response to harsh conditions brought about by economic collapse; a map entitled "Eleanor Roosevelt's Travels, 1936–1937," illustrating the various states, cities, and towns visited by the First Lady in the period of just one year; and "The Declaration of the Rights of the American Youth," authored by the American Youth Congress in July 1936. Determined to use these sources to teach about the uniqueness of the New Deal era, the Boston team began the meeting by thinking about and articulating the big ideas of the time period and how they might relate to Cohen's recommendations.

Those present first spoke of the reality of the nation in the early 1930s and envisioned a nation depressed, battered by images of shantytowns and Hoovervilles made popular by the photographs of Dorothea Lange and Walker Evans. They juxtaposed this portrait of poverty to the wealth that still existed for some during the time, and explored how to problematize this paradox for and with students. The team spoke of the irony of a catastrophic depression following an on-the-surface time of roaring progress.

We also discussed the actions taken, decisions made, and beliefs held by those in power during the Great Depression and among the populace in general, and it became clear that within the context of the era there existed a number of potential lesson opportunities: one lesson might focus on the political transformation that occurred when Hoover, a laissez-faire–oriented Republican, was replaced by FDR, a Democratic man "of the people"; other lessons might focus on the ideological transformation incurred by the election of FDR, extending beyond politics into society. Another lesson might explore the concept of escapism and how the people looked to gambling, team sports, and movies to suspend reality for a moment, if only to remember what it meant to smile and feel hopeful; another might examine the processes through which a socially active people proved ready to stop at nothing to procure their rights.

The Boston team also recognized the importance of framing the unit through a lens of hope so as to emphasize optimism and faith in the potential of democracy. This decision was in no way independent of an awareness of the students our team was charged to teach in both cities. Their own socially located selves—living in urban communities and attending often under-resourced schools—necessitated that we illustrate the power of an active, determined people in a democracy to empower our own students to realize the possibility of change. It was necessary to paint for and with our students a portrait of a democracy in a dire state of affairs and to explore *what* was done to remedy the nation's ills, *how* it was done, and by *whom*.

It proved difficult to decide upon a question that would guide this unit. A number of possible themes emerged. The unit could focus on the economics of financial hardship; the socio-economics of Civil Rights; the collaborative spirit of the New Deal; the social mores with regard to political access and decision-making. After much discussion, the Boston group put the social, economic, and political wellbeing of the people at the forefront, and *initially* determined to construct a unit that would focus on the government's role, willed by the people, in the cultivation of these social, political, and economic benefits.

Upon further thought, however, this idea seemed somewhat contradictory to what Cohen had proposed. A singular focus on the government as the nurturer of reform seemed antithetical to the more socially active lens that the team had hoped might frame the unit. It was therefore critical to incorporate what the people of the nation had done to aid the country's political, economic, and social woes into an essential question. Ultimately, in order to balance both governmental as well as civic activism, the group members present settled upon the guiding question, "How can a democratic government and its people work together to remedy political, social, and economic ills?" as the essential lens through which to frame students' understanding of the time period, knowing that adaptations would be necessary in order to meet the needs and capacities of Tom, his school, and his students. This next section highlights the rich dialogue that brought this inter-city collaboration to life, and illustrates the dynamic process that joined experts from different areas of education to develop an enriching learning experience for students.

The Collaboration

In January 2008, the ideas developed in Boston were shared in New York with the entire group, consisting of Tom, Emily, Cohen, and our group leader, Shari Dickstein, herself a teacher educator and former social studies teacher. Cohen's presence throughout the planning process was invaluable: he was present at many of our meetings and made himself available through e-mail and phone whenever necessary.

At our first full group meeting in New York City, and throughout those that ensued, the initial ideas developed in Boston were built upon and, at times, modified. Tom, for example, expressed concern early on that, as written, the essential question's vocabulary might be difficult for his students, who were younger than their Boston counterparts and had less familiarity with the English language. Given this, we modified the question for Tower's eighth-graders. Whereas the Success students explored the unit via the question, "How can a democratic government and its people work together to remedy political, social, and economic ills?," Tower's students were guided by three essential questions, facilitating their clearer grasp of the unit's themes and enduring understandings: "How active should the government be in the lives of the people? Who does the government help? What is the responsibility of the people and the government to work together to improve society?" Once we settled upon on our essential questions, we devoted our meeting times to the creation of a final assessment and to the development of a variety of lesson plans and additional questions to pose for students, using the backward-planning methods advocated by Wiggins and McTighe in *Understanding by Design* (2004).

In an early spring meeting, Tom noted that he found "it interesting that textbooks tend to overlook the people-powered/grassroots element in this story. Do we not want our children empowered?" His comments illuminate the importance of highlighting the social history of the New Deal, and made clear that we approached this collaboration from similar pedagogical interests in civic empowerment (Dixson & Rousseau, 2005) and equity (Hollins & Guzman, 2005). As Emily noted:

> In the absence of any discussion of social reform and the relationship between civil society and those who lead us in our classroom textbooks, it is critical to create experiences for students to learn about them in other ways. The social story begs the question of where the impetus to stand up and demand change really comes from. While there is so much driving a person to push for reform, what comes across to students is sometimes unfortunately that those moments in history or that impetus in a person is both unusual and even unsustainable. While social reform is incredibly complicated, there are so many that contribute to every movement that we never really get to highlight.

When we began planning lessons using the documents recommended by Cohen, we quickly reached consensus that it would be as critical to speak of the era's social movements and the degree to which the government and people galvanized to remedy national woes as it would be to explore and analyze the effectiveness of their actions. Cohen had noted that often, during moments in U.S. history when people have a little bit of hope during a bad time, social activism increases. We thus collectively agreed that it would be important to highlight the idea that activism increased under the Roosevelt administration, as compared with the Hoover administration, because people had more faith in political change with FDR at the helm. The concept that more political activism might indicate more faith in government led us to other questions about contemporary perceptions of the New Deal. How might we measure the efficacy of the New Deal? How effective was the New Deal in addressing the needs of the people? In exploring the above questions, we not only solidified our final assessment, but also realized the beauty of our interdisciplinary collaboration.

As the conversation began to broach questions of the New Deal's effectiveness, Cohen suggested that we might also use his book *Dear Mrs. Roosevelt* (2002)—a collection of letters from children in the United States to the First Lady. We welcomed his suggestion. As Emily noted, *Dear Mrs. Roosevelt* "reveals both the plight of the American people at the time as well as their deep trust in the government's (with Eleanor Roosevelt as the proxy) willingness and ability to directly address the seemingly insurmountable problems of their circumstances." Looking at the letters, the pleas, and the circumstances of so many people would, she continued, "help students to both empathize as well as to critically conceive of their own relationship with government." Furthermore, by embedding the letters—which provide first-hand details of people's real lives and experiences—within a larger unit exploring the will of a people and a government to remedy the nation's ills, we would be able to help students perceive both the government's and their own ability to address social and economic woes in a democracy.

The collection of letters in *Dear Mrs. Roosevelt* helped us to create lessons wherein students explored the effect of New Deal programs on the lives of the people, and provided us with useful questions for our final assessment. We committed to create a culminating project that would have students (1) analyze the effect of the book's letters on the government; (2) explore the actions of citizens to influence government policy; and (3) consider the degree to which the woes and remedies of the New Deal are still felt today, so that they might (4) demonstrate their grasp on the era's short- and long-term impacts.

We decided to have students work in groups to choose letters and images that would aid in the creation of their own personal narrative on the era. Students would then showcase their learning through the medium of the iMovie. The choice to use group work, narrative creation, and technology as the venues through which students would present their learning had four overarching purposes:

- We wanted to develop participating students' abilities to collaborate; working in groups to create iMovies would necessitate collaboration.
- We wanted to encourage students to create their *own* narratives, much like those personified by the authors of the letters to Eleanor Roosevelt. This allowed for further alignment between the task in which we were asking students to partake and the essence of the letters themselves.
- Creating a final assessment in film form allowed us to use the rich technological resources available in both schools, a rarity in most urban contexts upon which we felt compelled to capitalize. We wanted students to become fluent in a new technology; in an era such as ours, technological literacy is critical to student success.
- Framing the assessment through a lens that asked students to analyze the *effectiveness* of New Deal policies both then and now would keep the history relevant and meaningful.

In the true spirit of backward design, having reached consensus on the style and scope of the final assessment we felt prepared to turn to concrete lesson planning—and it was at this point in the planning process that the true challenge of our inter-city, inter-disciplinary collaboration would manifest.

It would be incorrect to say that we agreed upon, and had worked out all of the kinks in, our New Deal unit from the outset of the project. From a distance, meeting online and over the phone, we continually adapted our lesson aims, tweaked various documents to make them readable and understandable across diverse reading levels, and thought deeply about where to place particular lessons within the unit. Throughout the planning process, however, we held to the collective aim that each lesson would focus on the following overarching instructional goals:

- We wanted students to understand that the government has an important role to play in a market economy, and that a deep economic crisis can occur even in the absence of a major disaster. Market failure might be a function of a crisis of confidence, or irresponsible and unrealistic financial practices. Given this, we aimed to deepen students' understanding of the nature of economic cycles and the role that public perception, especially confidence, might have in them. We also wanted to help students understand the effect of a market economy on culture, and the potential correlations between wealth and the arts.
- With regard to the role of the citizen in a democracy, we wanted students to understand that change in government occurs when people call for it, and that during the New Deal, there was a fundamental change in the relationship between the federal government and

civil society. The New Deal built a tradition of more governmental presence in the economy, including many of the economic constructs that still exist, such as the Securities and Exchange Commission, the Federal Deposit Insurance Corporation, the Social Security Administration, and the National Labor Relations Board. Democracy allows for an open dialogue between citizens and their government, and we determined to show students how the New Deal invited, encouraged, and responded to this dialogue.

In planning lessons with the above instructional goals in mind, we hoped that students would develop a basic understanding about the details of the era and its surrounding historical context, and a command of basic financial and economic concepts. Further, through our use of the letters, maps, and additional documents recommended by Cohen, we were able to highlight the social history of the New Deal to an even greater degree.

Use of the letters allowed students to explore the particular situations of the authors and their families, analyze what the children and young adults writing the letters believed that the government—using Eleanor Roosevelt as their proxy—could do for them, and explore the relationship between the American people and the government at the time. This led to rich discussion in both grades about the students' own lives, the social issues they experience, whether and if so to whom they might write letters, and for which problems they might request assistance. Students had to think critically about which problems they might like to see solved; whom these problems most affect; what some potential solutions might be; how to persuade others to see the critical nature of the problem; and how to motivate others to act.

Through an early unit lesson using a document entitled "Popular Protest in the Great Depression, 1933–1939," Tower and Success students were asked to consider what the map (Figure 5.1, p. 131) was telling them about the time period and to think about the kind of activity or demonstrations of activism they saw happening. Emily asked her Success tenth-graders to go one step further and think about which groups of people seemed most active in trying to bring about change. They were asked to speculate about why they thought such activism was occurring and why these particular groups of people might have been working toward change. Some of the documents recommended by Cohen proved harder to integrate into our lessons. We had trouble, for instance, with "The Declaration of the Rights of the American Youth." Tom noted early on that the language of the document would be difficult for his students to grasp. But Cohen insisted on the importance of this document; it powerfully conveys, he argued, the ways in which young Americans were using their voices to demand change during the Depression. He also stressed that it illustrates how students joined together and spoke collectively to demand change from the government. To address Tom's concerns, Cohen suggested that he not use the original document in the lesson, and offered a set of strategies to paraphrase the document's message for use in Tom's middle school classroom. Heeding Cohen's advice, Tom modified the document and distributed the edited version to his students, asking them to summarize each paragraph in their own words and then facilitating a conversation about the authors of the original document, its meaning, and its implications.

Reflections on the Collaborative Process and the Teaching of the Unit

Reflecting back upon our work, we identified four central insights gained through the process of collaborating as an inter-city, inter-grade, inter-disciplinary team. First, teaching social history is critical to understanding the meaning of the Depression and New Deal. Second, the technological aspect of unit was critical to its success. Third, this unit built upon the social, cultural, and academic capital of our students. And, fourth, collaboration transformed our teaching in surprising ways.

Social History as Critical to Understanding the Meaning of the Era

The decision to put social history at the center of the unit and use it as the lens through which to illuminate all content was an incredibly useful one. It made the focus of the unit more about political enfranchisement, and the actions, decisions, and personal experiences that so dramatically reshaped civil society's relationship with government.

Approaching the New Deal through social history helped to engage students' empathy and sense of citizenship, and the content was illuminated and sustained by the students' interest in personal economic security and the role that we all play in it. When approached strictly through the lens of political history, the New Deal seems like some laundry list package of experiments and reforms, quantifiable and easily forgettable. Using the lens of personal experience and social history made the classroom experience palpably relevant and made students' products genuine expressions about their beliefs in the role of government and the ability of civil society to demand that the role of government take a more populist shift.

Technology as Key to the Unit's Success

The final project video was a good medium to use in teaching this unit. It forced students to construct a meaningful narrative and then relate this narrative to the present day. Clearly, the more relevant history feels and the more authentic a particular task seems, the more students will connect with and understand the content. The students found the more contemporary technological medium of the iMovie to be an engaging way to demonstrate their knowledge. Because this unit dealt with issues of poverty and justice, and because the project was essentially a documentary film, there was high interest in what happened. It was a great vehicle through which students could collaborate with each other, demonstrate content knowledge and analysis, and transform the crush of events in the 1930s into compelling personal narratives. As a more practical matter, the students all had individual laptops at the Tower School, so the technological aspect of the unit was easier than it might have been. And the PhotoStory program used was very intuitive—assuming basic knowledge of how a computer works. Ultimately, the iMovies allowed students to show off their creativity and production skills, to develop technological literacy, and also to convey their empathy for and understanding of people who lived through this historical era.

From a pedagogical perspective, students not only engaged in stylistic elements of documentary filmmaking, but also learned about the major problems of the Great Depression and the dimensions of government interventions in times of economic crisis. Students developed a better sense of positive and negative aspects of government action. In class discussions, students started to move away from the idea that government should just do everything for us, or give everything to us. This would seem counterintuitive based on the time period studied, but, as Emily noted, "when students read the letters to Eleanor Roosevelt and saw what kids were asking for, and then debated whether or not answering these requests was appropriate for government, they began to understand the limits—and responsibilities—of government action."

Building upon the Social, Cultural, and Academic Capital of Our Students

Participation in this project built upon the social, cultural, and academic capital, and the overall life experiences, of the students in our classrooms. For example, although middle schools always have unique challenges and opportunities for learning, the student backgrounds at Tower presented more opportunities than challenges given the lens of this particular project. As Tom noted:

students could very much identify with the lives of those they read about possibly because they themselves were not from wealthy families. As New York City youth, they also see an active government around them everyday, so it may not have been such a mental leap for them to think about how FDR was helping during the New Deal.

Likewise, students who attend Success School are used to content-driven, structured lessons, but also do very well when they are put to a creative task. Using social history and narratives of events in U.S. history brought out compassionate responses from the students and provided a more nuanced understanding of the scope of those impacted by the era, and the depth of the impact. An initial goal in planning this unit was to first help students empathize with people from the time period, learn the content and feel that they had a good command of the material, and then to help them synthesize their impressions of the era, their creative energy, and their content knowledge. The final assessment of the iMovie became a valuable vehicle for showcasing all of these things. The students kept their daily lessons in their notebook along with daily formative assessments. In the end, students responded very well to the format and drew heavily on their notebooks to confirm their assertions. For example, in an attempt to give students a chance to express their opinions about the New Deal as a new direction in government, one formative assessment was to have students grade FDR and the New Deal programs in cooperative groups. This also produced very incisive and eloquent responses, and students enjoyed getting to interrogate the New Deal programs for how many sectors of the population they actually helped.

Collaboration as Transformative

The success of this unit of instruction drew largely on the variety of strengths that group members brought to the table as educators and historians. Many of the essential questions and themes that we developed in this curriculum were conceived in a dialogue about the centrality of social activism and shared civil experiences, rather than an effort to illustrate FDR's power to craft and implement New Deal legislation. Participating teachers were not necessarily clear about the degree to which the government was responding to the pleas of the people during the Great Depression, rather than proactively trying to address issues. They maintained their initial impressions that Roosevelt was aware of the poor economy and with his advisers drew up plans to ameliorate the situation.

Working with Robert Cohen on this unit gave the group an invaluable redirection for their thinking and approach to content development. As a social historian who has done very rich primary research into the era, Cohen brought many uniquely relevant primary materials to the project. The ability to collaborate with experienced teachers powerfully aided the planning process; being able to consult directly with an expert historian with such vast educational expertise when questions arose was invaluable. Because of the nature of this project, we could attack curriculum design by putting the nuance of an historical matter at center-stage. In practice, this was a big departure from planning by first honoring content standards and then simply encouraging students to articulate enduring understandings and the relevance of history to their own lives. We began with the latter and, as a result, the former was conveyed.

Implications of "Teaching the New Deal" for Today

The credit storm that has brewed over the last year into a full financial crisis and the election of Barack Obama as the nation's forty-fourth president make it imperative to develop deep understandings of the Great Depression and New Deal for our students. With the "D-word" (depression) being bandied about on radio and network news, students are constantly asking what it was like during the Great Depression and inquiring about whether we are headed for the same fate.

Given the current financial crisis, many of today's experts and pundits are speculating that the economy is collapsing because people got into financial situations that were beyond their command. While political commentators go back and forth on whether it is the fault of lax regulations or irresponsible citizens taking on debt they would never be able to pay back, the fundamental truth to both arguments is glaringly present: The economy is collapsing because millions of Americans did not have the financial knowledge and technical sophistication to perceive the danger of the loan agreements that they entered into. And still we do not teach financial literacy in our public schools.

Beyond that, Americans have been through a psychologically trying time, in which many good people have been doing what they believed to be right, but still ending up in dire economic straits. At the same time, we just saw the election of a president whose campaign mobilized a record number of people to grassroots political action and whose fundraising successes were so broadly based that they took on historic proportions. We are in a moment in history when civil society is feeling the need for reform and when the relationship of civil society with the government is about to experience a much anticipated and dramatic change.

It is essential that our schools provide students with the background knowledge to understand these trying times and the sense of history that helps them to see that civil society can ultimately be the master of its own fate. The way the New Deal era is often taught, students are invariably moved by the heroism of the individual. Units on the Great Depression and New Deal are often preceded by the study of the Progressive Era, and students are always moved by the biographies of such people as Upton Sinclair, Ida B. Wells-Barnett or W. E. B. DuBois—in part because they are everyday people who accomplished sweeping reform and increased broad-based public awareness just by telling the truth in a compelling way. Still, the idea that Lewis Hine stopped child labor cold with a camera in hand or that Ida B. Wells-Barnett personally shouldered the entire Anti-Lynching campaign is both inaccurate and also misleading. To the contrary, the portrait of reform that this unit paints is one of many, many voices calling out together for jobs, for justice, and for social welfare. And in this example, the pleas of many were responded to. A curriculum such as this is so important because it develops the skills for sophisticated political, social, and economic analysis, as well as the sense of agency to believe that individuals do have a relationship to and role within the actions of the federal government.

Being so steeped in and ruled by political, content-specific standards, it was difficult to give the social history of the Depression era its due. In many cases, state support or requirements for economics in the curriculum are absent. Since many of the enduring student understandings from the New Deal unit are economic in nature, the New Deal might be the only place where students are exposed to ideas having to do with the economic cycle and the stock market, investment, speculation, inflation, deflation, overproduction, unemployment, and even public assistance as a landscape of specific programs. Therefore, as previously mentioned, it becomes incumbent on history teachers to teach economics within the content in a very explicit manner and tie those understandings to current economic realities. The New Deal is the place in the curriculum for those goals.

Clearly, the Depression era is about much more than economics and political power-grabs. The social history of the New Deal is one that stays with many Americans, when our country experienced a huge reconfiguration of the relationship between the government and its people. It is also the time when so many Americans endured what they never thought imaginable and would forever view material wealth differently. Being on the cusp of an era in which the United States will grapple with hard economic realities, but also experience a change in the relationship between civil society and the federal government, it is important that students understand the role and power of the individual in such a political and economic climate.

Works Cited

American Youth Congress. (July 4, 1936). *The Declaration of the Rights of American Youth*. New York: Robert Cohen Personal Collection. Downloaded November 1, 2007, from http://www.newdeal.feri.org/texts/757.htm.

Cohen, R. (2002). *Dear Mrs. Roosevelt: Letters from Children of the Great Depression*. Chapel Hill: The University of North Carolina Press.

Dixson, A. & Rousseau, C. (2005). And we are Still not Saved: Critical Race Theory in Education Ten Years Later. *Race and Ethnicity in Education*, 8(1), 7–27.

Hollins, E., & Guzman, M. (2005). Research on Preparing Teachers for Diverse Populations. In M. Cochran-Smith & K. Zeichner (eds.), *Studying Teacher Education: The Report of the AERA Panel on Research and Teacher Education*. Mahwah: Lawrence, pp. 477–548.

Wiggins, G. & McTighe, J. (2004). *Understanding by Design*. Alexandria, VA: Association for Supervision & Curriculum Development.

CHAPTER RESOURCES

I. Lesson Framework—Teaching the Great Depression

Intended Learning Outcomes (Use NYS SS Standards)

Understandings (Big ideas):

- Students will understand that at different times in history, government actions have benefited different groups of people.
- Students will understand that at different points in history, government has been more or less involved in daily life.
- Students will understand that government has an important role to play in a market economy.
- Students will understand that change in government happens when people call for it.
- Students will understand that deep and endemic economic crisis can occur even in the absence of a major physical or diplomatic disaster.
- Students will understand that market failure can be a function of a crisis of confidence as well as irresponsible and unrealistic financial practices.

Essential Questions:

- How can a democratic government and its people work together to remedy political, social, and economic ills?
- How might we measure the efficacy of the New Deal?
- How effective was the New Deal in addressing the needs of the people?
- How active should the government be in the lives of the people?
- Whom does the government help?
- What is the responsibility of the people and the government to work together to improve society?

Understandings (Big ideas) (continued):

- Students will understand the nature of economic cycles.
- Students will understand the role that general confidence and public perception play in the economy.
- Students will understand that there was a fundamental change in the relationship between the federal government and civil society during the New Deal.
- Students will understand that the New Deal built a tradition of more governmental presence in the economy, and many of the economic constructs that we rely on today.
- Students will understand that democracy allows for an open dialogue between citizens and their government, and the New Deal invited, encouraged, and responded to this dialogue.

Content Knowledge:

- Students will command basic financial and economic concepts and vocabulary.
- Students will understand who the major players in the New Deal administration were (Franklin D. Roosevelt, Eleanor Roosevelt, etc.).
- Students will know who the critics and supporters of the New Deal were.
- Students will know about the stock market crash: what it was, why it happened, its economic effects; government did not regulate; bad investments.
- Students will know the effects of the depression—poverty, homelessness, unemployment, Dust Bowl.
- Students will know responses to Great Depression—focus on Works Progress Administration, Tennessee Valley Authority.
- Students will know why the government became the active at the people's request.

Skills:

- Use and analyze primary sources to construct larger historical understandings.
- Parse out the role of primary images, testimony, letters, newspaper articles to put together a conceptual historic landscape.
- Use technology to create an iMovie and/or photostory board.
- Learn how to decipher between descriptive and non-descriptive images and photos.
- Write engaging commentary for a documentary film.

Vocabulary:

- Speculation, Over-speculation, Buying on Margin, Stock Market, Banking Crisis, FDIC, Fireside Chats, Over-production, Capitalism, Social Democracy, Credit, Breadline, Hooverville, Dust Bowl, New Deal, Pension, FDR, Social Security, Great Migration, Laissez Faire, SEC, Social Security Administration, National Labor Relations Board

Learning Experiences:

- Interviewing people in Washington Square Park (NYC) to assess how involved they felt the government should be in their lives.
- Analyzing and empathizing with young people writing letters to Eleanor Roosevelt in the 1930s.
- Interrogation of the relationship between civil society and the federal government.

Resources:

- *Dear Mrs. Roosevelt* by Robby Cohen
- "Political Protest" and "Eleanor Roosevelt" maps
- Declaration of the Rights of the American Youth
- iMovie software and technology

II. Popular Protest in the Great Depression, 1933–1939

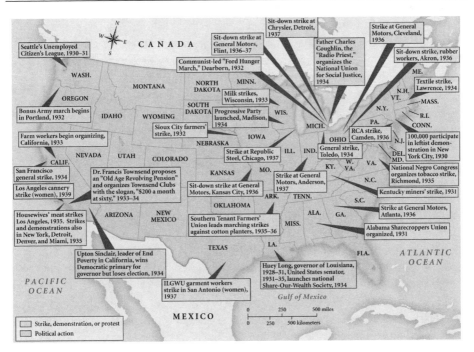

Figure 5.1 From *America's History*, 5th edn, by J. Henretta *et al*. Copyright © 2004 by Bedford/St. Martin's. Reproduced by permission of Bedford/St. Martin's.

III. Primary Document—American Youth Congress (July 4, 1936), The Declaration of The Rights of American Youth (Edited for Use with Students)

On the Fourth of July one hundred and sixty years ago our forefathers declared their independence from the King in order to get the rights to life, liberty, and the pursuit of happiness.—Today our lives are threatened by war; our liberties threatened by bad laws; and our right to happiness is nowhere to be found—Therefore, on this Fourth day of July, 1936, we, the young People of America, announce our own declaration—A Declaration of the Rights of American Youth.

We declare that our generation deserves a useful, creative, and happy life, including: full educational opportunities, jobs that pay well, help when we need it, civil rights, religious freedom, and peace.

We have a right to liberty! In song and legend America has been the land of the free, a safe place for anyone in need. Yet on every hand we see this freedom limited or destroyed. The Negro people are constantly abused. Workers who strike for a living wage are met with increasing violence.

We demand not only the maintenance but the extension of our elementary rights of free speech, press and assemblage. We think freedom of speech includes thinking what we want at school.

We have a right to happiness! Our country with its natural resources and mighty industries can more than provide a life of security and comfort for all. But today we are not provided with this security, we are not permitted to enjoy its comforts. We want to work, to produce, to build, but millions of us are forced to be out of work and bored. We graduate from schools and colleges, ready for careers and professions, but there are no jobs. You can find us along the highways, or in army-supervised camps, separate from friends and family. We refuse to be the lost generation.

We urge a system of unemployment and social insurance as an immediate improvement in the condition of unemployed youth, and we want to be paid what we deserve for our jobs. We who are employed express our dissatisfaction with the prevailing low wages, long hours and the intense speed-up which destroys health and stunts our development. We insist upon our right to higher wages and shorter hours. For the youth on the farms, the right to work means the right to security in the possession of their farms, free from the burden of debts. While we want the right to work for ourselves, we also want those people who can't work to get help from the government.

Education must be available to everyone without discrimination, poor as well as rich, Negroes as well as white, through free scholarships and government aid to needy students. Our educational system should provide for job training. We declare that the workers of hand and brain, the producers of our wealth, the builders of our country are the most important people in the country. We recognize that young people have the same problems as adults. We extend our hand in brotherhood to the youth of other lands who also strive for peace, freedom and progress.—We look at this country of ours. We love it dearly; we are its flesh and marrow. We have roamed its roads; we have camped in its mountains and forests; we have smelled its rich earth; we have tended its fields and dug its earthly treasures. We have toiled in it. Because we know it so well, we know that it could be a place of peace and security for everyone.

Therefore, we the young people of America, declare our right to life, liberty and the pursuit of happiness. With confidence we look forward to a better life, a larger liberty and freedom. To those ends we dedicate our lives, our intelligence and our unified strength.

IV. Primary Document—Letter from a Fifteen-Year-Old from Cleveland, Ohio, to Eleanor Roosevelt. Received January 17, 1935

Mrs. Roosevelt:

You may think I am very bold to write to you but since you seem so kind and everything I ever read about you seems pleasant I thought it would not be so very wrong to ask you for a little advice.

I am writing this secretly my father and mother don't know and I wondered if I could surprise them with your answer if you would possibly and kindly be able to send me one.

My father was not working for 5 years this being the cause of the great debt which we are now in.

My father started working now and since he works only two days in a week we could barely keep up with our present needs. But now the landlord whom we owe $312 and the grocer whom we owe close to $500.00 are constantly asking for money which we positively cannot afford to pay now I wonder if you could advise me and give a little information to whom I could turn for these bills. Who would be willing to help but we cannot repay right away?

I just can't stand anymore to look at the crying and thinking that my parents do.

I am just 15 years old and entered High-school. The teacher gave me a job through which I earn my schooling. If I ever succeed I would gladly pay back every cent to anyone who would possibly be able to help.

Please keep this letter a secret Mrs. Roosevelt and please, if possible soon and if it won't interfere with your affairs answer me.

Maybe you know of a contest or anything which would help me win. I could at least try.

Trusting in the confidence of God and in your kindness I will await an answer soon.

Oh please do not think I'm terrible for writing to you but I can't help. My heart just seems ready to burst.

May God Bless You

V. Final Assessment—"Dear Mrs. Roosevelt" iMovie Project

Objective: You will choose one of the letters to Eleanor Roosevelt and paint a picture (using iMovie) of the hardships that people faced and the assistance that they requested. Your movie should incorporate the following things:

- text from the letter to Mrs. Roosevelt;
- pictures and images that show the writer's situation;
- a narrative written by your group that shows:

  - an understanding of the causes of this person's hardship;
  - examples of people in similar situations;
  - an explanation of the government's response to the person's request;
  - an analysis of the person's thinking when writing to Eleanor Roosevelt;
  - an audio or video clip from the time period (for example, a WPA movie, a clip from a fireside chat, a protest song from the time period);
  - a script of your speech that will be given over the audio file;
  - a completed self-assessment sheet.

We will work on the following schedule:

Day 1: Intro to project: assign groups and roles.
Day 2: Pick letter, identify government projects associated, research background.
Day 3: Find pictures, clips, and upload them, research facts and write narrative.
Day 4: Record narrative and put finishing touches on iMovie.
Day 5: Present iMovie to class, hand in self-assessment sheet.

Team Member Roles:
- Research Coordinator: Images and Clips:_____
  Responsible for finding pictures and audio/video clips from the time period and making sure that they are uploaded to the iMovie file. This person will canvass the internet for good resources to include, and make sure they are uploaded. (Warning: this takes some time!!)
- Research Coordinator: Text and Facts:_____
  This person is responsible for collecting the facts to substantiate your iMovie. He/she will do research about the situations that people lived through, and the hands—from the government and from neighbors—who reached out to help them.
- Script Writer:_____
  This person will work with the research coordinator of text and facts to write the script that your group will record as the audio file that will be narrated along with the iMovie. A final draft of the script will be handed in. This person will work closely with the letter and narrate what was written.
- iMovie Director:_____

After the research coordinator for images and clips has uploaded the images from the first day, this person will be responsible for using the iMovie program, arranging the clips and images, and making sure that the project is completed in time.

VI. Relevant New York State and NAEP Standards: The Great Depression and the 1930s

New York State Learning Standards, U.S. History

Students should be able to:

- Consider the sources of historic documents, narratives, or artifacts and evaluate their reliability (MS.4A)
- Understand how different experiences, beliefs, values, traditions, and motives cause individuals and groups to interpret historic events and issues from different perspectives (MS. 4B)
- Compare and contrast different interpretations of key events and issues in U.S. history, and explain reasons for these different accounts (MS.4C)
- Describe historic events through the eyes of those who were there (MS.4D)
- Analyze historical narratives about key events in U.S. history to identify the facts and evaluate the authors' perspectives (HS.4A)
- Consider different historians' analyses of the same event or development in U.S. history to understand how different viewpoints and/or frames of reference influence historical interpretation (HS.4B)
- Evaluate the validity and credibility of historical interpretations of important events or issues in U.S. history, revising these interpretations as new information is learned and other interpretations are developed (HS.4C)

New York State Learning Standards, Historical Thinking

- Students describe the reasons for periodizing history in different ways (MS.2A)
- Students investigate key turning points in U.S. history and explain why these events or developments are significant (MS.2B)
- Students complete well-documented and historically accurate case studies about individuals and groups who represent different ethnic, national, and religious groups in the United States at different times and in different locations (MS.3A)
- Students gather and organize information about the important achievements and contributions of groups living in the United States (MS.3B)
- Students describe how ordinary people and famous historic figures in the United States have advanced the fundamental democratic values, beliefs, and traditions expressed in the Declaration of Independence, U.S. Constitution, the Bill of Rights, and other important historic documents (MS.3C)
- Students classify major developments into categories such as social, political, economic, geographic, technological, scientific, cultural, or religious (MS.3D)
- Students analyze the development of American culture, explaining how ideas,

values, beliefs, and traditions have changed over time and how they unite all Americans (HS.1A)

- Students develop and test hypotheses about important events, eras, or issues in U.S. history, setting clear and valid criteria for judging the importance and significance of these events, eras, or issues (HS.2B)
- Students compare and contrast the experiences of different groups in the United States (HS.2C)
- Students research and analyze major themes and developments in U.S. history (HS.3B)
- Students prepare essays and oral reports about the important social, political, economic, scientific, technological, and cultural developments, issues, and events from U.S. history (HS.3C)

Adapted from *New York State Learning Standards, U.S. History* (1996)

NAEP Learning Standards, U.S. History

Framework 1: Themes in U.S. History

- How have state and national governments responded to issues raised by economic developments and how have they participated in the economy? (3)
- What ideas, values, and practices contributed to the development of the American economic system? How has the economic system, including its ideas and values, adapted to changing conditions and changing demands? (3)
- How have the work lives and economic opportunities of various groups differed? (3)

Framework 2: Periods of U.S. History

- How did Franklin Roosevelt's New Deal legislation change the role of the federal government in relation to social welfare and individual rights? Which new agencies were created and which of them became a lasting part of American government? (7.1)
- What is the importance of the New Deal in American social reform? What were the key policies? Who developed the policies and who were the critics? (7.2)
- What caused the Great Depression? How did Herbert Hoover and Franklin Roosevelt respond? How did it alter ideas, values, and practices of the American economic system? What was its impact on the lives of ordinary Americans? (7.3)
- How did the Great Depression and New Deal influence economic theory and practice and the role of government in the economy? (7.3)

NAEP Historical Thinking Standards, U.S. History

Framework 3: Ways of Knowing and Thinking about U.S. History

1. HISTORICAL KNOWLEDGE AND PERSPECTIVE

Students should be able to:

- Name, recognize, list, identify and give examples of people, places, events, concepts, and movements
- Place specifics in a chronological framework and construct and label historical periods
- Define historical themes and give examples of the ways themes relate to specific factual information
- Describe the past from the perspectives of various men and women of the time
- Explain the perspective of an author of a primary source document
- Describe different perspectives related to a historical issue or event
- Summarize the contributions of individuals and groups to U.S. history
- Summarize the meaning of historical sources and link these sources to general themes

2. HISTORICAL ANALYSIS AND INTERPRETATION

Students should be able to:

- Specify and explain cause-and-effect relationships and connect contemporary events to their origins in the past
- Categorize information and develop strategies for organizing a large body of facts
- Examine multiple causes of historical developments
- Explain points of view, biases, and value statements in historical sources
- Determine the significance of people, events, and historical sources
- Weigh and judge different views of the past as advanced by historical figures themselves, historians, and present-day commentators and public figures
- Demonstrate that the interpretation and meaning of the past are open to change as new information and perspectives emerge
- Develop sound generalizations and defend these generalizations with persuasive arguments
- Make comparisons and recognize the limitations of generalizations
- Apply knowledge, draw conclusions, and support those conclusions with convincing evidence

Adapted from National Assessment Governing Board (2006)

Works Cited

National Assessment Governing Board (2006). *U.S. History Framework for the 2006 National Assessment of Educational Progress*. Washington, DC: U.S. Department of Education.
New York State Learning Standards, U.S. History (1996). Albany: New York State Education Department.

Six
The Civil Rights Movement

Framing the Questions: An Interview with Adam Green, conducted by Rachel Mattson

Adam Green is an Associate Professor of History at the University of Chicago. He is the author of *Selling the Race: Culture and Community in Black Chicago, 1940–1955* (2009) and co-editor, with Charles Payne, of *Time Longer than Rope: Studies in African American Activism, 1850–1950* (2003).

Adam Green: I think the single best way to look at the accelerated phase of black freedom—the era from the 1940s until at least the 1960s and possibly the 1970s— is to say that before you pay attention to leaders you have to pay attention to organizers. Of course, certainly it's important to think about the rank and file and the ways in which these were very much mass movements. But I think seeing the alternative to a leader-centric notion of history as being a mass-centric notion of history seems to me to be replacing one essentialism with another essentialism.

So, for example, for many, many years people thought about the Civil Rights movement as a pantheon of great male leaders, like Martin Luther King and Malcolm X—and then there was Rosa Parks, who is often represented as a woman who stood up momentarily, and basically through her humble, quiet dignity created a certain kind of turn or spark or paradigm shift that gave rise to the kind of mass component of the movement.

But one of the things that has to be understood in relation to making sense of Rosa Park's role was that she had been an organizer. She had been someone who had worked within the NAACP as a very important member. And she had a deep understanding of the full operation that had been waiting for a case, basically, to move the bus boycott campaign in Montgomery forward.

Through her example and through her historical presence, people began to identify other key figures, most notably a woman named Jo Ann Gibson Robinson, who was a professor at Alabama State, an historically black college located in Montgomery. She basically had in her head and on paper the campaign to leaflet thirty thousand different fliers asking people to observe the boycott if and when a case came up that was of sufficient gravity to inspire blacks in Alabama not to ride the buses. And out of this intervention, in relation to Montgomery, really has sprung out a broad range of very, very important works that have stressed the fact that that movement was the result of people's skill, dedication, sacrifice, and, most of all, persistence in relation to making sure that the conditions are on the ground to make a mobilization of a sufficiently large group of people possible.

Ella Baker is also important. She was the field secretary of the NAACP during the '40s, into the '50s, eventually became one of the founders of Southern Christian Leadership Conference. Then in turn she became one of the founders or at least one of the inspirers of the Student Non-Violent Coordinating Committee as a kind of counter to the hegemony or the, sort of, excessive authority that the Southern Christian Leadership conference was exerting over Civil Rights activism. Baker has been written about now by two different biographers. And she's been spoken about primarily as an organizer. And I think the thing that came through most powerfully in terms of Baker's story, to just name one of many, many stories of important organizers in relation to the '50s and the '60s among African Americans, is that it was Baker's persona and the way in which Baker thought about almost the ethics of how it was that people in a movement should relate to each other. What's the place of politeness in relation to the ways in which organizers work with members in the field or members in the grass roots and the rank and file? What's the importance of a sense of reciprocity? What's the importance of having a persistence in how you visit people and, at the same time, a kind of humility that you are there only at their invitation and only because of the fact that people want to hear you out and want to hear what it is that you have to say? And this kind of mixing of an intense ethical sensibility along with a political vision of what it is that people wanted to accomplish, this was foundational to what it was that Baker was able to accomplish in terms of building the NAACP, for example, from an organization that I think was under fifty thousand members to an organization that had close to ten times that amount of members by the time we get to the late 1940s. And, in turn, as we go into the 1950s, building these organizations that were actually going to prove foundational in relation to the kind of organizing and campaigns that came out of the 1960s.

So it was actually Ella Baker who first said that "Martin did not make the movement, the movement made Martin." The idea being that the movement could make a leader of that sort because the movement was based on such a radical vision of people building a better society, building a good society, building a democracy in many ways, based on their desire to participate collectively and struggle, and based on the ways in which people's commitment to struggle emerged out of very real interactions, very real trusts, very real relationships that were built over a long period of time.

And so now we know about Ella Baker's role and about Septima Clark's role and about Bob Moses's role. And now we know about Bayard Rustin's role and the fact that the March on Washington didn't simply emerge out of the ground but, in fact, was an infrastructural institutionalized operation of tremendous challenge that had to be put together in two or three months' time. Rustin by and large coordinated a small staff that was able to pull together all the resources to be able to bring 250,000 people to the Washington Mall area and to create the kind of stage that, in essence, instituted anti-racism in part as a kind of secular religion in relation to the United States. In some ways, with all of the kinds of contradictions and the problems that have emerged, certainly the ways in which King's speech at that march, on that day, is replayed again and again and again as a way of speaking about what it is that this country needs to re-dedicate itself to perpetually, that says something about the accomplishment of that organizing initiative.

What we see then is the antidote to a way of thinking about history simply as something either that great people and, usually, great men do or something that the mass of people naturally call up from themselves. The antidote, I think, to both of those kinds of essentialisms is to say, "How do we actually document and discuss the work involved with shaping people into a group and a community and a society committed to change?" This is really what we see during the 1960s.

Rachel Mattson: *How do you teach that?*

AG: Well, one, you teach social movements as an open story. And you teach social movements as something that should not be approached, at least initially, as a story in which there is a clear beginning and a clear end, a clear challenge, and a clear realization of a goal. But rather, like anything, a successful relationship, a positive process of parenting, an effective kind of approach to teaching, it's an everyday process. These were not things that were epiphanies, by and large. These were not things that reached some kind of sudden and dramatic end. And, sad to say, these are not things that can be represented as clear and unambiguous stories of victory in terms of some set of lasting accomplishments that then is able to stay and endure past all sorts of forms of backlash, all kinds of forms of reaction. I mean, much of what we've seen over the last twenty to thirty years in this country politically has told us how much of the gains that could be won through this organizing and through this mobilizing is stuff that also can be lost according to the ways in which politics shift and turn. This is really a story of how some people, mainly because of the ways in which they committed themselves to the work of bringing about change, encouraged many other people to similarly dedicate themselves to working for change.

Just think about that in terms of one example: How do you teach the Montgomery Bus Boycott as a kind of chapter in movement organizing and in freedom struggle on the part of African Americans? Before Martin Luther King got up before a church and gave a speech, and before the newspapers came down to record the story, Jo Ann Gibson Robinson was sitting at a mimeograph machine literally running off thirty thousand leaflets along with a couple of students and doing so with the knowledge that she was not authorized to use that equipment in the school to do that. And she came very close to being fired by the president of the college as a result of having used school equipment to engage in that kind of campaign. She was absolutely right to do it. History has vindicated her for doing it. The president of that university ultimately said, "You know, this was something that I understood that you needed to do." But at that moment in time, a very mundane decision and a very mundane act was something that had profound consequences politically.

Had she been terminated, had she been prevented from being able to use that equipment, those leaflets would not have gone out, and there probably would not have been a Montgomery Bus Boycott. Sometimes it's a very, very mundane set of things that allow a campaign to reach its critical mass and realize the kinds of gains that it's able to do. And although it may seem at first glance challenging to tell a story in such everyday ways, I firmly believe that the only way to teach social change is in some kind of proportional relationship to how the majority of people actually live out their lives. Lots of people use mimeograph machines. Lots of people make choices about how to get to work. Lots of people have tried to figure out how to get a large group mobilized with many, many different agendas and then inspire them to think about how they do things in coordinated ways. Lots of people have seen the power of courtesy, respect, and dignity in relation to how it enhances their ability to work and relate with other people in their lives. All of these things were just as foundational to the Civil Rights movement, to black nationalist struggles, to revolutionary groups during the late 1960s. All of these things were just as crucial to the progress of those movements as anything that any inspirational leader did. So I say teach in a way that corresponds to the conditions of most people's lives. Because then they can respect their own capacity and their own potential if they put the work in and if they are consistent and dedicated. They can understand their own capacity similarly to bring about social change.

RM: *Can you be a little bit more specific about what you actually do in the classroom?*

AG: You get stories other than the ones that have to do with the immediately identified leaders. Jo Ann Gibson Robinson's story is present in a memoir that she published called the *Montgomery Bus Boycott and the Women Who Started It*. Ella Baker's story is present in two biographies now that have been done on her. Bayard Rustin's story is present in John D'Emilio's (2004) biography, plus a film called *Brother Outsider* (2002). The story of Mississippi organizing is present in an absolutely brilliant book by Charles Payne called *I've Got the Light of Freedom*, which, by the way, makes clear this distinction between the mobilizing dimensions of political struggle and the organizing dimensions of political struggle. And it emphasizes very, very strongly that organizing was really about the everyday work of building trust among people who are coming in and trying to inspire or compel political change and those that lived locally in the community that were trying to find ways to link up those older activists who had been working with those communities, in this case in the delta of Mississippi and nearby Jackson for decades before anybody had come from the outside from the North or elsewhere to try to really sort of accelerate the process of encouraging Mississippi voting.

Thankfully at this point in time, the resources are really all around us. And I think the only thing to my mind that really constitutes a significant barrier to using those resources is the fear on the part of the teacher that by making the story too complicated, by bringing too many people in, that it's somehow going to lose the attention of the student.

And, yet, my experience has been, without exception, whether talking to high school students, to college students, to people outside of an academic context, that if you bring stories in that correspond to the conditions of their lives, people remain interested. And people actually learn something, not only about the great change that was accomplished by these individuals, but also what kinds of possibilities exist for them to create change themselves.

Works Cited

D'Emilio, J. (2004). *Lost Prophet: The Life and Times of Bayard Rustin*. Chicago: University of Chicago Press.
Kates, N. and Singer B. (2002). *The Life of Bayard Rustin* (videotape). San Francisco: California Newsreel.
Payne, Charles (2007). *I've Got the Light of Freedom: The Organizing Tradition and the Mississippi Freedom Struggle*. Berkeley: University of California Press.
Robinson, Jo Ann Gibson (1987). *Montgomery Bus Boycott and the Women Who Started It: The Memoir of Jo Ann Gibson Robinson*. Knoxville: University of Tennessee Press.

Essay: The Transformational Properties of the Mundane: Teaching the Civil Rights Movement through the Lens of Community Organizers

By Diana Turk, with Stacie Brensilver Berman and Ryan Mills

Sometimes it's a very, very mundane set of things that allows a campaign to reach its critical mass and realize the kinds of gains that it's able to do. And although it may seem at first glance challenging to tell a story in such everyday ways, I firmly believe that the only way to teach social change is in some kind of proportional relationship to how the majority of people actually live out their lives. Lots of people have tried to figure out how to get a large group mobilized with many, many different agendas and then inspire them to think about how they do things in coordinated ways. Lots of people have seen the power of courtesy, respect, and dignity in relation to how it enhances their ability to work and relate with other people in their lives. All of these things were just as foundational to the Civil Rights movement, to black nationalist struggles, to revolutionary groups during the late 1960s. All of these things were just as crucial to the progress of those movements as anything that any inspirational leader did. So I say teach in a way that corresponds to the conditions of most people's lives. Because then [students] can respect their own capacity and their own potential if they put the work in and if they are consistent and dedicated. They can understand their own capacity similarly to bring about social change.

Dr. Adam Green

Ask most middle- and secondary-level students what they have learned about the Civil Rights movement, and most likely they will tell you a story of great leaders who, through their bravery and inspiring words, led millions to stand with them in the struggles for freedom, equality, and Civil Rights. The names Martin Luther King, Jr. and Malcolm X will come up, occasionally accompanied by groups such as the NAACP or Freedom Riders. In general, the stories will be simple and teleological: They will begin with the *Brown* vs. *Board of Education* decision, will continue with King and his calls for action in Selma and Washington DC, will recount, perhaps, the transformation of the movement from one led by the "moderate" King to one led by the "militant" Malcolm X, and will note the assassination of both. The conclusion of the story is often assumed, as though the end of mass protests coincided with the end of all oppression. Through all, the focus will be on a great leader giving a call to action, the masses responding, and change occurring. Little attention will be paid to what happened after 1968. Instead, the movement will probably be presented as a neat and clean story of progress.

This is an easy story to tell, and it makes sense why it would be the dominant narrative of the Civil Rights movement. There are so many interesting heroes, such as King, Malcolm X, the Little Rock Nine, Rosa Parks, the NAACP lawyers, and others who played prominent roles in the public events of the era. And, of course, there are also the villains, in the form of white segregationists. The beginning and end of the struggle seems clear and uncontested. But of course this simplified narrative masks a far more complex and nuanced historical reality, and as engaging and inspiring as this tale of brave and inspiring leaders may be, much is lost when we look at history as a story of only a few individuals and their acts of heroism. As Dr. Adam Green, an historian of the black Civil Rights movement in the United States, importantly argues, great leaders don't get very far unless they have great organizers behind them; someone needs to plan and announce boycotts and marches, set up rallies, arrange for speeches and press coverage, and spread the word about the events that together make up movements. Thus, a useful way to approach a watershed era such as the black freedom struggles of the twentieth century is through the lens of the organizers: the people who drew together the masses and created the moments where the great leaders could inspire. Not only can a focus on organizers give students a sense of some of the important—and often forgotten—forces that helped shape history, but such an approach also can empower students to see how seemingly small, localized, and unheralded actions can truly change the course of human events.

The group that came together to focus on teaching the black freedom struggles of the twentieth century included a social studies education professor and historian and ethnographer, who served as the group leader, and three experienced teachers: Kevin, a seven-year veteran teacher who was offering an elective on the Civil Rights movement; Suzie, also in her seventh year, who was offering an Advanced Placement U.S. history course; and Danielle, an experienced middle school teacher who now served as a curriculum coach at a small alternative school. A doctoral student in literacy education and urban schooling at New York University also joined us for several of our planning meetings.

The group used as its starting point two in-depth interviews that had been conducted with Dr. Adam Green in preparation for this book. In these interviews, Green discussed what he considered to be the most compelling recent scholarship addressing the Civil Rights movement: those that focused on the efforts and achievements of organizers. Using his arguments as our springboard, our group created a series of lessons that would help students go beyond the leader-centric narrative they would read in their textbooks, toward a closer examination of the actions and achievements of the organizers of some of the major events and efforts of the Civil Rights movement. Such an approach would allow us to examine the local struggles that everyday people participated in to help effect important change on a national level—and give us something to help inspire our own students to take steps to effect change on a local level. All members of the group shared a deep commitment to using the lessons to inspire civic engagement on the part of students, and thus we hoped to build in assignments that would encourage students to develop their voices and propel them to begin to see themselves as players in democratic civic processes. At the same time, though, we needed to ensure that the lessons would enable students to be able to master enough of the "basic facts" of the Civil Rights movement to pass the high-stakes tests many of them would take only a month or so later.

How Mimeographs Enabled a Boycott and a Movement

According to Adam Green, important scholarship from the past several years has poked deep and meaningful holes into the standard narrative of the Civil Rights movement as a story of the actions of a handful of great leaders. The historian Charles Payne's (2007) *I've Got the Light of Freedom: The Organizing Tradition and the Mississippi Freedom Struggle*, in particular, has done much to shed light on the role of what Green called the "organizing dimensions" of political struggles. Payne's study, according to Green, showed very strongly that "organizing was really about the everyday work of building trust among people," laying the foundation of commitment and support among "ordinary people" so that when events compelled action, "mobilizing" forces could call whole communities to act in concert. With reference to some of the organizers whose efforts helped bring about the Montgomery Bus Boycott and the 1963 March on Washington DC, Green argued

> What we see, then, is the antidote to a way of thinking about history as something simply either that great people and, usually, great men do, or something that the mass of people naturally call up from themselves. The antidote, I think, to both of those kinds of essentialisms is to say, "How do we actually document and discuss the work involved with shaping people into a group and a community and a society committed to change?"

Pointing to the organizing efforts of individuals such as Jo Ann Gibson Robinson, Bayard Rustin, Ella Baker, and others who helped bring into being the events of the Civil Rights movement that proved so pivotal in the course of history, Green prompted us to see the black freedom struggles of the mid-twentieth century as a movement that "emerged out of very real interactions, very real trusts, [and] very real relationships that were built over a long period of time." As Ella Baker famously noted (and Green reminded us), "Martin [Luther King, Jr.] did not make the movement; the movement made Martin." This notion proved enormously compelling for our group, as we began to consider how we would structure lessons around movement organizers and the organizing process in general.

As our group worked through the transcripts from Green's interviews, we became struck by another argument he made, that "sometimes it's a very, very mundane set of things that allow a campaign to reach its critical mass and realize the kinds of gains that it's able to do." We came to call this idea "the transformational properties of the mundane," as our way of noting the small and seemingly insignificant building blocks that together can build a societal movement for change. Green recounted the story of Jo Ann Gibson Robinson, a professor at historically black Alabama State College in Montgomery, who had access to a mimeograph machine and whose efforts were chronicled in her memoir, *The Montgomery Bus Boycott and the Women Who Started It*. Robinson's "mundane efforts" in copying thirty thousand fliers and preparing blacks in Montgomery for an eventual boycott if and when a case of sufficient gravity to inspire action came up proved enormously important in bringing into effect the successful Montgomery Bus Boycott. "Before Martin Luther King, [Jr.] got up before a church and gave a speech and before the newspapers came down to record the story [of the Montgomery Bus Boycott]," Green argued:

> Jo Ann Gibson Robinson was sitting at a mimeograph machine literally running off thirty thousand leaflets along with a couple of students and doing so with the knowledge that she was not authorized to use that equipment in the school to do that. And she came very close to being fired by the president of the college as a result of having used school equipment to engage in that kind of campaign. She was absolutely right to do it. History has vindicated her for doing it. The president of that university ultimately said, "You know, this was something that I understood that you needed to do." But at that moment in time, a very mundane decision and a very mundane act was something that had profound consequences politically. Had she been terminated, had she been prevented from being able to use that equipment, those leaflets would not have gone out, and there probably would not have been a Montgomery bus boycott.

Through Robinson's actions, Green argued, and through those of others like her, whose seemingly small efforts brought about real effects, we can see that, in Green's words:

> the movement was the result of people's skill, dedication, sacrifice, and, most of all, persistence in relation to making sure that the conditions are on the ground to make a mobilization of a sufficiently large group of people possible.

Our group found the example of Robinson inspiring and eagerly took Green's recommendation that we use Robinson's book as a way to show the transformational effects that "mundane efforts" can have. This source would, we felt, help inspire in students a sense of civic engagement and might enable them to begin to see how Robinson's actions could be a model for themselves, as they made small efforts to bring about change in their own communities and environs.

Turning Academic Arguments into Curriculum: The Planned Lessons

Because we all agreed on what aspects of the Civil Rights movement, and, in particular, the Green interviews, we wanted to focus on, our group did not have a difficult time determining the essential questions we wanted to use for the lessons we would develop. Harder, though, was finding actual time to meet as a group; we ended up doing much of our planning using "Google Docs" and allowing the two high school teachers to take a strong lead in determining what particular sources and topics to address in which lessons. We ended up developing a four-pronged approach to examining this era in American history, centering on: (1) the role of organizers and the "organizing process" in effecting change; (2) the role of the media in bringing the stories of the Civil Rights era to national attention; (3) the "transformative properties of the mundane"—how small actions can bring about large effects; and (4) the timeless quality and "never ending" nature of the black freedom struggles. As a way of framing our lessons, we chose the following essential questions, each targeted toward one of our themes, for the unit:

- What roles did the leaders, organizers, and masses all play in the movements of the Civil Rights era and how can we evaluate their relative importance to the success of the movements?
- In what ways did the print, radio, and television media of the time help move the localized events of the time to national attention?
- How can "the mundane" be transformative? What does it mean to argue that the power of the Civil Rights movement developed from "mundane" efforts and what are the implications of such an argument?
- Why do we say that the Civil Rights movement is never ending?

In addition to our content-related essential questions, we also chose to center the lessons around several conceptual and skills-related goals:

- to consider multiple perspectives on issues;
- to remember that history is not a collection of dates and names, but rather an argument about the meaning of the past;
- to read primary source documents critically, for their arguments;
- to consider competing opinions and not select only sources that "agree" with our arguments;
- to recognize that photographs can and should be read as "texts" with complex meanings, authorial intention, and intended audiences, and therefore to ask of them questions similar to those we ask of written texts; and
- to consider the ways that media images and offerings can affect perceptions of reality and therefore shape public opinion on important issues.

Armed with these guiding principles and essential questions, the teachers in our group worked independently, in the case of the middle school teacher, and together, in the case of the high school teachers, to map out their lessons: They designed assessments to guide teaching and learning within the unit, creating projects that included student-designed newspapers and research projects linking action within the Civil Rights movement to action on current issues today. Following steps laid out in Grant Wiggins and James McTigh's (2005) *Understanding by Design*, the teachers planned backwards for the unit, moving from our essential questions to aims for each lesson to sources and activities that would help students build toward enduring understandings of the topic. Along the way, the teachers shared their works-in-progress lessons with the rest of the group and elicited feedback and input. Because Green had provided a clear lens through which to examine the subject matter and the group had spent careful time crafting the essential questions and instructional goals, all members remained on the same page as to what we hoped to achieve, thereby allowing for a level of trust that made the planning process smooth.

The Taught Curriculum

Planned curriculum is sometimes very different from taught curriculum. Teachers may have the best-laid plans of what they want to share with their students, but factors related to the real-world nature of schools and classrooms often mean that changes have to be made, sometimes at the last minute. Owing to complex circumstances largely beyond her control, Danielle, the middle school teacher, proved unable to devote the kind of attention to the lessons that she had hoped to be able to give. She was unable to carve out the time necessary to offer the lessons in sequence and to allow learning to build from day to day. In addition, an overseas move shortly after teaching the unit also prevented Danielle from engaging with the rest of the group in an in-depth debriefing and processing. As a result, this section on the "taught curriculum" will focus on the secondary-level classrooms only.

Few visitors could help being impressed by the high school: its physical size, the volume of its course offerings, and the energy of its students. The school is known throughout the city for its academics; 90 percent of its graduates go to college, a rate far beyond the norm for secondary schools in its urban environs. The qualifications of the teaching staff are impressive: 80 percent have taught in the school for more than two years, and almost 60 percent hold a masters degree or have completed additional graduate work, including earning a doctorate. In an urban setting in which roughly 70 percent of high school students qualify for free or reduced lunch, fewer than 30 percent of the school's students meet such designation. The school boasts a population of more than four thousand students that is roughly 35 percent white, 28 percent black, 15 percent Hispanic, and 20 percent Asian/Pacific Islander. About 10 percent of the students are English language learners, and 12 percent require special education. Two-thirds of the students are girls, possibly the result of screened admissions programs in art, theater, and music. There are no organized sports offered at the High School at all.

Upon entering the massive building, a visitor will be stopped by a security officer who will sign you in and give you a name tag. When I, the group leader, arrived to observe the two high school teachers as they taught selected lessons from the black freedom struggles unit, it took two tries to remember the directions the officer barked out at me. As I worked my way down the hallway, however, I became less intimidated by the massive expanse of the school and more caught up in its community feel.

The pea-green and yellow painted hallways were bright with student artwork; the faces of student self-portraits smiled or frowned at me as I looked up at them while waiting for the elevator. Notices of assistance programs—both for students and for charity—adorned the walls. The energy of the students traveling to and from their classes gave the place a humming feel.

Taking the elevator to the second floor, I disembarked into a red painted hallway, also decorated with lively student work, and followed seemingly endless twists and turns to the social studies department and then down a long corridor to the last classroom at the end. With a lunchroom that is way too small to accommodate the number of students enrolled, the school has chosen not to have a set lunchtime but instead provides students with free periods in which to eat. As a result, students lounge on the floor outside of classrooms throughout the building, their backpacks spilling their contents into the thoroughfares. To enter the classroom at the end of the hall, I had to step carefully over the legs of students clustered outside. The students seemed to take this in stride, however, and were remarkably friendly, greeting me, a total stranger, unprompted, in a friendly manner uncharacteristic of most high school settings.

The teacher desk in Suzie's classroom sits at the front of the room, with the students' desks formed into two U's, an inner and an outer, facing the teacher desk with the tops of the U's open to the front. The thirty-two juniors enrolled in this section of Advanced Placement U.S. History sat in rapt silence as Suzie explained the segment of the acclaimed documentary film series *Eyes on the Prize* that they would be viewing shortly. Despite the fact that the lights had been dimmed for the showing, the room was sunny and bright. The deep level of engagement of the students, the quality of the student artwork on the walls, and the plentiful texts and blow-ups of primary source documents posted around the room all came together to paint a picture unlike most other urban public high school classrooms I have visited in my near-decade of observing in urban schools.

Kevin's class proved very similar, despite being a regular education (not Advance Placement) course for thirty-two juniors and seniors taking a Civil Rights movement elective. Here, too, the students listened attentively and followed the lesson and teacher's instructions closely. In this classroom, as in Suzie's, a nearby subway train roared by every few minutes, requiring speakers to pause mid-sentence or else to raise their voices and those nearest the open windows to hold their hands over their ears for a few seconds. The students and teachers in both classes seemed to take this in stride, however, and continued their discussions without missing more than a beat.

In their classrooms, both Kevin and Suzie appeared to move with ease among their students, bantering lightly as they segued from topic to topic, gently prodding students to take their comments deeper, asking increasingly probing questions about the material in question and listening closely to the answers. In both classes on the day of observation and in the subsequent lessons of the unit, as well as with Suzie's two additional sections of Advanced Placement U.S. History, the teachers' instruction progressed largely according to plan, with surprisingly little variation from the written outlines that the teachers had planned in advance. Both Kevin and Suzie presented the primary source materials we had chosen with fluidity and ease; their students asked and answered their questions with skill and evident interest. Both students and teachers paid close attention to the comments of others students; when no student volunteered an answer to a query, both teachers called on members of the class, the quality of the answers of those called on no different from those who had volunteered their answers.

"Imagine 99 percent of people in New York City decided to boycott public transportation," Suzie posed to her class. "In order to do so, what would we need to put in place to ensure our success?" Writing "bus boycott" in a center circle, she drew lines radiating out from the center, each line marking a different aspect that would need to be planned. "A team to lead," one student offered. "A charismatic leader," another followed. "People to join the group," a third proposed. "Funds for alternative transportation and for publicity" another put forth. Each of these, along with "clearly outlined goals," "widespread publicity," and "communications network," Suzie wrote next to a single spoke emerging from the center circle. "Is this the job of one person?" she asked. A chorus of "no!" filled the room. "We need a lot of people!" "We need a leader!" "We need a hierarchy!" "We need technology!" "OK, now let's apply this to the whole Civil Rights movement," Suzie proposed. "Were the masses as important as the leaders? What about the organizers? What does it take to have a successful movement?" Discussion fairly flew from there.

In both classes, the teachers led students from a generic discussion of "organizing" to one specifically focused on the role of the Women's Political Council (WPC) in the Montgomery Bus Boycott. Using letters, excerpts, and photographs drawn from Robinson's (1987) *The Montgomery Bus Boycott and the Women Who Started It*, Kevin and Suzie walked their students through an exploration of how the background organization of the WPC, the groundwork that had been laid in preparation for a stand against the treatment of African Americans by the Montgomery city bus lines, and the networks that swung into action when the call to act went out, all enabled the singular act by Rosa Parks of refusing to give up her seat—an act with which the students were all familiar but the context for which they had never considered—to spark a successful city-wide boycott.

The lesson on the Montgomery Bus Boycott, and the strong message of the power of organizers to effect change, fed into an examination the next day in class of the question: Does organization ensure success? In this lesson, Kevin and Suzie prompted their students to examine the efforts, tactics, and relative achievements of several Civil Rights era groups: the Student Nonviolent Coordinating Committee (SNCC), the Congress of Racial Equality (CORE), and the Southern Christian Leadership Conference (SCLC). Both teachers divided their classes up into small groups and provided each group with primary source documents related to one of the above organizations. The teachers then had the students use a graphic organizer (see Chapter Resources III, p. 159) to consider the circumstances each organization faced, how the group confronted its particular circumstances, what the key events were in each group's timeline, and what the outcomes were of each organization's efforts, including its relative successes and failures. As the small groups presented their analyses of each organization's efforts to the rest of their classmates, they each taught their classmates about their chosen group's efforts in a pedagogical approach called "jigsawing." Each group's contribution provided additional pieces to a larger class "puzzle" that when put together helped paint a complex portrait of the mission, efforts, and tactics of different groups within the Civil Rights movement. The classes as a whole then considered the commonalities and differences between SNCC, CORE, and the SCLC, as well as the extent to which the students believed that the efforts of each group could have been successful without the massive organizations that supported them. The classes then considered the extent to which they thought each organization had achieved its goals, with students in both classes disagreeing on their findings and arriving at different conclusions as to whether organization ensures success.

Additional lessons in the unit explored the significance of the role of media in garnering support for the Civil Rights movement, and the lasting struggles of African Americans for political and social equality in the United States. Kevin and Suzie used excerpts from the celebrated *Eyes on the Prize* series to show how national television coverage of the Birmingham protests in 1963, when Public Safety Commissioner Bull Connor's use of fire hoses and dogs on protesting children shocked many northerners and whites out of complacency and helped rally support—in terms of boots on the ground, as well as emotion and money—for protesters' causes. In both teachers' classrooms, students recognized the continuing struggle for political and Civil Rights faced by minorities in this country today. In projects completed in groups that painted poignant pictures of racial relations in the United States, students showed that they recognized the enduring struggles of the Civil Rights movement—and how battles for equality are still being fought.

In Suzie's classes, students worked together in groups of five students to create newspapers that detailed a major event of the Civil Rights movement, with a particular focus on the efforts of the three organizations the classes examined in depth: SNCC, CORE, and the SCLC. Students within the small groups wrote news articles that detailed the background, unfolding, and significance of particular events, while others wrote editorials in which they evaluated the significance and lasting impact of the events. These newspapers not only served to reinforce for students the important messages regarding organizing and background efforts that had inspired the early lessons in the unit, but they also showed in very real ways the effects that members of the media could have on shaping their readers' impressions and understandings of the events they chronicled.

In Kevin's class, the students used their learning in these lessons to begin ambitious projects that would engage them for the remainder of the semester: the creation of a direct action plan that would, according to the instructions given to students, "use many of the 'organizing' strategies employed in the [Civil Rights] movement." In a process that took several weeks to complete, students came together in groups and selected an issue, problem, or struggle that the members of each group considered an "injustice" within their communities. They brainstormed ideas and weighed the reasons offered by each member for tackling particular causes or efforts. After settling on an important cause or issue, they explained the "issue/injustice" they saw, noted why it was important to their group, and discussed ideas for ameliorating its effects. After receiving approval from Kevin for their topic, each group researched the background of the issue, identified the main debates and concerns related to it, isolated the reasons and causes for it, and considered how the issue affected people, both locally and beyond. They then created an "information board" to be posted within their school to raise awareness among students about their issue, and also created an information pamphlet to distribute to the public, as a means of motivating people to act (see assignment, pp. 160–162).

The "injustices" selected by the students revealed a wide range of concerns: animal testing, the high cost of college, the effects of a nearby oil spill, police brutality, tax issues affecting minors, and the overwhelming presence of fast food establishments in low-income urban communities. The students researched their topics and planned steps that individuals might take to combat their selected "injustice." All of the groups spent enormous energy and efforts creating their triptychs (three-piece poster boards) and pamphlets for distribution and community education. Several groups chose to spend weekend and after-school time handing out their pamphlets at nearby subway stations and on street corners (see student pamphlet, pp. 163 and 164, Figures 6.1 and 6.2).

Both Suzie and Kevin drew on a wide range of source material for their lessons and as background for the projects they assigned. In addition to assigning excerpts from Faigher *et al.*'s (2000) *Out of Many* textbook and from Kennedy and Bailey's (2002) sourcebook, *The American Spirit*, the teachers also shared with their students a wide array of photographs of sit-ins, lunch counter protests, and boycotts; newspaper articles detailing events of the time from a variety of locations (both northern and southern); statements by participants in the sit-ins and protests; the mission statements of groups such as the SCLC, SNCC, and CORE; excerpts from speeches by Martin Luther King, Jr., and other movement leaders; video excerpts from *Eyes on the Prize*; music and songs of protest by Chuck Berry, Sam Cooke, Ray Charles, and other artists; excerpts from Robinson's (1987) *The Montgomery Bus Boycott and the Women who Started It* and from Howell Raines's (1983) *My Soul is Rested: Movement Days in the Deep South Remembered*; and excerpts of transcripts of the interviews done for this book with Adam Green.

The Experienced Curriculum: What Teachers and Students Learned through the Lessons

In Kevin and Suzie's classes (as well as in Danielle's middle school class, as reported by the teacher), the students eagerly engaged in the topics and issues raised in the lessons that grew out of our group's consideration of the black freedom struggles. The teachers created dynamic lessons that both framed the issues Adam Green had raised about the Civil Rights movement in his interviews, and also inspired student participation and investment. According to my own observations of the high school teachers' lessons and to reflections done by Kevin and Suzie, as well as by Danielle, the middle school teacher, the students in all the classes were able to identify with the goals of the black freedom struggles and with the people who organized and participated in the movement, especially as they saw that children and college students were so central to the events of the era. In very real ways, students of all levels and abilities were able to, in the words of one of the teachers, "put themselves in the roles" of the historical actors whose efforts they examined. And they were able to see, as Green had hoped, that the Civil Rights movement is an "open-ended story," one that is still being written today.

Kevin and Suzie, the two high school teachers, effectively involved their students through practical, student-led activities that required organizing participants and information based on the examples set by SNCC, CORE, and the SCLC. Both teachers had students write platforms and/or news articles in which they put themselves into the roles of historical actors, bringing to fruition what Adam Green himself had predicted, that if students are encouraged to see the actions of the historical actors they are studying as akin to those they themselves might take, then they will come to see themselves as capable and important actors. As Green noted:

> My experience has been, without exception, whether talking to high school students, to college students, to people outside of an academic context, that if you bring stories in that correspond to the conditions of their lives, people remain interested. And people actually learn something, not only about the great change that was accomplished by these individuals, but also what kinds of possibilities exist for them to create change themselves.

"Sometimes it's a very, very mundane set of things that allows a campaign to reach its critical mass and realize the kinds of gains that it's able to do," Green had told us, as we have already noted above. "And although it may seem at first glance challenging to tell a story in such everyday ways, I firmly believe that the only way to teach social change is in some kind of proportional relationship to how the majority of people actually live out their lives." For all of the teachers, this statement proved accurate. In Kevin's class in particular, as the students focused on the important effects that "ordinary people" had on the course of events in the black freedom struggles, they seemed to understand that they too had a role to play in effecting events in their own communities and willingly threw themselves into righting what they perceived as "injustices" surrounding them.

Both high school teachers reported that this project took a lot more time than they normally spent on curriculum development and required a great deal of extra work, but both argued that their participation in the project brought strong rewards to themselves as teachers, as well as to their students as learners. Suzie reported that she "enjoyed teaching this way more than the traditional way" and that she found the lessons "more effective" than those on the Civil Rights movement she had taught in the past. Students "got beyond the facts" and "learned so much about the movement and what it was trying to accomplish." Suzie also noted that the lesson on television and radio media was extraordinarily relevant for her students and argued that they could really identify with the movement participants as a result of the sources she shared with them: "They went so far beyond 'this is a sit-in'; they focused on why it happened and what was accomplished and that it wasn't just African Americans but whites were involved too." Reflecting back on the lessons nearly a year later, Suzie reported:

> I do work with some of my students from last year, and we were speaking the other day about the Montgomery Bus Boycott lesson because one of the questions they have to answer is about freedom to associate, assemble, and petition, and we got into a whole conversation about the role of the average person in effecting change. As a class, we've also discussed sit-ins, student movements, and media as a tool. It makes me so happy when they recall what they learned [nearly a year ago]. I feel like I actually had an impact. I don't know that the students would be very eloquent with their lasting impressions, but the mere fact that they remember what they learned, when I also

know that there are so many things they've already forgotten, is gratifying for me. I also know that I fully intend to teach these lessons in exactly the same manner this year, and I do not plan to return to the way that I used to teach the subject.

Reflecting later on using a more group-centered approach to teaching as opposed to a standard "received" narrative focusing on major leaders and their actions, Suzie reported, "I try to do that with other units now, as well, and I credit my lessons on the black freedom struggle with giving me the impetus to do so."

Kevin, too, took great satisfaction from the process of creating and teaching these lessons, though he also noted that the project required a great deal of extra work. He was teaching a new course with new students, so he did not have as much knowledge of his students' abilities and prior understanding of the freedom struggles as Suzie did. Kevin chose to begin each day by discussing a quote from Green's interview with his students, as a way of setting up his essential questions for each lesson, and he argued that this new approach to a topic he had taught several times before forced him to re-think and re-study a lot of ideas, a challenge he appreciated enormously. Both teachers found that their students came away from their lessons with an excellent understanding of the themes they had presented as well as solid understanding of and ability to assess and evaluate the roles of leaders, ordinary citizens, and organizers of the movement. The lessons also met the National Assessment of Educational Progress (NAEP) as well as New York State content standards for the topic.

Overall, both teachers found their students successful in being able to identify and explain the dynamic relationship between organizations and leaders, as demonstrated on their end of year exams. They were able to discuss the role and value of both and demonstrate their understanding of the powerlessness of one without the other. In both the multiple choice and essay-based question portions of the state's high-stakes test that dealt with the events or players in the Civil Rights movement, the students in both high school teachers' classes reported ease in answering the questions. One hundred percent of the students in both teachers' classes who took their state's exam in U.S. History in the month following these lessons passed it.

That said, the teachers certainly encountered challenges in their teaching of the lessons. For both Kevin and Suzie, the lessons' focus on organizers and organizing in some ways detracted, they felt, from the presentation of what they called the "grand narrative" of the Civil Rights movement. Following a more traditional approach to teaching, they argued, would allow a more sweeping sense of what had happened and the progress that was made through the events of the era. In addition, the lessons as conceptualized took a lot of time, both to prepare and to teach, and both teachers found it a challenge to spend so much time on one topic (Danielle, the middle school teacher, had certainly felt this way as she had struggled, as previously noted, to even find the time to teach the lessons). In Kevin's class, for example, the decision to model the efforts of the organizers whose actions they were studying, by having the students organize themselves into committees and then teach each other the materials, took enormous time and energy that a more straightforward, teacher-centered approach would not have required. In his class's case, though, picking some of the highest achievers to go first when the students did their presentations to "teach each other" about particular groups within the movement proved a helpful strategy, as the rest of the class saw strong models and were able to emulate them. While recognizing the riskiness of relying on students to teach and lead each other so much, Kevin still found that the topic and the class's focus on organizers inspired students to take on the role of organizers themselves in an effective way. Still, what "should have been" four days' worth of lessons, for Kevin's class, turned into seven. The effort proved worth the extra time taken, he felt, but all of us recognize that other teachers may not have the same luxury he had.

In addition, as we stepped back and analyzed the unit as taught, although it was clear that students grasped the importance of organizers and organizing to the success of the Civil Rights movement and that they grasped the important role the media played in inspiring support for the protesters among whites and those outside the South, less clear was the extent to which students in both classes really grasped the "unending" nature of the Civil Rights movement. Green had admonished against the teaching of social movements such as the Civil Rights movement as "a story in which there is a clear beginning and a clear end, a clear challenge, and a clear realization of a goal." Rather, he argued, these must be taught as "an everyday process:"

> These were not things that were epiphanies, by and large. These were not things that reached some kind of sudden and dramatic end. And, sad to say, these are not things that can be represented as clear and unambiguous stories of victory in terms of some set of lasting accomplishments that then is able to stay and endure past all sorts of forms of backlash, all kinds of forms of reaction . . . Much of what we've seen over the last twenty, thirty years in this country politically has told us how much of the gains that could be . . . won through this organizing and through this mobilizing is stuff that also can be lost according to the ways in which politics shift and turn. This is really a story of how some people, mainly because of the ways in which they committed themselves to the work of bringing about change, encouraged many other people to similarly dedicate themselves to working for change.

The very nature of an educational unit, with a beginning, middle, and culminating project, in many ways flew in the face of this important reminder. The fact that the oppression of certain groups is less institutionalized today can mean for some students that it is less apparent or even less urgent to combat. Certainly, Kevin's project on "injustices" today helped show students that struggles against inequality and oppression still continue. Yet the extent to which students came to understand or appreciate this point, even though the teachers addressed it in their instruction, is not something we were able fully to grasp.

Reflecting Back the Following Year

Despite the extra time and effort the unit took and the fact that the lessons may have fallen short of meeting all their goals, all participants of our group still considered the black freedom struggles project largely successful. Reflecting back the following school year on the process of planning and teaching the unit, Suzie wrote:

> the way we taught the Civil Rights movement provided the students with a much more profound understanding than the way that we usually teach it. They had the opportunity to understand how massive the movement really was versus looking at it as two men [here, referring to Martin Luther King, Jr. and Malcolm X] with opposing views leading an entire race.

She also noted that for her students:

learning about the student involvement in the movement proved incredibly beneficial because it made the movement real to the teenagers I teach who live in a world where, although racism exists, it isn't as widespread and institutionalized as it was in the South in the '50s and '60s.

Suzie also felt that for a teacher of an Advanced Placement course who works in an environment in which she is expected to spend much of her time "teaching to the test," this unit proved among the most enjoyable she had had the opportunity to teach: "I truly witnessed one hundred students learn," she wrote, "and I watched their faces as they started to understand the depth of the organization and events. It was really incredible." She added:

> The thing that I really used from Adam Green was where he said, "I firmly believe that the only way to teach social change is in some kind of proportional relationship to how most people live their lives." So much of history is foreign to the people who learn it, especially when it is simply an educational requirement. Having students see that every little action can be important and that anyone can be an agent of change was my goal and that quote from Green drove that point home.

Kevin also reflected back on his lessons on the black freedom struggle months after completing the unit and noted that using Green's interviews as a starting point for each lesson raised students' expectations by challenging them to re-contextualize the movement. The greatest achievement of the unit, according to Kevin, was that it "introduced the intricacies and nuances that challenge the typical textbook story and test-based version of history that usually reach students [prior to] their college years." It gave his students a taste of the way more advanced students—those in college and even graduate school—get to learn and think about the discipline of history, which proved exciting for both students and teacher.

As our group considered the deep investment prompted by the lessons on the part of students, we were reminded of what the historian Charles Payne (2007) wrote in the introduction to his book, *I've Got the Light of Freedom*. Referring to organizers whose actions brought about such profound change during the Civil Rights movement, Payne noted:

> Part of the legacy of people like Ella Baker and Septima Clark is a faith that ordinary people who learn to believe in themselves are capable of extraordinary acts, or better, of acts that seem extraordinary to us precisely because we have such an impoverished sense of the capabilities of ordinary people. If we are surprised at what these people accomplished, our surprise may be a commentary on the angle of vision from which we view them.

(p. 5)

Ultimately, a central goal of our lessons was to highlight the capacities of ordinary people to perform basic yet brave and crucial acts at key points in history. We hoped that through experiencing them, students would see—and take to heart—the notion that the role of the transformer is not reserved only for those with extraordinary gifts or abilities. Through small efforts, through the "mundane actions" of everyday people, students can see that they too can become important players in the histories of their own times and movements.

Works Cited

Eyes on the Prize: Awakenings, 1954–1956 (DVD edition, 1999). Alexandria, VA: PBS Video.

Faigher, J. M., Buhle, M. J., Czitrom, D., & Armitage, S. (2000). *Out of Many*, 3rd edn. London: Prentice Hall.

Kennedy, D. & Bailey, T. A. (2002). *The American Spirit*, 10th edn. New York: Houghton, Mifflin.

Payne, C. (2007). *I've Got the Light of Freedom: The Organizing Tradition and the Mississippi Freedom Struggle.* Berkeley, CA: University of California Press.

Raines, H. (1983). *My Soul is Rested: Movement Days in the Deep South Remembered.* New York: Penguin Press.

Robinson, J. (1987). *Montgomery Bus Boycott and the Women Who Started It: The Memoir of Jo Ann Gibson Robinson.* Knoxville, TN: University of Tennessee Press.

Wiggins, G. & McTighe, J. (2005). *Understanding by Design.* New York: Prentice Hall.

CHAPTER RESOURCES

I. Unit Framework—The Civil Rights Movement

Intended Learning Outcomes (Use NYS SS Standards)

Understandings (Big ideas):

- Analyze the roles that the leaders, organizers, and masses all played in the movements of the Civil Rights era.
- Assess the relative importance of each group to the success of the Civil Rights movement.
- Analyze the effectiveness of different types of protest and consider the role that "organization" played in each type of protest's success or failure.
- Evaluate whether organization guarantees success.
- Evaluate the power of various forms of media to reveal the plight of African Americans and its significance to the Civil Rights movement.

Essential Questions:

- Were the masses as important as the leaders in the Civil Rights movement?
- How does the structure and detail of the Montgomery Bus Boycott reflect the need for mass support and organization throughout the boycott?
- Why do historians focus on Rev. Dr. Martin Luther King, Jr.'s role over the contributions of the masses?
- Does organization ensure success?
- What did SNCC, CORE, and the SCLC have in common? How were these organizations different? Why do you think they sought equality in such different manners?
- Could these protests have happened without the massive organizations that supported them? Why or why not?
- Did these organizations achieve their goals in the long run? Provide evidence to support your answer.
- How significant was the role of the media in the Civil Rights movement?

Essential Questions (continued):

- Would the Birmingham protest have been as effective without the presence of television cameras and the dissemination of these images?
- Why are songs, and music in general, integral to the Civil Rights movement?
- Why did Black Power and the Black Panthers appeal more to television producers than nonviolent protest? How does this represent the confluence of social reform and economic necessity?

Content Knowledge:

- Identify Rosa Parks, Jo Ann Robinson, the Women's Political Council, the Montgomery Improvement Association, and Martin Luther King, Jr.
- Discuss the role of the masses, as well as the planning and organization necessary, in the Montgomery Bus Boycott.
- Evaluate Martin Luther King's role in the boycott and his legacy as its leader.
- Discuss the common goals of SNCC, the SCLC, and CORE.
- Describe the sit-ins, Freedom Rides, protests in Birmingham and Selma, and Freedom Summer and explain what each organization wanted to accomplish.
- Discuss how various branches of the Civil Rights movement used the media to influence public opinion.
- Describe and analyze the multiple roles that radio played in the Civil Rights movement.
- Analyze images significant to the Civil Rights movement, including nonviolent and Black Power protests.

Skills:

- Reading and analyzing primary source documents.
- Deciphering the significance of photographs and contextualizing the images.
- Verbally expressing ideas.
- Working cooperatively.
- Written assessment of material.
- Synthesizing thematically linked sources and ideas.
- Applying lessons to current events and modern-day problems.
- Analyzing maps.
- Evaluating political cartoons.

Vocabularly:

Non-violence, Children's Crusade, Boycott, Black Power, Masses, Black Panthers, Sit-in, Black-oriented radio, Freedom Ride, Activist, SCLC, SNCC, CORE

Learning Experiences:

Bus Boycott Lesson:
- Group Work—analyze transportation, finances, newsletter.
- What did they do?

Resources:

- Jo Ann Robinson, *The Montgomery Bus Boycott and the Women Who Started It*

Learning Experiences (continued):

- Why was this work necessary to perpetuate the boycott?
- How does this reflect the need for mass support and organization throughout the boycott?

Organization Lesson:

Prior to class, students will be divided into six groups. Each group will be assigned one organization, the SCLC, SNCC, or CORE, and the group will study the organization and the protest it organized. Each group will be responsible for reviewing the material and writing an article in which they discuss the protest and its effectiveness. There will be two groups for each organization. One group will write an objective news article while the other will write an editorial in which they take a stand on whether or not the organization and its protest furthered the goal of the Civil Rights movement. Students will present their work when it is completed and all work will be collected. When students return from break they will receive a full newspaper with all of their articles included. We will refer to this work when we discuss the role of the media in the Civil Rights movement.

Media Lesson:

- Group activity—students will listen to songs for which they have lyrics on their handouts. After songs are played each group will be assigned one song (six groups, two groups per song).
- How does this song reflect the ideas/goals/issues of the Civil Rights movement?
- Is the artist advocating a solution? If so, what is it?
- Many African-American artists, including Chuck Berry, Ray Charles, and Sam Cooke, owned the rights to their own music. How might this have impacted the images they relayed?
- Why are these songs, and music in general, integral to the movement?

Resources (continued):

- Howell Raines's biography of Rosa Parks, *My Soul is Rested: Movement Days in the Deep South Remembered*
- Martin Luther King, Jr., MIA Mass Meeting at Holt Street Baptist Church
- Ralph Abernathy, from Jo Ann Robinson, *The Montgomery Bus Boycott and the Women Who Started It*
- Photographs of segregated buses, Rosa Parks' arrest, African Americans participating in the bus boycott
- Cover of the *Montgomery Advertiser* from December 1955
- I. F. Stone, *I. F. Stone's Weekly* (June 4, 1962)
- James Peck, Freedom Rider (1962)
- Quotes from Freedom Riders
- Norman Thomas, Committee of Inquiry Report (May 1962)
- James Farmer, interviewed by C. David Heymann, *A Candid Biography of Robert F. Kennedy* (1998)
- Freedom Rider's account—David Fankhauser
- Map of the Freedom Rides
- Photographs of burned buses and protesters on the buses
- Photographs of the three phases of the march from Selma to Montgomery
- Quote from Jackie Robinson
- Speech by Martin Luther King (March 25, 1965)
- George B. Leonard, *The Nation* (March 8, 1965)
- Images from Greensboro, Nashville, and Atlanta sit-ins
- Reactions from people involved in the sit-ins
- "Movement by Negros Growing; No Service Given Students," *Greensboro Daily News* (February 4, 1960)
- "New Protests Are Followed By Arrests," *Greensboro Daily News* (February 24, 1960)
- Footage of Birmingham protest and Children's Crusade

Resources (continued):

- Music: "Change is Gonna Come" by Sam Cooke; "The Promised Land" by Chuck Berry; "What's Going On?" by Marvin Gaye
- Martin Luther King, Jr., Speech to the National Association of Radio Advertisers
- Images from 1968 Olympics
- Daniel Schorr, CBS News Correspondent (quote)
- Brian Ward, *Radio and the Struggle for Civil Rights in the South*

II. Lesson Framework—The Civil Rights Movement

Intended Learning Outcomes (Use NYS SS Standards)

Understandings (Big ideas):

- Analyze which group, leaders, or masses sacrificed and/or contributed more to the success of the boycott.
- Assess whether the masses were as important as the leaders in the Civil Rights movement.

Essential Questions:

- Why was this quantity of work necessary to perpetuate the boycott? How does this reflect the need for mass support and organization throughout the boycott?
- Who was more important to the success of the movement: the masses or the leaders? Why?
- Why do historians focus on Rev. Dr. Martin Luther King, Jr.'s role over the contributions of the masses?

Content Knowledge:

- Identify Rosa Parks, Jo Ann Robinson, the Women's Political Council, the Montgomery Improvement Association and Martin Luther King, Jr.
- Discuss the role of the masses, as well as the planning and organization necessary, in the Montgomery Bus Boycott.
- Evaluate Martin Luther King's role in the boycott and his legacy as its leader.

Skills:

- Reading and analyzing primary source documents.
- Deciphering the significance of photographs and contextualizing the images.
- Verbally expressing ideas.
- Working cooperatively.
- Written assessment of material.
- Synthesizing thematically linked sources and ideas.
- Applying lessons to current events and modern-day problems.
- Analyzing maps.

Vocabulary:
Non-violence, Boycott, Masses, Segregation

Learning Experiences:

- Motivation: Boycott Web. On the board at the front of the room was an empty web with the words "NYC Bus Boycott" in the center. Students were asked to elucidate the components of a successful boycott as well as assess whether one leader could do this work alone.
- Group Work: Analyze transportation plans, finances/budget, newsletter disseminated to participants. Based on these sources students determined what the so-called "masses" did to make the boycott start and continue for 381 days. Students also evaluated whether all of this work was necessary to perpetuate the boycott and how this vast amount of work necessitated and reflected the need for mass support and organization throughout the boycott (six groups, two per source). Students then presented their work to the class.

Resources:

- Jo Ann Gibson Robinson's letter to the mayor of Montgomery (copy of original)
- Jo Ann Gibson Robinson, *The Montgomery Bus Boycott and the Women Who Started It*
- Howell Raines' biography of Rosa Parks, *My Soul is Rested: Movement Days in the Deep South Remembered*
- Martin Luther King, Jr., MIA Mass Meeting at Holt Street Baptist Church
- Ralph Abernathy, from Jo Ann Gibson Robinson, *The Montgomery Bus Boycott and the Women Who Started It*
- Photographs of segregated buses, Rosa Parks' arrest, African Americans participating in the bus boycott
- Cover of the *Montgomery Advertiser* from December 1955

III. Graphic Organizer for Taking Notes on Student Presentations

	EXPLAIN the background/ problem and goals	EXPLAIN the main events of the movement	DESCRIBE the resolution of the movement	EVALUATE the extent to which this movement was or was not successfully organized
SIT-INS				
SNCC				

Freedom Rides
CORE

Voting Rights
SCLC

IV. Civil Rights Project Assignment, Eleventh- and Twelfth-Grade U.S. History

Your unit project is a learning experience directly related to the Civil Rights movement. As we will be learning throughout the unit, the movement was collection of small movements with famous figures as well as average and ordinary people. Most importantly, this movement was a collection of organizers and organizations. (Some examples are The Student Nonviolent Coordinating Committee, Congress of Racial Equality, and The Southern Christian Leadership Conference.) So, you will organize your own *direct action plan* that will exercise many of the important skills and use many of the "organizing" strategies employed during the movement in the 1960s.

A threat to justice anywhere, is a threat to justice everywhere.

MLK

Pre-Meeting—Organizing Your Organization (HMWK Assignment)

(Due Friday 18 April)

Choose a topic: Select an issue, problem, or struggle that your group sees as an injustice in our community today. Brainstorm your ideas, make a list, and weigh the reasons offered by the people of your group. Think a lot before you settle on an issue/cause. Cooperate and give each person a voice in your discussion. Create a group name based on your cause. Submit an outline that:

- explains what issue/injustice you choose and its importance to your group;
- brainstorms a list of ideas for addressing the issue;
- brainstorms your roles and the specific responsibilities for each role and assign roles for each member.

**** Share all your contact information: names, email and phone numbers. ***

Part One—Research and Investigation (20 Points)

(Due Friday 9 May)

Gather information about your topic by researching important information and interesting facts about your topic. You should consult a variety of sources, including one magazine and one newspaper article. Each person must bring three articles about your topic to your group meeting on Friday 2 May. Delegate the responsibility and share your information. Organize your information neatly in these categories: Submit in a folder (provided):

- background on your issue;
- main issues and concerns of your issue;
- reasons and causes for your issue;
- explanation of the impact/importance of your issue.

*** Think of your "direct action plan" for people. ***

Part Two—Information Board (30 Points)

(Due Friday 16 May)

You and your group will create a triptych (three-piece poster-information board) to RAISE AWARENESS on your issue. This will be displayed for others in the school to see and will serve as the reason for your group's existence. You will have space in the school to educate, motivate, and activate your peers for the remainder of the school year. This board should feature the main ideas of your research and clearly explain your action plan for others to have an impact on your issue.

You should:

- clearly present research and investigation;
- use images and creativity to gain attention and give information;
- include simple actions that people should be encouraged to take.

Part Three—Pamphlet (30 Points)

(Due Friday 23 May)
Create an informative pamphlet that you can distribute to the public to motivate them to act. It must:

- contain most of the information from the information board above;
- inform and enable others to act;
- be clear and concise with ideas of how to act simply to combat the injustice/issue you selected.

Part Four—Work Log (10 Points)

(Due Friday 23 May)
Each person in the group should use the work log to show me (or the investors that will give you money for your campaign) all the work that you have done. This will be a form I will give to you and you should trace your actions and the actions or inactions of your group. Also complete the reflection on the backside of work log.

FAIR FOR JUSTICE—Attendance and participation is also mandatory for our "Fair for Justice," which will present our ideas to the school during the school day in June. 10 points deducted for unexcused absence.

EXTRA CREDIT—You will also receive extra credit for documenting your time educating the public beyond our school.

You may meet with members of your group and pass out your fliers and document this with photos.

I have read and understand the group work requirements for my/my child's cycle project.

_____

Student Signature

_____

Parent Signature

V. Student Pamphlet, Front

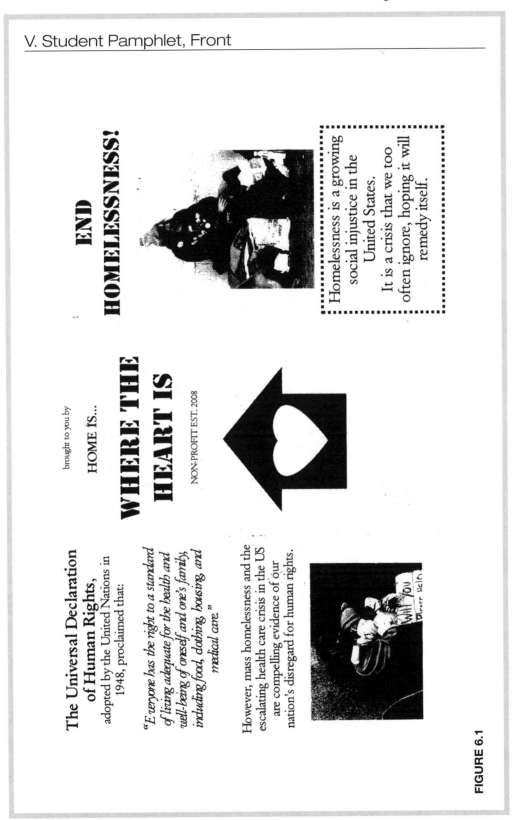

END HOMELESSNESS!

Homelessness is a growing social injustice in the United States.
It is a crisis that we too often ignore, hoping it will remedy itself.

brought to you by

HOME is...

WHERE THE HEART IS

NON-PROFIT EST. 2008

The Universal Declaration of Human Rights, adopted by the United Nations in 1948, proclaimed that:

"Everyone has the right to a standard of living adequate for the health and well-being of oneself and one's family, including food, clothing, housing and medical care."

However, mass homelessness and the escalating health care crisis in the US are compelling evidence of our nation's disregard for human rights.

FIGURE 6.1

VI. Student Pamphlet, Back

STATISTICS

On any given night in US, anywhere from 700,000 to 2 million people are **homeless,** according to estimates of the National Law Center on Homelessness and Poverty.

3.5 million people (1.35 million of which are children) will experience homelessness in a given year.

Single men comprise 44% of the homeless, **single women** 13%, **families with children** 36%, and **unaccompanied minors** 7%.

The homeless population is about 50% African-American, 35% white, 12% Hispanic, 2% Native American and 1% Asian.

Veterans are 40% of the homeless pop.

1 in every 5 homeless persons has a severe or persistent mental illness.

42% of homeless children are under the age of five.

Poverty and **lack of affordable housing** are the principal causes of homelessness.

STOP CRIMINALIZING, start sympathizing

The main causes of homelessness are poverty and a lack of affordable housing yet society often pegs the homeless individuals as criminals. More often than not, homeless people are victims of circumstance. Victims of disease or mental illness. Victims of HIV and AIDS. Victims of unemployment. Instead of criminalizing them, we must rise up and organize to help these unfortunate victims.

HOW TO HELP

Americans everywhere must ensure that homelessness does not become a family tradition. Use the facts and statistics provided to make a difference in your community.

- *Volunteer for local homeless organizations.* HOUSING WORKS is a New York City based organization that provides housing, medical, prevention & support services for the homeless in NYC. Go to **www.housingworks.org** for more info on how to get involved.

- *Advocate for community-based treatment and support services* for families which enable them to find homes, receive appropriate physical and mental health treatment, and rebuild their lives in the community.

- *Inform your local and state governments* that if these services are not funded and successfully implemented, the social and economical costs to society will have a devastating impact on everyone's future.

FIGURE 6.2

VII. Relevant New York State and NAEP Standards

New York State Learning Standards, U.S. History

- Students explore the meaning of American culture by identifying the key ideas, beliefs, and patterns of behavior, and traditions that help define it and unite all Americans (MS.1A)
- Students interpret the ideas, values, and beliefs contained in the Declaration of Independence, the United States Constitution, Bill of Rights, and other important historical documents (MS.1B)
- Students describe the reasons for periodizing history in different ways (MS.2A)
- Students complete well-documented and historically accurate case studies about individuals and groups who represent different ethnic, national, and religious groups in the United States at different times and in different locations (MS.3A)
- Students gather and organize information about the important achievements and contributions of groups living in the United States (MS.3B)
- Students describe how ordinary people and famous historic figures in the United States have advanced the fundamental democratic values, beliefs, and traditions expressed in the Declaration of Independence, United States Constitution, the Bill of Rights, and other important historic documents (MS.3C)
- Students classify major developments into categories such as social, political, economic, geographic, technological, scientific, cultural, or religious (MS.3D)
- Students analyze the development of American culture, explaining how ideas, values, beliefs, and traditions have changed over time and how they unite all Americans (HS.1A)
- Students describe the evolution of American democratic values and beliefs as expressed in the Declaration of Independence, U.S. Constitution, Bill of Rights, and other important documents (HS.1B)
- Students discuss several schemes for periodizing the history of the United States (HS.2A)
- Students develop and test hypotheses about important events, eras, or issues in U.S. history, setting clear and valid criteria for judging the importance and significance of these events, eras, or issues (HS.2B)
- Students compare and contrast the experiences of different groups in the United States (HS.2C)
- Students compare and contrast the experiences of different ethnic, national, and religious groups, explaining their contributions to American society and culture (HS.3A)
- Students research and analyze major themes and developments in U.S. history (HS.3B)
- Students prepare essays and oral reports about the important social, political, economic, scientific, technological, and cultural developments, issues, and events from U.S. history (HS.3C)

New York State Learning Standards, Historical Thinking

- Consider the sources of historic documents, narratives, or artifacts and evaluate their reliability (MS.4A)
- Understand how different experiences, beliefs, values, traditions, and motives cause individuals and groups to interpret historic events and issues from different perspectives (MS.4B)
- Compare and contrast different interpretations of key events and issues in U.S. history, and explain reasons for these different accounts (MS.4C)
- Describe historic events through the eyes of those who were there (MS.4D)
- Analyze historical narratives about key events in U.S. history to identify the facts and evaluate the authors' perspectives (HS.4A)
- Consider different historians' analyses of the same event or development in U.S. history to understand how different viewpoints and/or frames of reference influence historical interpretation (HS.4B)
- Evaluate the validity and credibility of historical interpretations of important events or issues in U.S. history, revising these interpretations as new information is learned and other interpretations are developed (HS.4C)

   Adapted from *New York State Learning Standards*, U.S. History (1996)

NAEP Learning Standards, U.S. History

Framework 1: Themes in U.S. History

- What individuals and groups have been important in maintaining, testing, and changing America's institutions? Which democratic institutions and procedures made change possible? (1)
- What core civic ideas have influenced American society? What individuals and groups have maintained, tested, and influenced the evolution of these ideas? (1)
- What major issues and controversies arose about issues of diversity and unity? (1)
- How have work lives and economic opportunities of various groups differed (e.g. racial groups)? (3)

Framework 2: Periods of U.S. History

- How was the U.S. Constitution changed after the Civil War? How did the changes affect democratic ideas and practices and contribute to achieving democratic ideals? (5.1)
- What were the goals of the radical and moderate reconstructionists? How and why did they succeed and fail? (5.1)
- What actions did African Americans take before, during, and after the Civil War to secure their freedom and rights and citizens? (5.1)
- How did postbellum black communities differ from slave and antebellum free black communities? (5.2)
- How did Reconstruction change the economic life of the South? (5.3)

- What gains and losses in individual rights resulted between the Civil War and World War I? How did these changes relate to other reform efforts? Who was left out of these reform efforts? (6.1)
- How did politics in the 1920s reflect both the advancement and retreat of important democratic principles? (7.1)
- How have the ideas of the founding period about the nature of liberty been maintained and changed? Why do important core civic ideas of individual rights, equal rights under the law, and popular sovereignty continue to be forces in American society? (8.2)
- What political issues have been most significant in contemporary America? How have these issues and controversies been resolved in the American democratic political system? (8.1)

NAEP Historical Thinking Standards, U.S. History

Framework 3: Ways of Knowing and Thinking about U.S. History

1. HISTORICAL KNOWLEDGE AND PERSPECTIVE

Students should be able to:

- Name, recognize, list, identify and give examples of people, places, events, concepts, and movements
- Place specifics in a chronological framework and construct and label historical periods
- Define historical themes and give examples of the ways themes relate to specific factual information
- Describe the past from the perspectives of various men and women of the time
- Explain the perspective of an author of a primary source document
- Describe different perspectives related to a historical issue or event
- Summarize the contributions of individuals and groups to U.S. history
- Summarize the meaning of historical sources and link these sources to general themes

2. HISTORICAL ANALYSIS AND INTERPRETATION

Students should be able to:

- Specify and explain cause-and-effect relationships and connect contemporary events to their origins in the past
- Categorize information and develop strategies for organizing a large body of facts
- Examine multiple causes of historical developments
- Explain points of view, biases, and value statements in historical sources
- Determine the significance of people, events, and historical sources
- Weigh and judge different views of the past as advanced by historical figures themselves, historians, and present-day commentators and public figures

- Demonstrate that the interpretation and meaning of the past are open to change as new information and perspectives emerge
- Develop sound generalizations and defend these generalizations with persuasive arguments
- Make comparisons and recognize the limitations of generalizations
- Apply knowledge, draw conclusions, and support those conclusions with convincing evidence

Adapted from National Assessment Governing Board (2006)

Works Cited

National Assessment Governing Board (2006). *U.S. History Framework for the 2006 National Assessment of Educational Progress.* Washington, DC: U.S. Department of Education.
New York State Learning Standards, U.S. History (1996). Albany: New York State Education Department.

Seven
U.S. Imperialism

Framing the Questions: An Interview with Laura Briggs, conducted by Rachel Mattson

Laura Briggs received her PhD from Brown University's Department of American Civilization and is currently an Associate Professor of Women's Studies at the University of Arizona. She also holds affiliate appointments in History, Anthropology, and Latin American Studies. Briggs is the author of *Reproducing Empire: Race, Sex, Science, and U.S. Imperialism in Puerto Rico* in which Briggs argues that Puerto Rico provides the perfect lens through which to examine the history of U.S. imperialism because it has been a place where, for over a century, the United States has developed its approach to expansionism. Briggs is now currently working on a book on transnational and transracial adoption.

Rachel Mattson: *What would you call your primary area of specialization?*

Laura Briggs: I think these days I say transnational history.

RM: *What, for you, are the most exciting debates in this field right now?*

LB: I think the central question that people struggle over is: What are the approaches that one might use to thinking through war and U.S. imperialism? It used to be the case that the biggest struggle was over whether or not to use the word *imperialism*, to describe the United States's role as a world power. In the early '90s when the term *globalization* was all the rage, that was the fight. But as Amy Kaplan (2004) pointed out about four or five years ago in her address to the American Studies Association, that is no longer the big question because with the beginning of the wars in Afghanistan and Iraq, the Neo-Cons began to use the term *imperialism* very straightforwardly as their term for U.S. foreign policy. And so all of a sudden that debate got rendered irrelevant—

because if the people enacting policy are going to call what they do imperialism, then there's not so much to fight over.

One of the specific historical questions that very much fascinates me now is: How do we bring questions of gender and sexuality and intimacy to the forefront of our study of war and U.S. imperialism? The more I sit with that question, the more persuaded I am that it is a critical question. Sometimes it erupts quite straightforwardly, like when Laura Bush says "we have to go to war in Afghanistan in order to save Afghani women." Then it's really clear that women are on the agenda. But other times it seems like the folks who want to talk about the economy or militarism as the central questions about U.S. foreign policy or imperialism often seem to have the most persuasive case. And it seems to me that there's a really persistent undertone about how much it matters to our account of ourselves as engaging in a kind of benevolent supremacy—that phrase is not mine, it's from a policy document called NC168—and it's not what people took out of it. But that's what we should be aiming for in the aftermath of World War II. Our benevolent supremacy is a lot about women and forms of family, just as it was for the British—questions of genital cutting, of the veil, of sutee, of overpopulation.

The other question that really interests me is: Can we write history that doesn't take the nation as its automatic frame? On the one hand the answer is straightforwardly, institutionally: No. But especially when you get into the colonial period, you realize how much the nation is an ideological construct that's imposed on much more heterogeneous and complex histories—because of course there's no such thing as, for instance, colonial Guatemala. At that time Guatemala didn't belong to an entity or a world in which things were formed as nations.

I think historians have been really enlisted in a nationalist project of naturalizing the nation, of making us believe that national boundaries somehow always were there and make logical sense, and that nationality is something etched onto geography or populations. And for people for whom that narrative doesn't fit or in places, like the Southwest—the Borderlands—where that narrative doesn't fit, the nation makes not that much sense. Or *sometimes* it rises to prominence and sometimes it doesn't. But if we take the nation as the naturalized thing, then we never notice when it rises to prominence and when it recedes.

RM: *Which raises the question for me: How do you even begin to think about teaching the idea of the nation as a constructed entity?*

LB: Some of that is regional, I really think. When you think about the American Southwest in general, the struggle to make it actually part of any nation has been an ongoing one. It was only poorly part of Mexico and now it's only poorly part of the United States.

But where I would start right now is by talking about immigration, because that's so much on people's minds. And to think about all the hybrid nationalities that people occupy and the circular migrations from Mexico, Guatemala, the Philippines, and people are also perhaps a little bit aware that China's influence in Africa has vastly expanded and the number of Chinese and Japanese businessmen running U.S. maquiladoras in Latin America is huge.

And then of course you can point to the moments and places where the nation is very much questioned—should Puerto Rico, for example, be part of the United States? Why? How?

RM: *I'm interested in hearing your thoughts on teaching Puerto Rico in particular because there's so little good history that's accessible to K–12 teachers and students. In a city like New York, where there are so many Puerto Rican students, that is a serious problem.*

LB: I know.

RM: *So I'm wondering if there's maybe a debate or an overarching historical question in this vein that is specific to U.S. imperialism/colonialism in the Puerto Rican context that we can talk about.*

LB: I think we teach more easily about Cuba than we teach about Puerto Rico, ironically enough—ironically, because probably many more of us have been to Puerto Rico than are ever going to go to Cuba. Okay, I'm going to tell this story backwards but I think it makes sense this way. In the aftermath of World War II and the decolonization struggles of that period, one of the things that policy-makers came to believe is that decolonization had to be a prerequisite for development, and it became very normalized. The decolonization movements were something that the United States backed—never mind the odd assassination by the CIA here and there—but officially we talked about the American Revolution as an echo of decolonization struggles in the aftermath of World War II. And that's the moment at which the history of Puerto Rico became literally sort of unspeakable, because Cuba had fought a decolonization struggle against Spain and then was deeply resistant to the U.S. presence and the United States didn't last long there. The Philippines, actually, we should be more excited about because they fought this long and fabulous war against the United States that was bloody and horrible and in many ways a run-up to some of the war-fighting policies of Vietnam—reconcentration camps, model villages, and so forth—but we don't really talk about the war that the United States fought to subdue the Filipinos because that was actually ugly, and people in the United States were deeply troubled by it. So we tell the story of Cuba because it sort of fits our happy paradigm. The United States was sort of imperialist but really in the service of Cuban anti-imperialism, and then we got out of there fairly quickly.

Puerto Rico was a much more hybrid kind of place to begin with in the sense that many of the people who were royalists in Spain, who had fled the slave uprising in Haiti, who actually had left other anti-slavery movements, came to Puerto Rico. So while there was an anti-Spanish imperialist movement in Puerto Rico, it was not strong and it was very, very elite. And the masses of working people in Puerto Rico never particularly identified with it. And so the United States' troops were greeted happily in Puerto Rico and then the United States stayed, and stayed—and stayed. And so we don't have either the strong narrative of anti-imperialism—although I would make the argument that there was plenty chafing against U.S. rule in Puerto Rico, it just rarely took overtly political or military forms. But the other thing is the United States brought with it a set of ideologies that were deeply embraced by working people in Puerto Rico—everything from a labor movement to enfranchisement of landless and illiterate people, and eventually the enfranchisement of women, that built strong support for some of the ideals of the United States. Now, it was a much more optimistic version of what the United States stood for than was ever lived out in the United States. But one of the best examples of that kind of collaboration was between the Socialist party in Puerto Rico (which was very strong after the United States arrived, and which enfranchised working-class people), and its connection to the Socialist movement in the United States. Puerto Ricans were from the outset a very cosmopolitan people who took up the terms of U.S. social justice struggles, but not necessarily anti-imperialism. I don't want to say that there hasn't been an anti-imperialist movement in Puerto Rico—there has, and it came to a head in the middle of the Depression in the '30s when the people were truly starving in Puerto Rico, and the New Deal had not come, and the independence movement was very strong and the US repressed it extraordinarily harshly. And what many Puerto Ricans took out of that is that there are better ways to get what you want out of the United States than to resist it.

RM: *Have you found any effective teaching methods for getting students to understand these and the other sorts of arguments that transnational historians are making?*

LB: One of them is through social movements. The other one is more obvious and potentially less disruptive: It's just to teach U.S. policy. One of the things that I've enjoyed teaching this last year was Greg Grandin's book, *Empire's Workshop* (2006), which suggests that U.S. involvement in Central American wars from the '50s through the '90s was a rehearsal of policies and practices that have come to the fore in the context of U.S. military policy in Iraq and tracing those kinds of connections—just like what I just said about the relationship of the war in the Philippines to the war in Vietnam. And that seems really riveting and to engage people in thinking about how U.S. policy moves.

This is not a bad time for me to whip out a document. I want to look at a piece of writing by Helen C. Wilson on Reconcentration in the Philippines—which includes an extended account of what it meant that U.S. forces in 1906 were trying to stop what was basically a guerilla war by putting people in camps. It was quite similar to the model villages policy in Vietnam. It was also practiced in El Salvador and Guatemala in the '80s. A couple of things seemed interesting to me about this document. One of them is, it's 1906—women don't yet have the vote. It seems really significant to notice how much women were engaged as political actors even before they had the vote. Wilson wrote this piece for a small local paper, *The Springfield Republican*. It's an account of atrocities—which is a tactic borrowed from the anti-slavery movement to really hold up the horror of the impact of a policy. And the other thing is: Wilson was a member of the Anti-Imperialist League. We forget how strong an anti-imperialist movement there has been in the United States—when we talk about the age of imperialism or when we try to connect the notion of imperialism to wars in Vietnam or Iraq, either we tell them in the most depressing possible way or, in the case of textbooks, in a hopelessly optimistic way. The United States was briefly engaged in imperialism, then it got better. No mention of the strong anti-imperialist movement in the United States—which is why we don't admit, in U.S. history courses, the hugely significant role of the anti-war movement in putting an end to the war in Vietnam. We cultivate this despair among students, who believe there's nothing that they can do.

The story that we tell K–12 students, or really high school students, about American democracy is that it came from the Constitution and its gradual unfolding over time—not that American democracy is something that's been endlessly fought for. And so we're not allowed to talk about American democracy. I think it's those moments where democracy feels alive—during a struggle, or a protest—that are absolutely thrilling to some of us and terrifying to others, but that is not the content by and large of what social studies is supposed to contain.

RM: *Can you look at this document that you've just shown me and describe it? Just describe it: Describe what it is and what is interesting and useful about it.*

LB: OK. First, it starts with a chart that tries to show change over time—which is interesting to me because this is a moment when social science is emerging as a way to tell a story, and it's quite a compelling story that this chart tells, if you can figure out how to read it. It becomes quite clear that the effect of the war in the Philippines has been absolutely devastating on the countryside and then it follows with quite a long narrative. One of the things we know from looking at it is that newspapers were different in the beginning of the twentieth century, in 1906—because this is almost as long as a *New Yorker* piece. These days, you would have to have a magazine to do that. The other thing is it's written by a woman at a moment when women's role in public life is being very much debated—there's a suffrage struggle in the streets. And it's a very moving kind of narrative—she writes about "we started out here and then we went there and this is what we saw and these were some of the horrors visited on people in terms of malnutrition in these places, their fear, their connection or non-connection with the rebels." And it's a travel narrative—you also get a sense that you wouldn't necessarily have from a lot of what you read that women went places—the idea that women only after World War II or something were very involved in public life. No. This is quite an intrepid story of "I waded through the mud and went to this scary place and there's a war on." But more than anything what strikes me about this document is the kind of outrage that it expresses that U.S. policy is doing this. And a belief in what America could be, should be, that U.S. policy ought to be as something better and different from this. That has been the reservoir of social movements, not just in the United States—but this dream of democracy, of justice, of fairness to all people, of anti-racism. She writes these words absolutely believing that they will move people and that it can change policy.

Works Cited

Grandin, G. (2006). *Empire's Workshop: Latin America, the United States, and the Rise of the New Imperialism*. New York: Metropolitan Books.

Kaplan, A. (2004). Violent Belongings and the Question of Empire Today. *American Quarterly* 56(1), 1–19.

Wilson, H.C. (1906). *Reconcentration in the Philippines*. Boston: Anti-Imperialist League.

Essay: Pivotal Failures: Experiments in a Secondary History Classroom

By Rachel Mattson, with Jill Jeffery and Terra Lynch

> The practice of failure is pivotal . . . Failure signals a project that may no longer be attempted, or at least not on the same terms.
>
> Kamala Visweswaran (1994, p. 99)

Over the course of the 2007–2008 academic year, I participated in a wonderful, collaborative curriculum development project. In doing this work, I was part of a team of committed educators that collectively studied a set of historical questions, developed a primary document-based lesson meant to teach a group of public high school students to think critically about these questions, and then subsequently taught that lesson to those students. The project yielded inventive solutions to difficult historical and pedagogical questions and resulted in teaching days that provoked students to engage in critical writing and discussion; to closely examine primary documents; to deploy higher-order thinking skills; and to develop their own opinions about the meaning of the past. The fact that students were able to do such careful and critical work was, to us, a sign of our success, since engaging students in this kind of historical enterprise was among our central objectives (just as they are, quite often, key elements of best practices for the K–12 social studies classroom, nationwide). In short, this project could be called a "success"—an experiment in curricular development that achieved its objectives.

And yet, reflecting on the work of this group in the months after the project ended, I began to grow uneasy with this kind of evaluative statement. Not because, using the standard criteria listed above, the project was not a success—it most certainly was. But as the months rolled on, I began to wonder if perhaps we were using the wrong set of criteria altogether. Or at least, if we were using only one small subset of the criteria we ought to use to judge critical instructional work in the history classroom. That is to say, I began to wonder if, in fact, this instructional moment could not also be considered a "failure." Indeed, it seemed to me that there might be some deep practical use—for me, and for other educators and scholars—in exploring the question of whether, and where (or how) this project did fail—and what those failures might reveal about the larger effort to "reform" history education more generally.

The idea that there might be something to be gained by examining failed research projects is not a new one. Especially among anthropologists, the idea of inspecting and writing about failed encounters has gained some popularity in recent years, and among those who offer thoughtful and useful models for thinking productively about investigative failures is the feminist anthropologist Kamala Visweswaran. In an essay entitled "Feminist Ethnography as Failure," Visweswaran considers one occasion when her efforts to interview a woman who participated in the Gandhian freedom struggle went terribly awry. In an attempt to conduct an ethnographic interview by the rules—and indeed, precisely because she stuck so closely to the rules—Visweswaran's efforts ended up a miserable failure, one that generated very little in the way of useful data. But as she attempted to make sense of this failed encounter, she realized that it suggested something larger about the flawed assumptions that structure the field of inquiry within which she is engaged. "There is a sense in which any discussion of methodology," she writes, "diverts attention from more fundamental issues of epistemology." As a result, instead of looking for ways to improve her interview technique—her "methodology"—she re-evaluates the broader assumptions and goals—the "epistemologies"—that she and her fellow feminist anthropologists have created for themselves.

Visweswaran's reflections, though far afield from the concerns of educational research, are easy enough to translate. Like Visweswaran, we might also see the failures in our projects as invitations to inspect the core "assumptions" and "strategies" that guide our work and the field of inquiry within which we labor (Visweswaran, 1994, p. 98). In this essay, I take her suggestions to heart. Using the curricular project that started me thinking about these questions as an opportunity, I inquire, here, into the question of failure and success in the history classroom in a broad frame. How *do* we define success and failure in the middle and secondary history classroom? And what do our working definitions of success and failure obscure about the assumptions and strategies that guide this work? In what ways do they prevent us from seeing new possibilities for what a history classroom can be and do? And what kinds of alternate criteria might we develop for evaluating our history educational projects?

In this, it is not my intention to dismiss the very valuable work of critical history educators working in the middle and secondary context—or the importance of thinking about and developing effective pedagogical methodologies. Nor, like Visweswaran (who rejects the "politics of despair") do I mean to contribute to public despair about the current state of K–12 history education. On the contrary, I mean to raise a set of questions that often—at least to my mind—seem to be off-limits, and to inquire into the mechanisms that limit our ideas about the meaning of success in the history classroom. For me, these questions are very important, because I believe that history education has the potential not simply to develop, in the oft-repeated phrase, "engaged participants in democracy." I also believe that it holds the power to teach young people to understand *how power works*, and *how change happens*. This might appear to be a subtle distinction, but I believe that the two statements reflect significantly distinct propositions. History education, at least in theory, holds great potential to teach young people not only that they can be "active participants" in our democracy, but also to see the limitations of that democracy—and to transform it.

"Its Just Really Frickin' Hard": Teaching the History of Imperialism in a Tenth-Grade Regents Classroom in New York City

Visitors often get lost trying to find their way to New York High School. Although the school sticks out among the many shorter buildings that surround it, it is located on a short backstreet that very few New Yorkers—even those residents who have lived there a long time—have ever heard of. But once you arrive at the school itself, it is not difficult to find your way. At the entrance sits a friendly security guard (no metal detector) ready to direct visitors to their intended destination. And the route to Ms. X's classroom is pleasant. The hallways are clean, orderly, and decorated with neatly organized bulletin boards. Before arriving at Ms. X's room, you will pass a gym, a dance studio, and several friendly teenagers goofing around with a math teacher or an Assistant Principal. The majority of the school's students come from immigrant families. Of the school's 478 students, over half are Latino and 27 percent are Asian. The rest of the student body is composed largely of African-American students (15 percent) and white students (4 percent). Nearly 90 percent of all the school's students qualify for free lunch. Performance on standardized tests varies, but overall, in 2007, 66 percent of the school's students earned "proficient" marks on the statewide reading tests, and 74 percent earned "proficient" marks on the statewide math tests.

Ms. X's tenth-grade Global Regents class more or less reflects these demographics. Predominantly Latino, the class also contains African-American, South Asian, and white students, of whom two are immigrants from Eastern Europe. By Ms. X's accounting, the classroom also contains one chronically depressed student, one painfully shy student, three students who are repeating the class after failing it the previous year, one student who hasn't been able to come to class in weeks because he's in jail, and four students with documented learning disabilities. Some of her students spend class time slumped in their chairs, with their faces on their desks. But mostly, her students are lively, attentive, and actively participatory during class. The vast majority of them want to go to college, and they are motivated to pass the Regents Exam that looms over the entire school year, like a dark, rain-filled cloud waiting for them at the end of June. Ms. X, a white woman in her mid-thirties, has been teaching for six years—this makes her one of the more experienced teachers at New York High School. She is a wonderfully creative teacher, interested in finding ways to engage her students' minds and curiosity without giving up on teaching them the skills and knowledge they'll need to know for the Regents.

The Working Group

The working group that would, ultimately, create a lesson for use in Ms. X's classroom was small, but effective. Consisting of fewer than six participants, it included historians, educational researchers, and classroom teachers, including Ms. X. One member—NYU graduate student Jill Jeffery—brought to our work special pedagogical and scholarly knowledge about the teaching of writing skills and the relationship between student writing and performance on standardized tests, knowledge that would be very useful to our work. Other members—including Ms. X herself—were experienced in the art of combining instruction in writing and historical thinking skills in a social studies class. The energy of the group was friendly, enthusiastic, hard working, and cooperative. We frequently met over dinner, in somebody's living room, on a Friday night. Over meals that were usually ordered in, our conversations ranged widely. We discussed historical ideas, pedagogical questions, the state of public education, and the contours of our own lives. These Friday night dinners went a long way to add depth and a sense of excitement to our work; to create a sense of friendship; and to provide time for us to extensively debate questions about history, pedagogy, and method.

This group had been charged with developing a lesson of any length about the history of U.S. imperialism, and to get us started we were given a transcription of an interview with the historian Laura Briggs. In the course of her interview, Briggs introduced a wide range of fascinating and provocative ideas—ideas that our working group labored very hard to integrate into our instructional plan. Among the most compelling, and difficult, ideas that Briggs offered us was the notion that we might take a transnational approach to history education: "I think historians have been really enlisted in a nationalist project of naturalizing the nation," she said, "of making us believe that national boundaries somehow always were there and make logical sense." Instead of confining ourselves to teaching history as a series of national stories, she suggested, we might teach about the invention of nations, or we might teach the history of regions as inter-related wholes. "Can we teach history in a way," she wondered, that "doesn't take the nation as its automatic frame?" Briggs was not cavalier about this proposition: In some ways, she observed, the answer to this question "is straightforwardly, institutionally: No." But, she continued, the idea that nations are inventions created by historical events is so important that we really should try.

But this was not the only set of concerns that Briggs raised. She also spoke about the importance of teaching with a gendered lens, and about teaching in a way that situates the United States within the larger history of global imperialism. She suggested one specific primary document that she thought might be useful in anchoring a classroom discussion of these ideas—an article entitled "Reconcentration in the Philippines." Written in 1906 by an anti-imperialist American woman named Helen Wilson (and published in a small local paper, *The Springfield Republican*), the piece described atrocities that the U.S. army committed against Filipino civilians as part of the United States's attempt to subdue the Filipino nationalist movement and acquire the Philippines as an imperial possession.

In Briggs's view, the document presented several interesting teaching opportunities. First, it offered an opportunity to discuss competing nationalisms—American imperialist nationalism, American anti-imperialist nationalism, and revolutionary Filipino nationalism. It also offered an opportunity to discuss questions about democratic participation—especially the sort of democratic participation that does not rely on the vote. Written by an American woman before American women had yet won the right to vote, the document highlighted, in Briggs's words, how actively "women were engaged as political actors even before they had the vote." Moreover, because Wilson was a member of the Anti-Imperialist League, the document invites exploration of the history of U.S. anti-imperialism. This is important, Briggs noted, because often, "when we teach about the age of imperialism":

> either we tell them in the most depressing possible way or, in the case of textbooks, in a hopelessly optimistic way. [. . .] No mention of the strong anti-imperialist movement in the United States. [The result is that] we cultivate despair among students, who believe there's nothing that they can do. The story that we tell [. . .] high school students about American democracy is that it came from the Constitution and its gradual unfolding over time—not that American democracy is something that's been endlessly fought for.

In our small working group, we struggled with Briggs's ideas and suggestions. How, we asked, could we integrate her ideas with the constraints of Ms. X's class? In the first place, the lesson that we would teach would take place just a few weeks before Ms. X's students took the Global History Regents Exam. This was a time when, traditionally, Ms. X turned her attentions quite explicitly toward making sure her students developed the kinds of skills that they would need to pass the Regents. Moreover, the subject of U.S. imperialism—which was the subject of Briggs's interview—is not tested on this exam (it appears, instead, on the U.S. History Regents Exam, which students would not take until the eleventh grade). Finally, many of Ms. X's students were struggling readers who would not be able to succeed—or, really, learn much—in the context of a reading-heavy lesson.

We gave up almost immediately any ambition to design a lesson that could investigate some of the most provocative of Briggs's suggestions. Instead, we shifted our focus to questions about how we might use this particular primary source document in Ms. X's classroom. We believed that if we used the history of U.S. imperialism in the Philippines as the primary content for the lesson, then we would be on our way toward integrating her ideas into our work. We came up with an approach that was, in many ways, an ingenious solution to this challenge: Although this particular content would not be tested on the Regents, we could use it to reinforce questions about imperialism that *would* appear on the Global exam. Teaching it within a larger unit on European and Asian imperialism, and Third World nationalist struggles, we could design a lesson meant to support the unit's instructional goals. Additionally, we could use this material to reinforce Ms. X's efforts to prepare students to write Regents-level document based question (DBQ) essays. Thus, we decided to make this lesson a "skills-focused" one. We would introduce the history of U.S. imperialism in the context of helping students understand the document-based essay portion of the Regents Exam. We did not want to give up on entirely on Briggs's suggestions, and we thought that this was a good compromise.

The Regents as a Frame for our Work

Because the Regents loomed so large in our considerations of how to teach this material, it might be helpful to explain the general structure of New York's History Regents—and in specific, the writing portion of those exams. Whereas nearly every other U.S. state includes essay items *only* for their English language arts writing assessments, New York includes essay items on both of its high school social studies exams, global and U.S. history—one is a "thematic essay" using "prior knowledge"; the other is a "document-based essay," in which students are asked to draw from multiple primary documents provided within the exam. Although these two essays account for only 30 percent of the total exam score, they can prove especially challenging for students with below-grade-level literacy skills (which many of Ms. X's students were). It was for this reason that preparing her students to earn passing marks on the essay portion of the Regents was an important goal for Ms. X.

Teachers working with underprepared students often express frustration about the question of how to prepare their students for these aspects of the exams. They often view the work they have to do in order to prepare students for the Regents Exam as standing in direct conflict with the task of cultivating historical thinking and understandings—and feel forced to choose between the two. For teachers of students who read below grade level, the conflict is even more acute. Since the teacher has a responsibility both to the school, which can face serious consequences for poor exam performance, and the student, who needs a passing score to graduate, the temptation to focus instruction on the essentials of test preparation—even if these support neither authentic historical thinking nor the school's mission of preparing every student for college-level work (not to mention the larger goal of teaching students to think broadly about their lives)—can be overwhelming.

Research indicates that preparing students for the history Regents writing tasks can be antithetical to teaching students to think historically. A study of students' retrospective accounts suggests that many of them are not engaging in history as an interpretive process when responding to high-stakes essay prompts designed to assess historical knowledge (Beck & Jeffery, 2009). It sometimes has the effect of teaching students that history is "just the facts," as opposed to a process in which students empathize with historical subjects (Seixas, 1996), understand primary sources as potentially biased interpretations (Hennings, 1993), and compare multiple perspectives to construct coherent accounts of historical events (Wineburg, 1991). In other words, Regents preparation focused on the basics of producing an acceptable essay is likely to reinforce students' misconceptions of history as static, impermeable, and dead, rather than dynamic, interpretive, and continuous.

But this does not have to be the case. The Regents history essays ask students to "describe" and "discuss" historical information. Although "describing" is a fairly straightforward process—defined on both tasks as "to illustrate something in words or tell about it"—"discussing" is far more flexible. The Regents explains that this includes making "observations about something using facts, reasoning, and argument; to present in some detail." In short, "discussing" invites, if not requires, students to interpret information and present coherent arguments. And, indeed, an examination of the rubrics used to score these responses supports the idea that demonstrating the ability to think broadly about historical questions—as opposed to just regurgitating facts—can earn a student high marks. To obtain a 5 (out of 5) on either essay, students must produce writing that is "more analytical than descriptive (analyzes, evaluates, and/or creates information)." A score point 3 essay, conversely, is one that is "more descriptive than analytical (applies, may analyze, and/or evaluate information)"; a 4 demonstrates both. So, whereas it may not be a requirement that students critically examine historical content to succeed on the test, the invitation is certainly there. And an informal look at the samples of high-scoring student essays suggests that those who organize their responses around a debatable thesis do well on these tasks.

Moreover, students' ability to achieve higher exam scores with such responses may have to do with the relationship between essay organization and the construction of a working historical argument. Students who organize their responses around an arguable thesis may find it easier to devise "a logical and clear plan of organization," a requirement for score points 4 and 5, than students who do not devise a unifying theme. Either way, the essay tasks seem deliberately structured to accommodate two visions of historical understanding: static and dynamic. If so, it's up to teachers to decide which vision they emphasize when preparing students. There is really no reason, then, to see the Regents Exam preparation as antithetical to teaching students to think critically, historically; to closely read primary documents; or to form arguments about the meaning of the past.

Ms. X's experience in the classroom reflects these ideas. Although she did, sometimes, feel frustrated with the competing demands of teaching historical thinking skills versus teaching exam-taking skills, she also learned over her years of teaching that she does not have to choose between these two distinct goals. Indeed, as she explains to her students, she believes that the exam sets too low a bar for their efforts. "I want you to be able to do more than what the test asks," she tells her students every year. Thus our group agreed that we could devise a lesson that would help students pass the Regents while still teaching them to read and think critically about the past, the present, text, and image.

Our Lesson

Our group designed a lesson that would take place over the course of several days in early May 2008. Organized around two overarching essential questions—How might the amount of power a person has shape his or her views about imperialism? And how might we read text and images critically?—we planned a sequence of instructional activities that would take students step by step through the process of examining primary source documents; considering those documents in the context of a topical question; and then, using the documents they had examined, composing an argument-driven "document-based essay" of the sort they would face on the Regents. But our goal was not simply to prepare students to pass the exam. We also hoped to give students the tools to critique this test—that is, to read the Regents Exam itself as a text that, like any document, was written in a particular moment in time and reflective of a particular set of beliefs about the meaning of the past and the present.

We taught this lesson over three instructional days. On day one we introduced students to the work they would be doing over the next several days and to the method we wanted them to use when, the next day, they would be asked to do close readings of primary source documents. Then, in order to get them thinking about the Regents Exam, we asked them to write a little bit about what they already knew of the Regents. In specific, we asked them to answer each of the following questions:

- What do you know about how you should approach the short answer section of a Regents document-based question (DBQ)?
- What are the elements of a good DBQ essay?
- What should you look for when reading an historical primary source document?
- What is your opinion of the Regents Exam and standardized testing more generally?
- Who do you think benefits from standardized tests such as the Regents, and how?

On days two and three, we divided students into small groups and gave each group a separate primary document related to the history of U.S. imperialism in the Philippines. We asked each group to collectively analyze their document by answering a series of questions designed to help them think about the relationships between an author's social position and his or her views on imperialism (see Resources II, p. 186). For this exercise, we had selected documents that featured a range of voices, from the Filipina anti-imperialist Clemencia Lopez to President William McKinley, which showcased a diversity of opinions in the debate that raged about U.S. imperialism in the Philippines in the early twentieth century, and which displayed the range of kinds of documents they might encounter on the exam (poems, political cartoons, and speeches) (see the Resources section of this chapter, p. 185, for a full list of these documents). Then, we asked students to "jigsaw" their work: that is, after they had done a close reading of this initial document with their small group, we asked them to create several entirely new groups, each group consisting of one member from each of the original groups. In these new groups, students were asked to adopt the role of an "expert" and present the document from their first group to the new group. We concluded this lesson by asking students to write short essays using the documents they had all analyzed in small groups. Having already considered each of the assembled documents in the context of the lesson's essential question—How might the amount of power a person has shape his or her views about imperialism?—we now asked them to gather their thoughts and to write a coherent essay addressing this same question.

We initially intended to continue our lesson into a fourth day, during which we would return to questions about the Regents Exam and ask them to critically consider the test's agenda and implicit assumptions. But a school-wide change in schedule disrupted our effort, and in the end, there was no room in Ms. X's busy end-of-the-year schedule for this extension. So our lesson ended with the essay-writing exercise, and then the class moved on to explore British and Japanese imperialism, and to continue their end-of-the-year test preparation.

How We Initially Evaluated Our Work

In evaluating our work in Ms. X's classroom, we consulted a range of materials, including student writing generated during the lesson; a loose transcript of in-class discussions; meeting and planning notes we had generated in the months leading up to the lesson; and our own memories and impressions of the work.

Although we had some concerns about our accomplishments, our initial evaluations were positive. In an email she wrote to the group a few days after the conclusion of the lesson, Ms. X remarked that she thought it "was one of the best classes this year for student output/thinking. I felt like the academic level was wonderfully high." Our lesson, she noted, even managed to motivate a student who had been consistently too shy to participate. Engaged throughout most of the instructional tasks we gave him, this student, she reflected, even stayed late to finish writing his essay. Ms. X attributed our success, here, in large part, to the fact that there were three extra "teachers"—two participants from the book project, and a student teacher—circulating around the room, facilitating students' small group conversations. This, she said, "made a difference" and seemed to bring about "a turning point."

Another participant reflected that she "felt despair" throughout the class periods—worrying that students were finding the primary documents inaccessible—but that as the lesson wound down, she could see that we had managed to accomplish our overarching objectives. And we did accomplish many of our goals. As we reviewed our planning documents, we recalled that we had designed this lesson around several instructional goals. We wanted students to:

- develop skills that would ultimately enable them to write a "document-based" essay of the sort that would earn them passing marks on the year-end Global History Regents Exam;
- learn a range of critical reading and historical thinking skills; specifically, we wanted them to understand that history is not a collection of dates and names, but rather an argument about the meaning of the past—and we wanted to give students practice taking a stand, making an argument about the past, verbally and in writing;
- consider multiple perspectives on an issue, and to gain experience with reading primary source documents critically, for authorship, bias, and argument;
- learn that the United States maintained a brutal imperial presence in the Philippines in the late nineteenth and early twentieth centuries; that Americans were engaged in a serious debate over the meanings and effects of U.S. imperialism; and that both women and men participated in these debates;
- gain skills that would help them pass, and think critically about, the Regents Exam.

We accomplished most of these goals. Even in the limited amount of classroom time we had— we taught this material over the course of three 45-minute class periods—we managed to get students to think about and articulate what makes a successful answer to Regents DBQs and to practice writing these sorts of essays. We got students talking about the meaning of imperialism, the many perspectives that Americans, Europeans, and Filipinos had on U.S. intervention in the Philippines; and we did have success in teaching students to read critically a broad set of primary source documents and articulate their findings to each other. We taught students both important critical historical thinking and essay-writing skills. We were also successful in staging some critical discussions between students and among students and adults. One team member had a fantastic discussion, for instance, with a young man who was struggling with the language in Rudyard Kipling's "The White Man's Burden." What began as a discussion about vocabulary—and the meaning of words, such as "burden," that are crucial to understanding Kipling's arguments— turned into a discussion about the effects of imperialism and the ideologies that have historically supported it.

That is to say, we were able to design a lesson that would both prepare students for the Regents and teach them to think critically about historical events. In one post-instructional evaluation, one of the participants wrote that she thought our lesson "demonstrated that teachers do not have to choose between test preparation and engaging students with complex historical understandings." By choosing an open-ended prompt for the lesson's culminating writing task, we had asked students to do the very same thing that they would be asked to do on their Global History Regents—that is, use documents to support a mini-argument on a historical question. But we also, as this team member noted, "went beyond direct test preparation": we provided students with "opportunities to interact with historical content and with their peers" and "to draw their own conclusions by analyzing the documents and using details from these as evidence to support their conclusions." Overall, then, the skills involved in our lesson helped prepare students to write a DBQ essay while asking them to do more than the Regents requires.

Rethinking the Evaluation

Doing all this was in many ways a great accomplishment. Teaching historical ideas in a way that is practical and engaging is, as Ms. X wrote in an email, "really frickin' hard." "You can want to teach historical thinking skills all you want—but it's easy to get caught up in the emotional needs of yourself and your kids," she reflected at the conclusion of our lesson. "And then there's always so much else going on—there's the trouble of absences, lack of time and space and no air conditioning. So even if you want to be a purist and always teach good historical thinking, it's a real challenge." And, certainly, there are innumerable secondary classrooms where students never have the opportunity to work with primary documents; where they are never asked to consider a set of historical documents and then offer their own opinion about what they thought; and where students are never introduced to the idea that, for instance, colonized people have frequently contested the conquest of their nations eloquently. We managed to integrate into our lesson a range of opportunities for students to do each of these things, and in that sense, the work was successful.

And yet, using another set of criteria, you could also say that this lesson accomplished far too little. In the first place, we did not achieve one of the other goals we had set for ourselves. We wanted to equip students to do a critical reading of the Regents Exam itself. Throughout all of our planning conversations, members of our team rebelled against simply teaching students to learn to pass the Regents. This, we thought, was too depressing, too mechanical. Instead, we aimed to teach students to see the Regents as a text in its own right—one that, like all texts, betrays one idea about truth, an idea that is part of the larger public debate about truth, and the past, and the politics of history education. We even came up with a do-able activity that we should have been able to integrate into our lesson: We would ask students to spend one class period studying several Regents questions and then writing a letter to the editor expressing their opinion about these questions and their experience studying for the test. But time constraints forced us to drop this aspect of our plan. You could call our failure to accomplish this one goal predictable. This was the sort of activity and instructional goal that sounds fun and critically engaging in the planning stage, but, in the context of a classroom that, as Ms. X noted, "has so much else going on," seems like a luxury. Predictable or not, it bears observation that we "failed" to accomplish this task—even though accomplishing it was important to all of us.

There were other things we failed to accomplish with this project—goals we never even set for ourselves, goals we left behind in the first meeting, goals we could never have conceptualized. In the first place—and this seems important to mention in a book that seeks to bridge the divide between the ideas of professional historians and the teaching of history at the secondary level—we had a hard time translating many of the most interesting aspects of Briggs's offerings into work that could be used in Ms. X's tenth-grade classroom. Almost immediately, we found that in order to keep up with Ms. X's rigorous Regents prep schedule, we would have to abandon the question, for instance, of how to get students to question the naturalness of contemporary national boundaries.

Another related topic that we never even began to approach was the subject of Puerto Rico. Part of the reason that the editors of this book chose to approach Laura Briggs, specifically, as the consulting historian on the question of teaching the history of U.S. imperialism was because she had written a wonderful book on the history of Puerto Rico. The question of how to teach Puerto Rico in the context of Regents-aligned curricula is a vexed one. Despite its centrality to the Age of Imperialism (which is, in itself, an important part of state and federal history content standards), and its significance in the context of both New York City immigration history and the lives of New York City public school students, students in the New York City public schools receive, on the whole, very little instruction on the history of U.S. imperialism in Puerto Rico. Indeed, when I interviewed Briggs, I asked her to speak specifically about the history of Puerto Rico—we're interested in this history, I explained, specifically "because there's so little good history that's accessible to K–12 teachers and students. In a city like New York," I continued, "where there are so many Puerto Rican students, this is a serious problem." In her book-length historical treatment of sex and science in early U.S. intervention in Puerto Rico, *Reproducing Empire*, Briggs had written: "How many non-Puerto Ricans in the United States could describe the island's status vis-a-vis the mainland?" The fact that most U.S. Americans do not know much about the U.S. territory of Puerto Rico, she writes, "is not an accident": it is "produced and maintained" through "the teaching of U.S. history" (Briggs, 2002, p. 2). Thus, I had hoped that Briggs would offer critical intellectual structures and primary source documents that we could use to teach public school students about the history of U.S. imperialism in Puerto Rico.

But Briggs had a hard time coming up with effective and classroom-appropriate ideas for teaching this material. In her interview, she spoke much more eloquently and practically about teaching the history of U.S. imperialism in the Philippines. Indeed, when asked directly about Puerto Rico, she agreed that this was an important subject. But the conversation drifted quickly away from this topic. "I think we teach more easily about Cuba than we teach about Puerto Rico," she explained, and then began to discuss post-World War II U.S. foreign policy in the Americas. "That's the moment at which the history of Puerto Rico became literally sort of unspeakable," she explained:

> because Cuba had fought a decolonization struggle against Spain and then was deeply resistant to the U.S. presence and the U.S. didn't last long there. The Philippines, actually, we should be more excited about because they fought this long and fabulous war against the United States . . . Puerto Rico was a much more hybrid kind of place to begin with [and] while there was an anti-Spanish imperialist movement in Puerto Rico, it was not strong and it was very, very elite. And the masses of working people in Puerto Rico never particularly identified with it.

"I don't want to say that there hasn't been an anti-imperialist movement in Puerto Rico," she concluded, "There was, and it came to a head in the middle of the depression in the '30s when the people were truly starving in Puerto Rico . . . But what many Puerto Ricans took out of that is that there are better ways to get what you want out of the United States than to resist it." These ideas are, to me, begging to be introduced to the young students studying in New York City's (and more broadly, in the United States's) public schools. But because Briggs couldn't boil her ideas about U.S. imperialism in Puerto Rico into standards-aligned chunks or translate her ideas into teachable primary documents, our team found it nearly impossible (given our time constraints) to adapt Briggs' ideas into a lesson about Puerto Rico that would be appropriate to the classroom context in which we found ourselves.

Perhaps this says something about the gap that divides university-level historical inquiry from secondary history education. It is naive to expect a university-based historian to know, without any exposure to the limitations guiding high school history instruction, how to translate his or her long-considered ideas about episodes from the past into the sorts of resources and ideas that can be best put to use in secondary classrooms. This is a deep divide that begs for attention, one that is long overdue for rectification. But it turns out that this was not the case with Briggs herself: as she explained to me in a subsequent conversation, Briggs knows quite a bit about the demands of a high school classroom—indeed, before earning her PhD, she worked as a high school history teacher in a public school in Boston—and remains committed to engaging with these questions in her work teaching undergraduates at a state university. Maybe the trouble was that I expected too much from one hour-long, taped conversation about a set of complicated and broad subjects. After reading an earlier version of this essay, Briggs remarked that, to her mind, the reason she offered less commentary about the history of Puerto Rico was due both to the way I had framed the conversation ahead of time ("in your email beforehand," she noted, "you asked me [to speak] about U.S. imperialism") and to the questions that were more pressing for her at that precise moment. "When we talked," she later recalled, "I hadn't worked on Puerto Rico in six years, and my head was deep in Guatemala (for research) and the war in Iraq (in life). The Philippines was on my mind because it was the site of the development of counterinsurgency warfare, torture, and a vigorous anti-imperialism movement (which seemed so missing in the United States at that time)." As a result, she explained, "the urgency in my head was about developing lessons about imperialism that stressed students' responsibility to participate in critical debates about the making of U.S. imperial policy." In retrospect it seems the trouble lay in the structure of our dialogue, and in the fleeting nature of our conversation. In large part because of the distance between Briggs's home (in Arizona) and our group's (in New York), our encounter was truncated. It seems important to observe, then, that, if we wish to foster real and effective dialogue among and between historians and high school history teachers, we will have to endeavor to create the conditions whereby these conversations can be ongoing, sustained, and long-term. (This kind of sustained dialogue is featured in Chapter 5 of this book—in which, in part because of geographical proximity to both of the teachers and the genesis and production of this project, the consulting historian was able to maintain ongoing involvement in the curricular project.)

More to the point, the work of our group was most deeply limited by the content and scope of state and federal curricular standards. These mandates sculpted the very scope of what our working group could imagine and create. National and state standards create a closed world of topics that students are expected to know about, a closed world of what "counts" as U.S. history. The history of nineteenth- and early twentieth-century U.S. imperialism has made it onto that list, but the specific contours of U.S. colonization in Puerto Rico and the Philippines have not. When questions about the nineteenth-century "Age of Imperialism" appear on New York State U.S. History Regents Exams—and generally these exams include, at most, two questions about this topic per year—they tend to be wide-ranging and broad, and rarely require students to know much in the way of details about these events. The multiple choice section of the June 2006 exam, for instance, merely asked test-takers to identify the "United States policy" that was "most closely associated with the annexation of Hawaii and the Philippines": Was it (a) neutrality, (b) isolationism, (c) imperialism, or (d) international cooperation?

But even given all of this, reflecting back, I am struck by how easily—and confidently—we sacrificed some of the most compelling ideas suggested by Briggs's interview and by the larger subject of U.S. imperialism. Finding her comments about the Philippines to be the most concrete and adaptable, we decided to focus the content of our lesson upon U.S. intervention there. But in doing so, we gave up any attempt to invite students into a sustained conversation about their conclusions about the meaning of the U.S. historical imperial adventures. We failed to ask students to inquire into deeper questions about subjugation, abuse of power, and the idea of self-determination—all of which are central to any comprehensive understanding of the local or global history of imperialism. We refused even to consider raising, with these students, questions about the naturalness of the United States's national boundaries. Indeed, in the end, we only deployed the barest shadow of Briggs's ideas—including the idea that was, perhaps, the most far-reaching among the ideas she offered us: that is, her critique of the project of K–12 history education in the United States. "The story that we tell high school students about American democracy," Briggs noted, "is that it came from the Constitution and [is gradually] unfolding over time—not that American democracy is something that's been endlessly fought for."

If it is true, as the anthropologist Kamala Visweswaran suggests, that examining the failures in our projects offers us the opportunity not simply to tinker with our methodologies, but, more importantly, to examine the core assumptions that silently guide our efforts, then this project demonstrated just how out of reach genuine questions about democracy are in many of our urban classrooms. Although middle and secondary social studies educators, school administrators, politicians, and other observers often argue that one of the primary purposes of K–12 history and social studies education is the creation of strong democratic citizens and the promotion of "civic competence" (NCSS, 1994, vii), we rarely engage students either in truly democratic processes or in considerations of the contradictions in the history of the United States as a democracy. We certainly do not, as Briggs notes, teach students that "American democracy is something that's been endlessly fought for." Likewise, very few opportunities exist for educators or administrators to inquire into the task of educating students for democratic citizenship. What does it mean, we might ask, to teach young people to be strong citizens, exactly? Does it mean we ought to teach students to be good future jurors, military draftees, drivers who pause at yellow traffic lights? To be thoughtful, critical voters? If history education is about creating engaged citizens, what about the students in our classes who aren't, and may never become, U.S. citizens—or (more pertinently) those who, residing in, or hailing from, the United States's colonial territories, have had only partial access to the rights of U.S. citizenship? The broad concepts of "Americanness" and "citizenship" are deployed, in the social studies and history content areas, very frequently—and with great gravity. But what, really, do these terms mean? Is the job of an engaged "citizen" perhaps bigger than simply knowing and observing the law? Asking about the naturalness of the United States's national boundaries and about the history and contemporary context of American imperial adventures could, if we would only make space for it, provide us with multiple opportunities for genuine engagement with questions about the meaning of democracy—and for inquiry into what tactics we, as educators, might use in our efforts to educate "strong citizens."

On one hand, clearly, our lesson was no failure. Not only did we engage a group of struggling students to ask complicated historical questions, to critically read primary source documents, and to write document-centered persuasive essays, but we also introduced them to a slew of new historical ideas. We did, at least implicitly, suggest to Ms. X's students that national belonging is not everything; that there have existed anti-imperialist movements in the United States; that women were politically involved long before they got the vote in either the United States or the Philippines; and that opinions regarding imperialism are dependent on the perspective from which one views it. But the lesson can be considered a success only if we use a narrow framework for evaluating our work. One of our group's members concluded, at the end of our experiment, that our work proved "that it is possible to engage students in historical thinking while preparing them for Regents essay tasks." True enough. But can we not set our sights higher? Can we not decide that we want history classes to be laboratories of sustained debate about the meaning of the past? A place where we begin to teach young people to develop their own opinions about ideas and events; to grow accustomed to *not believing* everything they see in print; to raise questions about who can legitimately tell stories about, and interpret the meanings of, U.S. pasts; and to stretch their imagination? That is to say: Might we actually begin to imagine a history classroom and curriculum that would provoke students to think about what it means to be genuinely democratic—at home, and abroad; in school, on the street, and in the workplace; locally and globally? To my mind, it is simply not enough to demonstrate that one can, while preparing students for a high-stakes standardized exam, get students to think critically about texts and ideas for thirty minutes. The trouble with that idea of success is that it obscures other possibilities, other mechanisms for teaching students to interpret the world; to be truly literate; and to understand how power works, how change happens, and what possibilities might exist in a genuinely democratic society.

Works Cited

Beck, S. W. & Jeffery, J. (2007). Genres of High-Stakes Writing Assessments and the Construct of Writing Competence. *Assessing Writing*, 12, 60–79.

Briggs, L. (2002). *Reproducing Empire: Race, Sex, Science and U.S. Imperialism in Puerto Rico.* Berkeley: University of California Press.

Hennings, D. G. (1993). On Knowing and Reading History. *Journal of Reading*, 36(5), 362–370.

National Council for the Social Studies (1994). *Expectations of Excellence: Curriculum Standards for Social Studies.* Silver Spring, MD: National Council for the Social Studies.

Seixas, P. (1996). Conceptualizing the Growth of Historical Understanding. In Olson, D. & Torrance, N. (eds.), *The Handbook of Education and Human Development.* Oxford, UK: Blackwell, pp. 765–783.

Visweswaran, Kamala (1994). Feminist Ethnography as Failure. In *Fictions of Feminist Ethnography.* Minneapolis: University of Minnesota Press, pp. 95–113.

Wineburg, S. S. (1991). Historical Problem Solving: A Study of the Cognitive Processes Used in the Evaluation of Documentary and Pictorial Evidence. *Journal of Educational Psychology*, 83(1), 73–87.

CHAPTER RESOURCES

I. Lesson Framework: U.S. Imperialism

Intended Learning Outcomes (Use NYS SS Standards)

Understandings (Big ideas):

Students will learn:
- to consider multiple perspectives on an issue;
- that history is not a collection of dates and names, but rather an argument about the meaning of the past;
- how to both pass and critique the standardized test in U.S. history.

Essential Questions:

- How might the amount of power a person has shape his or her views about imperialism? (How does one's access to power determine one's perspective on the effects of imperialism?)
- How might we read text and images (both historical and contemporary documents) critically?

Content Knowledge:

Students will know:

- that the United States maintained a brutal imperial presence in the Philippines in the late nineteenth and early twentieth centuries;
- that in the nineteenth century, there were deep debates over the meanings and effects of U.S. imperialism.

Skills:

Students will learn:

- how to write a document-based essay that would earn them passing marks on the Regents Exam;
- to read primary source documents critically, for their arguments, as well as to interpret statistics and charts, and to consider competing opinions.

Vocabulary/Important Concepts:

Imperialism, Anti-imperialism, Feminism, the Philippines, Primary source document, Document-based question, Power

Learning Experiences:

- Primary source document analyses in groups. Each group answers the following questions about their document:
  - Who is the author of this document? When was it created?
  - On a scale of 1 to 5 (1 being the least, and 5 being the most) how much power did the creator of this document have (in terms of race, gender, economic/class, education, and so on)?
  - How does the author of the document view the impact of imperialism?
- Culminating writing assignment: thematic document-based essay

Resources:

- Clemencia Lopez's 1902 Address to Annual Meeting of the New England Women's Suffrage Association
- Political cartoons from U.S. newspapers in 1899 ("Recommended by Hoar" and "The White Man's Burden")
- A pro-imperialism speech by President McKinley (1899)
- Lewis H. Douglass on African-American opposition to McKinley's imperialist policies (1899)

II. In-Class Questionnaire: Student Ideas about the Regents Exam

- What do you know about how you should approach the *short answer section* of a Regents DBQ?
- What are the elements of a good *DBQ essay*?
- What should you look for when reading a *historical primary source document*?
- What is *your opinion* of the Regents Exam and standardized testing more generally?
- *Who do you think benefits from* the standardized tests such as the Regents, and how?

III. Relevant New York State and NAEP Standards: U.S. Imperialism

New York State Learning Standards, U.S. History

- Students explore the meaning of American culture by identifying the key ideas, beliefs, and patterns of behavior, and traditions that help define it and unite all Americans (MS.1A)
- Students investigate key turning points in U.S. history and explain why these events or developments are significant (MS.2B)
- Students understand the relationship between the relative importance of U.S. domestic and foreign policies over time (MS.2C)
- Students analyze the role played by the United States in international politics, past and present (MS.2D)
- Students classify major developments into categories such as social, political, economic, geographic, technological, scientific, cultural, or religious (MS.3D)
- Students analyze the development of American culture, explaining how ideas, values, beliefs, and traditions have changed over time and how they unite all Americans (HS.1A)
- Students develop and test hypotheses about important events, eras, or issues in U.S. history, setting clear and valid criteria for judging the importance and significance of these events, eras, or issues (HS.2B)
- Students compare and contrast the experiences of different groups in the United States (HS.2C)
- Students analyze the United States's involvement in foreign affairs and a willingness to engage in international politics, examining the ideas and traditions leading to these foreign policies (HS.2E)
- Students compare and contrast the values exhibited and foreign policies implemented by the United States and other nations over time with those expressed in the United Nations Charter and international law (HS.2F)
- Students research and analyze major themes and developments in U.S. history (HS.3B)
- Students prepare essays and oral reports about the important social, political, economic, scientific, technological, and cultural developments, issues, and events from U.S. history (HS.3C)
- Students understand the interrelationships between world events and developments in U.S. history (HS.3D)

New York State Learning Standards, Historical Thinking

- Consider the sources of historic documents, narratives, or artifacts and evaluate their reliability (MS.4A)
- Understand how different experiences, beliefs, values, traditions, and motives cause individuals and groups to interpret historic events and issues from different perspectives (MS. 4B)

- Compare and contrast different interpretations of key events and issues in U.S. history, and explain reasons for these different accounts (MS.4C)
- Describe historic events through the eyes of those who were there (MS.4D)
- Analyze historical narratives about key events in U.S. history to identify the facts and evaluate the authors' perspectives (HS.4A)
- Consider different historians' analyses of the same event or development in U.S. history to understand how different viewpoints and/or frames of reference influence historical interpretation (HS.4B)
- Evaluate the validity and credibility of historical interpretations of important events or issues in U.S. history, revising these interpretations as new information is learned and other interpretations are developed (HS.4C)

Adapted from *New York State Learning Standards, U.S. History* (1996)

NAEP Learning Standards, U.S. History

Framework 1: Themes in U.S. History

- What were the causes and consequences of key events that marked American involvement in world affairs? (4)
- How have the geographical location and resources of the United States, its ideals, its interests, and its power influenced its role in the world? How and why has that role changed? (4)
- What primary documents and historical sources record the key developments in shaping United States foreign policy? (4)
- How have the interests, institutions, ideologies, individuals, power, and activities of the United States affected other nations? (4)

Framework 2: Periods of U.S. History

- What was the idea of Manifest Destiny? Who were its supporters and opponents? (4.4)
- What was the debate over American ownership of colonies after the Spanish–American War, and what was the influence of this debate on the nature of American government? (6.1)
- Why did the United States expand its role in world affairs in the late nineteenth and early twentieth centuries? (6.3)
- Who were the champions and critics of expansion? (6.4)
- In what ways did the United States expand its territory, its diplomatic importance, and its military power? (6.4)
- In what ways did other nations respond to the expanding role in world affairs? (6.4)
- How and why did the United States become the preeminent economic and military power in the world? (7.4)

NAEP Historical Thinking Standards, U.S. History

Framework 3: Ways of Knowing and Thinking about U.S. History

1. HISTORICAL KNOWLEDGE AND PERSPECTIVE

Students should be able to:

- Name, recognize, list, identify and give examples of people, places, events, concepts and movements
- Place specifics in a chronological framework and construct and label historical periods
- Define historical themes and give examples of the ways themes relate to specific factual information
- Describe the past from the perspectives of various men and women of the time
- Explain the perspective of an author of a primary source document
- Describe different perspectives related to an historical issue or event
- Summarize the contributions of individuals and groups to U.S. history
- Summarize the meaning of historical sources and link these sources to general themes

2. HISTORICAL ANALYSIS AND INTERPRETATION

Students should be able to:

- Specify and explain cause-and-effect relationships and connect contemporary events to their origins in the past
- Categorize information and develop strategies for organizing a large body of facts
- Examine multiple causes of historical developments
- Explain points of view, biases, and value statements in historical sources
- Determine the significance of people, events, and historical sources
- Weigh and judge different views of the past as advanced by historical figures themselves, historians, and present-day commentators and public figures
- Demonstrate that the interpretation and meaning of the past are open to change as new information and perspectives emerge
- Develop sound generalizations and defend these generalizations with persuasive arguments
- Make comparisons and recognize the limitations of generalizations
- Apply knowledge, draw conclusions, and support those conclusions with convincing evidence

Adapted from National Assessment Governing Board (2006)

Works Cited

National Assessment Governing Board (2006). *U.S. History Framework for the 2006 National Assessment of Educational Progress.* Washington, DC: U.S. Department of Education.
New York State Learning Standards, U.S. History (1996). Albany: New York State Education Department.

Concluding Thoughts

Research on Teaching and Learning History: Teacher Professionalization and Student Cognition and Culture

Terrie Epstein

Over the past twenty years, there has been an outpouring of empirical research on teaching and learning history in elementary and secondary schools. This is significant because, although comparable research on math, science, and literacy education has had long-established traditions, research on history education, often encompassed under the broader umbrella of social studies education, often became bogged down in internecine arguments about whether to organize the social studies curriculum around the academic disciplines of history and the social sciences or around interdisciplinary themes or persistent public issues. In recent years, however, history and social studies educational researchers have focused greater attention on how history teachers teach and learn the subject and how young people learn about history in classrooms and other settings. Consequently, researchers have examined the contexts in which pre-service and in-service teachers have learned to teach history from historians, educators, and their prior experiences as students; provided portraits of typical and extraordinary examples of classroom teaching and learning; and defined and analyzed teachers' and students' understandings of history as an academic discipline and how that knowledge can be enhanced. This book builds upon and extends this work in new ways.

What this research reveals is both discouraging and encouraging. On the one hand, recent surveys of teaching practices in public schools (Hicks, Doolittle, & Lee, 2004; Levstik, 2008; National Assessment of Educational Progress, 2006; Ragland, 2007) suggest that many history classrooms conform to the Ferris Bueller stereotype of the history teacher to which Robert Cohen and Michael Stoll referred in their introduction: a teacher who asks only dry and irrelevant questions, and relies on textbooks, classroom recitations, and worksheets organized around information to inculcate into the minds of the young traditional celebratory narratives of U.S. history (NAEP, 2001, 2006; VanSledright, 2008). The widespread use of standardized high-stakes testing has contributed to this pattern and also has had deleterious effects on teaching history as an academic discipline.

Contrary to policy-makers' intentions of using the tests to promote more rigorous instruction and deeper learning, high-stakes tests have encouraged some history teachers to "dumb down" their lessons, provide less creative pedagogy, present historical methods and skills as routine *vs.* intellectually engaging practices, and rush through 500+ years of the past in order to "cover the curriculum" and potential test questions (Grant, 2006; Segall, 2006; van Hover, 2006).

On the other hand, however, there have been some laudable (and sometimes well-funded) efforts to support the professional development of history teachers, restructure learning experiences so that teachers have greater time and resources to teach history well, and promote young people's abilities to connect to and construct rather than merely consume historical texts. This exciting body of work holds the potential to begin transform history education into a relevant, inquiry-driven enterprise.

Research on History Teachers' Professional Development

Historian–Teacher Collaborations

In her chapter on professional development in the *Handbook of Research in Social Studies Education*, Stephanie van Hover (2008) noted that studies on social studies teachers' professional development describe the fragmented nature of most professional development efforts, taking the form of two-hour, one-day, or summer-long workshops, with little follow-up after the teachers return to their schools. Most teachers who have participated in professional development reported on the satisfaction they gained in learning from historians or other content specialists and in collaborating with other teachers in planning new lessons and units. At the same time, researchers have not followed the teachers into the classroom to assess if or how they used workshop content, materials, or instructional models and if or what students gained as a result of teachers' professional training.

Since 2001, the Department of Education's Teaching American History (TAH) grants have become the most high-profile and well-funded professional development efforts for elementary and secondary history teachers. The federal government has offered competitive grants to school districts, which in collaboration with historians, professors of education, museum educators, and master teachers implement summer- and year-long institutes and workshops to deepen the historical and pedagogical knowledge of history teachers. Many of the programs follow a model in which historians give lectures and present primary sources related to specific historical questions or topics and experienced teachers and/or professors of education give demonstrations of effective ways to incorporate content, activities, and primary sources into elementary, middle, and secondary classrooms. Participating teachers also collaborate to develop and share lesson and unit plans based on what they learned in the workshops.

Published research on the effects on teacher learning and development of the TAH grants has reported mixed results. A government-funded evaluation of the program (Humphrey *et al.*, 2005) found that the majority of participants were certified teachers with undergraduate history majors and many years of teaching experience. Teachers learned a good amount of historical content, but possessed little ability to analyze and interpret historical evidence. Studies of individual TAH institutes also reported disappointing results. In two separate Institutes, teachers wanted more historical content to be taught, particularly on the specific subjects they planned to teach (Mucher, 2007; Warren, 2007). Some felt that lectures about newer historical scholarship or a historian's specific area of expertise were peripheral to what their students were required to learn. Other, experienced teachers were critical of presentations that focused on teaching history to promote young people's historical thinking, believing that their students were not capable of engaging in the types of historical inquiry presented by institute personnel.

Other evaluations of individual TAH institutes found more positive results. Teachers in Colorado reported using primary sources and the internet more often than they had before the institute, and engaged students in activities such as perspective taking and counterfactual questioning, which promoted analysis and synthesis of historical questions and sources (Ragland, 2007). The teachers also used more thematic rather than topic-oriented approaches to teaching historical periods and included more student-centered and critical-thinking activities, in which students learned to question and analyze primary and secondary texts.

Whereas the focus of most research on collaboration is on what teachers have learned from historians, a few historians have written about what they've learned from teachers. Carol Berkin, a distinguished historian who teaches at the City University of New York, found first and foremost that she gained great respect for teachers: "teachers who participated in these institutes had a far clearer understanding of the goals of teaching and far greater knowledge of how to do it well" (2006). She used what she learned from working with teachers to reform her own teaching. She expanded her aims for lectures and courses from moving beyond disseminating content for students to digest to providing analytic tools for students to connect the past and present and develop greater curiosity and empathy (Berkin, 2006; Woestman, 2008). Further, she scaffolded lectures and discussions for student learning by including explanations of terms and concepts that immigrant or underprepared students might not know. By following the lead of effective teachers in planning instruction around goals of student learning that were greater than simply mastering historical content, Berkin became a better teacher.

The editors of the present volume endeavored to invite middle and secondary teachers into a process that would avoid the pitfalls that researchers found to be a problem in many of the TAH professional development projects, while still capitalizing upon the benefits of collaborations between classroom teachers and historian. Sustained engagement with university-based historians deepened participating teachers' content knowledge, and their ability to teach historical content through thematic frameworks. Teachers incorporated new content into their lessons and units, used primary sources to illuminate concepts and themes, and required students to analyze and synthesize primary and secondary sources to answer significant questions about the past. They did this first by presenting historical content about a period that set the stage for interpreting historical questions. They then asked students to analyze the primary sources in light of the historical content and questions. The teachers also used their expertise to relate the newer perspectives on historical periods presented by historians to more traditional ones found in the learning standards and Regents Exams. Overall, the teachers learned historical content and perspectives from the historians and used their skills as experienced teachers to turn new disciplinary knowledge into academically challenging, innovative, yet utilitarian classroom lessons that met the developmental needs of their students, the rigors of new historical perspectives, and the demands of high-stakes testing (Grant, 2003).

Participating historians also learned from their experiences with classroom teachers. Although the historians who worked on this volume might not have revised their teaching in light of what they learned from the middle- and secondary-level history teachers who participated in the New York History Teaching Collaborative, many did come away with an important change in their views. As noted in the introduction, several historians gained new respect for the knowledge and skill of history teachers, many of whom work under less-than-ideal conditions. In contrast to the many professional collaborations that are organized implicitly if not explicitly as a one-way street—in which historians are the "real professionals" who provide the knowledge that teachers and students must master, and teachers "simply" deliver information or develop activities for the dissemination of historical knowledge—the collaborations that led to the essays in this volume expressly recognized the special skills and expertise of all parties. The fact that the historians recognized the professional expertise of teachers in planning and implementation—and the complexity and skill it takes to be an effective teacher—made it possible for the teachers in this project to find the collaboration both "educational and egalitarian." Although this may seem like a small matter, teachers in large under-resourced urban low-income schools often must battle for respect; the fact that participants recognized each other's professionalism was a key aspect of a successful collaboration.

Research on History Teachers' Routine and Exemplary Practices

Recent surveys have found that a majority of teachers continue to rely on textbooks, teacher-dominated recitations, and worksheets as standard tools and practices to transmit traditional content about nation-building actors and events (Hicks, 2004; NAEP, 2006; Warren, 2007). At the same time, over half of the teachers in Hicks's survey also reported using primary sources to teach history. Most, however, used the sources to provide additional information on actors and events that fit into the traditional narrative of national progress, rather than to complicate traditional narratives. Most teachers also have not used primary sources as historians do and as history educators advocate. Historians use primary sources as evidence and critically evaluate one primary source in light of other primary and secondary sources. They then organize and synthesize the fragmentary pieces of evidence to construct arguments or interpretations to answer significant historical questions (Wineburg, 2000). Most teachers have not had the training to undertake this level of disciplinary or ambitious instruction (Humphrey *et al.*, 2005). Critical use of primary source documents was a central goal of participants in this book. And the results, as demonstrated by the foregoing chapters, indicate the powerful, and exciting, effects that primary sources can have on history curricula when taught by educators who understand their critical uses, and who understand their relationship to larger historical questions and debates.

State-level history frameworks and learning standards tied to high-stakes testing also promote less ambitious pedagogies. Beginning teachers especially have felt pressure to "cover the curriculum" so that students pass the state-level history exams needed to graduate from high school (VanHover, 2006). More experienced teachers have tended to feel less pressure to teach to the test, and some have seen high-stakes testing as just one of many considerations to take into account when planning and teaching (Grant, 2003, 2006). Others, however, have felt constrained by the tests and align the historical content they teach to more closely match that which has appeared in state standards and tests (Grant, 2006; Segall, 2006). Although the jury is still out on whether high-stakes testing has produced greater learning about history (Grant, 2006), there is no evidence, at least among educational researchers, that the tests have encouraged more innovative approaches to teaching.

As the chapters in this volume have demonstrated, not all teachers have let testing, fears about controversy, or tendencies to reinforce routine practices constrain their practices. The teaching practices presented in these pages have shown how teachers managed to teach to and beyond the test, i.e., they presented newer historical scholarship in ways that promoted the skills and content students eventually would face on state exams. The chapters contribute to a literature of case studies of effective teachers who balanced demands of time constraints and testing to deliver challenging and innovative instruction. Just as the teachers in this volume approached teaching new historical content in a variety of ways, researchers who have written about effective social studies teachers have represented teachers whose educational philosophies and practices vary, thereby militating against a one-size-fits-all list of best or effective practices.

In two studies researchers (Grant, 2003; Wineburg & Wilson, 1988) presented examples of two high school history teachers whose perspectives and practices differed considerably. One teacher in each case had a more traditional view of teaching and a more traditional teaching style. The traditional teachers were more teacher directed than student oriented and spent a fair amount of classroom time lecturing about traditional topics. At the same time, each was a master teacher who began the lecture with examples that related the historical topic to students' lives or captured their imaginations. They then delivered the historical material in interesting ways, knowing the types of information and examples that best underscored important themes and the types of questions to ask throughout the lecture to engage and challenge students. Although each teacher was a master showperson in delivering lectures, each also included several other types of activities—group work, student presentations, etc.—that rounded out his or her repertoire and appealed to students' needs for diverse learning opportunities.

The researchers also presented portraits of effective teachers who used more innovative pedagogical strategies. Wineburg and Wilson (1988) highlighted the work of an eleventh-grade Advanced Placement teacher in an urban high school who had students interpret and synthesize primary historical documents in order to debate and answer significant historical questions. The authors portrayed a group of animated high school students who used primary sources to argue for and against the validity of the American colonists' claims about the need for a revolution against British rule. Grant (2003) provided the example of a teacher who used simulations and role-playing about contemporary examples of homophobia and other types of discrimination to enable students to compare contemporary issues to historical examples of racial segregation in the South. As the above-mentioned studies and the chapters in this volume illustrate, high-quality teachers in middle and secondary history classrooms can provide the foundation for student learning by teaching students to consider historical contexts, interpret and synthesize primary sources, and construct historical answers and arguments based on the evidence at hand.

Research on Cognitive Approaches to Teaching History

Teaching with Primary Sources

For over a century, reformers encouraged history teachers to use primary sources as historians do, i.e., as the building blocks constituting historical evidence and the glue with which historical narratives are constructed. Only recently, however, have researchers examined how history teachers have used primary sources and what students have learned from their engagement with them. Many history teachers have used primary sources and have done so for multiple purposes (NAEP, 2001, 2006). Some have used them simply to introduce historical actors or events, whereas others have used them to engage student interest (Hicks *et al.*, 2004; Warren, 2007; Yeager & Davis, 1996). Others have asked students to judge the accuracy of primary sources, determining whether or not a source is representative of "what happened" in the past (Epstein, 1994; Yeager & Davis, 1996). The problem with the first three approaches, some argue, is that they present primary sources as texts to be interpreted but not interrogated. The approaches required students to question the text, but only as a mirror image of the past, rather than as a trace of evidence about the past that may or may not provide reliable representation (Epstein, 2000; Gabella, 1998; Yeager & Davis, 1996).

The research on history education has included examples of teachers who have used primary sources to provide more complex and historically sound experiences (Epstein, 1994, 2000; Gabella 1994, 1998; Yeager & Davis, 1996). In these instances, teachers have considered primary sources as pieces of evidence that answer broad or significant historical questions about an event or period or illuminate people's intentions, motivations, and experiences. They have also provided instruction that enabled students to interpret and synthesize primary sources to answer historical questions and imagine the contexts in which people in the past thought and acted. As a result, students have learned to examine primary sources as evidence rather than simply as information, and to synthesize sources to produce historically sound and interesting representations of the past.

In working their projects, the teachers in the New York History Teaching Collaborative (NYHTC) used primary sources as evidence of people's perspectives on events and movements such as enslavement, abolition, immigration, the Progressive Era, the Great Depression, and Civil Rights. But they also used them as evidence of the *partial* and *perspectival* nature of primary sources. The chapter on immigration, for example, discussed how, through careful planning and questioning, the teachers in the group enabled their students to "read" photographs of nineteenth-century immigrants, as well as testimonies and interviews, not just in terms of what they revealed about immigrants' experiences but also as "tools of propaganda"—in other words, what they revealed about the social reformers who created, collected, and disseminated these visual and written documents. The students used the written sources to complicate and revise initial impressions they had constructed from the photographs of immigrant lives as having been harder in the United States than in Europe. Careful readings of the interviews and secondary materials enabled the students to recognize that the photographs were representative of but one moment in time and that in some cases, the photographer had literally staged the photographs for his own social reform purposes.

Teachers also use primary source documents to promote empathy. By *empathy*, historians and history educators mean the ability to gain an understanding of the perspectives or world view that people from an historical period constructed in response to the environments in which they lived. Unlike *sympathy*, or attempting to enable young people to "feel like" or "feel for" people in the past, historical empathy is meant to enable young people to understand the "ideas, beliefs, and values" under which people operated in societies or cultures unlike their own (Lee, Ashby, & Shemilt, 2005). Several teachers in this volume recognized the value of using primary sources as means to provide students with an understanding of the lives of others. In the chapter on the Progressive Era, for example, the teachers asked their students to reconstruct the views of historical actors through educational theater and debate. The teachers in this group recognized the dangers of "presentism"—the tendency to interpret historical actors and events from contemporary perspectives, rather than from the perspectives of historical actors—and worked very hard and successfully to teach in ways that stayed clear of it (Lee *et al.*, 2005; Wineburg, 2000).

Teaching and Learning History as Disciplined Inquiry

In addition to using primary sources as evidence and to promote empathy, researchers and teachers have used a range of approaches to teach history as an academic discipline. The approaches fall along a continuum in the degree of cognitive complexity that students are expected to exhibit. At the simplest level, disciplinary approaches are aimed at teaching students to interpret primary sources and relate them to historical topics and questions. More challenging approaches engage students in historical reasoning or argument about open-ended and debatable questions or topics. The most challenging approaches require students to comprehend the discipline's interpretive and tentative nature, recognizing how historians' constructions of concepts such as significance, agency, change, and continuity shape the interpretations of events embedded in historical narratives (Barton, 2008; Seixas, 1993).

In studies on teaching history as "disciplined inquiry" or as a means of promoting "thoughtfulness" (Newmann, 1990; Newmann, Marks, & Gamoran, 1996; Onosko, 1989, 1990), researchers examined instruction in secondary classrooms in which history teachers supported students in acquiring substantive and in-depth knowledge of an historical topic. Researchers analyzed the classroom practices of teachers who taught students to synthesize and evaluate historical sources and to construct arguments to answer analytic or speculative historical questions. They found that teachers who engaged students in disciplined inquiry covered a few chosen topics or themes in depth rather than many topics more superficially. These teachers related historical issues and themes to students' interests and experiences. They organized the curriculum around challenging questions and taught about the issue over several days or weeks. These practices gave students the time to become knowledgeable about the content, to interpret and synthesize evidence in relation to the issues, and to construct and critique alternative explanations or interpretations of an event or issue. Teachers also related the topic to previous and subsequent events and themes, as well as to students' interests and experiences.

In their classrooms, the teachers first asked questions to activate students' prior knowledge and then introduced new materials and tasks structured to assist students in answering open-ended and challenging historical questions. Once students had a grasp of new material or tasks, the teachers often used Socratic models of questioning, challenging students' analyses, arguments, and conclusions to ensure that their responses were based on sound interpretations of evidence, well-reasoned arguments, and historically valid or logical conclusions. The teachers encouraged creative or unconventional interpretations and arguments and included activities that encouraged students to question traditional authoritative sources such as textbooks. The teachers also modeled higher-order thinking or thoughtfulness by presenting and critiquing their own arguments and encouraging students to question the teacher.

Studies have shown that more than 75 percent of the students in these classes participated in discussions and a majority showed genuine interest in the activities (Newmann, 1990). Overall, teachers who taught for thoughtfulness and used disciplined inquiry considered student growth rather than content coverage as an important goal. They believed that depth rather than breadth of coverage was significant, even in the face of pressure from tests and administrators (Newmann, 1990; Onosko, 1989, 1990). Students also reported that they enjoyed classes organized around disciplined inquiry and were more engaged and challenged intellectually than they were in traditional classes.

There are numerous examples in this volume of NYHTC teachers presenting open-ended questions about historical periods or events to which there were no simple or clear-cut answers. In the chapter on U.S. imperialism, for example, the teachers organized instruction around the question, "How might the amount of power a person has shape his or her views about imperialism?" In the chapter on abolition, students pondered whether Frederick Douglass's change of heart and mind made him weak or strong. To answer debatable questions about the past, students examined primary sources from the multiple and conflicting perspectives and presented or wrote arguments in support of their views that used those primary sources as well as secondary materials. The teachers in this chapter recognized that the lessons, in addition to being among the most academically engaging and challenging presented throughout the year, provided opportunities for in-depth inquiry and discussion. They also found that they had met their goal of presenting historical inquiry as an argument about the meaning of the past and gave students practice in "taking a stand" and "making an argument."

Teaching and Learning History as Disciplinary Inquiry

The most ambitious attempts to engage secondary students in historical inquiry have included efforts that enable students to grasp the nature of history as an academic discipline, much as historians do (Ashby, Lee, & Shemilt, 2005; Lee *et al.*, 2005; Shemilt, 2000; Wineburg, 2000). This includes understanding that historical accounts are structured interpretations of the inter-relationships of historical actors and events and address concepts such as continuity and change over time, cause and effect, and empathy and moral judgment. Although historical accounts of the same actor or event may differ, history is not a relativist discipline in which any interpretation is as good as any other. Instead, historical accounts are judged on their comprehensiveness, strength of argument, and creativity, as well as on how well they critique or respond to competing accounts of the same events or phenomena.

For many years, secondary teachers in England have structured history instruction around teaching the subject as an academic discipline, but there are few published examples of this in the United States. One former high school teacher-turned-researcher (Bain, 2000, 2005) has written about his attempts to teach suburban high school students to understand historical narratives as interpretive accounts based on evidence, constructed according to the discipline's conceptual and procedural conventions. To accomplish this, Bain engaged tenth-grade students in a number of practices to challenge their preconceptions of history and extend their understanding of its interpretive and partial nature.

Bain (2000, 2005) concluded that his students responded positively to the more challenging tasks he set out. His students liked thinking about concepts of significance and empathy, and they responded well to a teacher who encouraged them to construct their own arguments about why events occurred in the past. They appreciated the teacher's emphasis that the textbook was no longer the major authority on history and gained confidence in refuting the text with their own interpretations of events. Some students, however, became overly critical of textbooks and other historical accounts, believing that there was no way to compare or judge the quality of secondary historical accounts.

Bain (2000) also found that students constructed a more complex understanding of history as an academic discipline than they had when they started the school year. Learning history became less about "covering the curriculum" and more about uncovering the motivations for people's actions, the reasons for change over time, and the consequences of change on societies and people's lives. Students took ownership of the idea of determining significance, rather than relying on an external authority to determine who and what was worthy of study. They also gained a deep understanding of the role of human agency—that people's actions made a difference—and of historical empathy—that people in the past acted in ways which made sense, even if these didn't accord with contemporary thinking.

Teaching high school students to "think like historians" has been a major pedagogical reform in England, where since the 1980s teachers have taught history as an academic discipline, with greater attention to the processes of constructing and critiquing historical narratives than to mastering historical facts and narratives. British researchers also have conducted extensive research into how this instruction has shaped students' ideas about historical evidence and accounts (Lee *et al.*, 2005; Shemilt, 1980, 2000). These researchers have investigated student understanding of what they refer to as "second-order" concepts such as significance, change, causation, and empathy and characterized students' understandings of historical epistemology in terms of progressions from less to more complex sets of ideas or concepts about the historian's craft.

At the lowest level and despite teachers' efforts to the contrary, some students and particularly younger ones considered historical narratives as factual reports or mirror images of what happened in the past. Slightly more advanced or sophisticated students understood that historians produced interpretive (versus factual or true) accounts from various primary sources but assumed that differences in accounts were due to an historian's bias and that there is no way to evaluate the credibility of different historical accounts. At the highest level of cognitive sophistication, students understood that historians have constructed interpretations that differ, but that criteria exist for determining if one historian's argument or interpretation is better reasoned or more comprehensive than another (Lee & Ashby, 2001).

British researchers also have characterized as a progression students' views of historical concepts of causation and empathy (Lee & Ashby, 2001; Shemilt, 2000). Younger or less sophisticated students considered historical causes as discrete and singular events, rather than as a result of ongoing and multiple processes. Older and more sophisticated students characterized causation as having developed out of a network of events and processes, rather than as a result of a singular and definitive action. Similarly, less sophisticated students explained people's actions in the past from their own viewpoint and considered people in the past to have been "stupid" in their decision-making (Lee & Ashby, 2001). More sophisticated or older students grasped that people in the past thought and behaved differently from people today and that they were products of their environments in the same way we are.

The research from England has provided an important look at how historical or disciplinary adolescents' thinking can become. The researchers have provided evidence that ambitious disciplinary approaches to teaching history enable adolescents at some level to grasp the evidentiary, interpretive nature of history, represented through narratives that address concepts of significance, causation, and empathy, among others. This is a leap forward from seeing history as a mirror image of the past or as equally valid and non-verifiable accounts based on a particular author's views or biases. At the same time, there are limits to most adolescents' abilities to think in the sophisticated ways of professional historians or to construct nuanced and comprehensive historical narratives from an array of primary and secondary historical sources.

Although the teachers in the NYHTC did not draw directly upon the approaches to teaching that Bain and the British researchers developed, they have in their lessons for this project done important work in developing new methods for teaching history critically and creatively. Practices such as presenting historical questions rather than historical texts as the starting point of inquiry may enable young people to think of history as an investigation into the past for which definitive answers or interpretations rarely exist. The analysis and synthesis of primary sources to construct more than one plausible answer to an historical question reinforces the idea of historical narratives as arguments that are constructed, rather than as truth or facts to be memorized or taken at face value. These types of activities may be seen as building blocks for engaging in more challenging approaches to teaching history as a disciplinary subject, with conventions and conversations unique to the discipline.

Research on the Political and Cultural Dimensions of Teaching History

Despite the outpouring of research on teaching and learning history, many teachers today continue to teach the U.S. history narrative as their predecessors did, i.e., an uncontested narrative of progress and inclusion. Part of this relates to what some teachers have considered to be the purpose of teaching U.S. history as transmitting a common "story of America" based on celebratory themes of economic, political, and social progress (Hicks *et al.*, 2004; Levstik, 2000; McNeil, 1988; VanSledright, 2008). History teachers in these studies believed a positive and progressive view of national history provided a unifying force across differences in student identities and ideologies (Levstik, 2000). Other teachers have stuck with teaching the traditional celebratory narrative because they eschewed teaching about controversy or conflict, wanted to avoid parental or administrative complaints, or feared the loss of classroom control (Levstik, 2000; McNeil, 1988). Others have avoided teaching about sensitive historical topics such as race relations for fear of upsetting students or saying the wrong thing, or because they believed they did not know enough about a particular topic (Bolgatz, 2005; Lewis, 2003).

A few examples exist of history teachers who have attempted to broaden students' perspectives about the course of national history by introducing them to the less celebratory aspects of the nation's past. In describing a series of classroom discussions about the Arab–Israeli conflict, Fine (1993) illustrated how a global history teacher navigated the difficult terrain of having adolescents debate contentious issues about historical origins and right to land. When one of the Jewish students in the class became defensive about another student's criticisms of Israeli policies, the teacher skillfully directed class discussions and after-class conversations with and between students to enable them to listen more openly to each other's views. As a result, the students in the class listened more patiently and with greater respect to their classmates' points of view, even when they contradicted their own.

Marri (2005) conducted a study of the teaching practices of three New York City high school history teachers, investigating how they promoted democratic and multicultural principles and practices within the context of the nation's history of inequality. Marri found that the three teachers shared three pedagogical strategies. First, they taught history from a critical perspective, which highlighted the struggles of marginalized groups to acquire freedom and equality. They also engaged students in thinking critically about change in history and the role of human agency in promoting some but not other courses of action. And, third, the teachers created classroom climates based on trust, classrooms in which students trusted their teachers and treated each other with respect, even in the face of disagreement and conflict.

Epstein, Mayorga, and Nelson (2009) examined how a teacher in a low-income urban school wanted students to understand the more subtle forms of racism historically and today. Students read *Twelve Angry Men* and focused on how the social contexts of racism in the 1950s shaped jury deliberation. They then compared the novel with contemporary trials of police officers accused of shooting or killing unarmed men of color in urban communities, events of which the students were painfully aware and toward which they felt anger and confusion. Students read legal documents explaining that jury members determined guilt or innocence based on the officers' states of mind and how subtle racism negatively affected their views of the motivations and potential violent actions of men of color in poor communities. Students also debated the merits of the verdict from both sides and read newspaper accounts of community protests during and after the trials. The teacher connected historical and contemporary events to the more subtle ways in which the legal system has protected the powerful at the expense of the less powerful, as well as provided knowledge about the legal system from which her students could profit.

Like the teachers described above, the teachers in the NYHTC thought deeply about ways to connect academic subject matter to the lives of urban low-income students of color, students who rarely see the histories and experiences of people like themselves reflected in mainstream historical texts and/or see them depicted primarily as victims of larger historical forces (Gutierrez, 2000). As shown in several of the chapters, in particular those focused on the New Deal and on the Civil Rights movement, many of the teachers who worked on this project considered students' marginalized racial, immigrant, and/or class identities as having represented "more opportunities than challenges." Many of the lessons and units discussed in the volume focused on the lives of ordinary and marginalized people and shifted the focus away from school-based historical narratives about political and economic elites. In doing so, the teachers broadened the national historical narrative not just in terms of which groups contributed to national development; they also inverted the narrative by framing events from the perspectives of, or in terms of the effects on, marginalized groups. In doing so, the teachers taught history not just for academic competency but also with an eye toward social justice by enabling young people to see people like themselves as having played an important role in shaping the nation (Epstein, 2009).

Several of the chapters also explored the agency that ordinary people had in resisting oppression and challenging powerful local or national interests to assert their struggle for freedom, dignity, and/or equality. The chapter on enslavement, for example, provided several examples of the overt and subtle forms of resistance to oppression that enslaved people used. The chapter on the New Deal represented a different kind of opposition, that based on social activism, as a means to promote government intervention to alleviate widespread suffering. Both approaches shifted the emphasis away from the government as the sole power responsible for positive historical change to that of marginalized persons and groups as individual or collective agents in promoting change. The focus on the historical agency of ordinary people has implications for citizenship in contemporary society, as evidenced in the chapter on the Civil Rights movement. Young people in one teacher's classroom selected, researched, and disseminated information on issues related to injustice in their community. The experience enabled the students to see that, like historical actors who struggled against injustice, young people themselves have a variety of means available to challenge the status quo and improve contemporary society (Banks, 2007).

Overall, this volume demonstrates how professional and dedicated teachers who have a solid grasp of history can make the subject responsive to the interests and intellects of young people, while at the same time meeting the demands of academic standards and accountability mandates. Balancing the many demands of teaching and learning history well, the teachers in the New York History Teaching Collaborative have demonstrated the possibilities as well as the limitations of the task in ways that are academically rigorous and culturally responsive. The purpose of presenting their successes and constraints is to provide aspiring and practicing teachers with realistic examples of good and great teachers who face the everyday challenges that classroom teaching presents. The hope is that the lessons learned by and from the teachers in this volume will motivate their colleagues to challenge themselves to teach history in ways that enable secondary students to engage in historical inquiry that broadens their minds, their lives, and the societies of which they are and will become a part.

Works Cited

Ashby, R., Lee, P., & Shemilt, D. (2005). Putting Principles into Practice: Teaching and Planning. In Donovan, M. S. & Bransford, J. D. (eds.), *How Students Learn: History in the Classroom*. Washington, DC: National Academies Press, pp. 79–178.

Bain, R. (2000). Into the Breach: Using Research and Theory to Shape History Instruction. In Stearns, P., Seixas, P., & Wineburg, S. (eds.), *Knowing, Teaching and Learning History: National and International Perspectives*. New York: NYU Press, pp. 331–352.

Bain, R. (2005). They Thought the World was Flat: Applying the Principles of How People Learn in Teaching High School History. In Donovan, M. S. & Bransford, J. D. (eds.), *How Students Learn: History in the Classroom*. Washington, DC: National Academies Press, pp. 179–214.

Banks, J. A. (2007). *Educating Citizens in a Multicultural Society*, 2nd edn. New York: Teachers College Press.

Barton, K. C. (2008). Research on Students' Ideas about History. In Levstik, L. S. & Tyson, C. A. (eds.), *Handbook on Social Studies Education*. New York: Routledge, pp. 239–248.

Berkin, C. (2006). Doing History: How the Worlds of the Scholar and Popular Historian Come Together. *Commonplace, 6*. Accessed online at <http://www.historycooperative.org/journals/cp/vol-06/no04/author/> on September 28, 2008.

Bolgatz, J. (2005). *Talking Race in the Classroom*. New York: Teachers College Press.

Epstein, T. (1994). The Arts of History: An Analysis of Secondary Students' Interpretations of the Arts in Historical Contexts. *Journal of Curriculum and Supervision, 9*, 174–194.

Epstein, T. (2000). Social Studies and the Arts. In Ross, W. E. (ed.), *The Social Studies Curriculum: Purposes, Problems and Possibilities*. Albany: SUNY Press, pp. 234–254.

Epstein, T. (2009). *Interpreting National History: Race, Identity and Pedagogy in Classrooms and Communities*. New York: Routledge.

Epstein, T., Mayorga, E., & Nelson, J. (2009). (How) Does Culturally Relevant Teaching Influence Urban Adolescents' Historical Understanding. Paper presented at the Annual Meeting of the American Educational Research Association, San Diego, April 13, 2009.

Fine, M. (1993). "You Can't Say that the Only Ones Who Can Speak Are Those Who Agree with Your Position": Political Discourse in the Classroom. *Harvard Educational Review, 63*, 412–433.

Gabella, M. (1994). The Art(s) of Historical Sense. *Journal of Curriculum Studies, 27*, 139–163.

Gabella, M. (1998). Formal Fascinations and Nagging Excerpts: The Challenge of the Arts to Curriculum and Inquiry. *Curriculum Inquiry, 28*, 27–56.

Grant, S. G. (2003). *History Lessons: Teaching, Learning and Testing in U.S. History Classrooms*. New York: Taylor & Francis.

Grant, S. G. (Ed.) (2006). *Measuring History: Cases of State-level Testing across the United States*. New York: Information Age Publishers.

Gutierrez, C. (2000). Making Connections: The Interdisciplinary Community of Teaching and Learning History. In Stearns, P., Seixas, P., & Wineburg, S. (eds.), *Knowing, Teaching and Learning History: National and International Perspectives*. New York: NYU Press, pp. 353–374.

Hicks, D., Doolittle, P., & Lee, J. (2004). Social Studies Teachers' Use of Classroom-based and Web-based Historical Primary Sources. *Theory and Research in Social Education, 32*, 213–247.

Humphrey, D. C., Chang-Ross, C., Donnelly, M., Hersh, L., Skolnik, H., & International, S. (2005). *Evaluation of the Teaching American History Program*. Washington, DC: United States Department of Education, Office of Planning, Evaluation and Policy Development. Accessed online at http:www.ed.gov/rschstat/eval/teaching/us history/teaching/exec-sum.html on July 24, 2009.

Lee, P. & Ashby, R. (2001). Empathy, Perspective Taking and Rational Understanding. In Davis, O. L., Foster, S., & Yeager, E. (eds.), *Historical Empathy and Perspective Taking in the Social Studies*. Boulder, CO: Rowman & Littlefield, pp. 21–50.

Lee, P., Ashby, R., & Shemilt, D. (2005). Putting Principles into Practice: Understanding History. In Donovan, M. S. & Bransford, J. D. (eds.), *How Students Learn: History in the Classroom*. Washington, DC: National Academies Press, pp. 29–78.

Levstik, L. S. (2000). Articulating the Silences: Teachers' and Adolescents' Conceptions of Historical Significance. In Stearns, P., Seixas, P., & Wineburg, S. (eds.), *Knowing, Teaching and Learning History: National and International Perspectives*. New York: NYU Press, pp. 284–305.

Levstik, L. S. (2008). What Happens in Social Studies Classrooms? Research on K–12 Social Studies Practice. In Levstik, L. S. & Tyson, C. A. (eds.), *Handbook on Social Studies Education*. New York: Routledge, pp. 50–65.

Lewis, A. (2003). *Race in the Schoolyard: Negotiating the Color Line in Classrooms and Communities*. New Brunswick, NJ: Rutgers University Press.

McNeil, L. (1988). *Contradictions of Control: School Structure and School Knowledge*. New York: Routledge Press.

Marri, A. (2005). Building a Framework for Classroom-based Multicultural Democratic Education: Learning from Three Skilled Teachers. *Teachers College Record, 107*, 1036–1059.

Mucher, S. (2007). Building a Culture of Evidence through Professional Development. *History Teacher, 40*, 265–273.

National Assessment of Educational Progress (NAEP) (2001). *The Nation's Report Card: U.S. History*. Washington, DC: U.S. Department of Education.

National Assessment of Educational Progress (2006). *The Nation's Report Card: U.S. History*. Washington, DC: U.S. Department of Education.

Newmann, F. (1990). Higher Order Thinking in Teaching Social Studies: A Rationale for the Assessment of Classroom Thoughtfulness. *Journal of Curriculum Studies, 22*, 41–56.

Newmann, F., Marks, H., & Gamoran, A. (1996). Authentic Pedagogy and Student Performance. *American Journal of Education, 104*, 280–312.

Onosko, J. (1989). Comparing Teachers' Thinking about Promoting Students' Thinking. *Theory and Research in Social Education, 17*, 174–195.

Onosko, J. (1990). Comparing Teachers' Instruction to Promote Students' Thinking. *Journal of Curriculum Studies, 5*, 443–361.

Ragland, R. (2007). Changing Secondary Teachers' Views of Teaching American History. *The History Teacher, 40*, 220–30.

Segall, A. (2006). Teaching History in the Age of Accountability: Measuring History or Measuring up to It? In Grant, S. G. (ed.), *Measuring History: Cases of State-level Testing across the United States*. New York: Information Age Publishers, pp. 105–132.

Seixas, P. (1993). Historical Understanding among Adolescents in a Multicultural Setting. *Curriculum Inquiry, 23*, 301–327.

Shemilt, D. (1980). *Evaluation Study: Schools Council History 13–16 Project*. Edinburgh: Holmes McDougall.

Shemilt, D. (2000). The Caliph's Coin: The Currency of Narrative Frameworks in Teaching History. In Stearns, P., Seixas, P., & Wineburg, S. (eds.), *Knowing, Teaching and Learning History: National and International Perspectives*. New York: NYU Press, pp. 83–101.

van Hover, S. (2006). Teaching History in the Old Dominion: The Impact of Virginia's Accountability Reform on Seven Secondary Beginning History Teachers. In Grant, S. G. (ed.), *Measuring History: Cases of State-level Testing across the United States*. New York: Information Age Publishers, pp. 195–220.

VanHover, S. (2008). The Professional Development of Social Studies Teachers. In Levstik, L. S. & Tyson, C. A. (eds.), *Handbook on Social Studies Education*. New York: Routledge Press, pp. 352–372.

VanSledright, B. (2008). Narratives of Nation-state, Historical Knowledge and School History Education. *Review of Research in Education, 32*, 109–146.

Warren, W. (2007). Closing the Distance between Authentic History Pedagogy and Everyday Classroom Practice. *History Teacher, 40*, 249–255.

Wineburg, S. (2000). *Historical Thinking and Other Unnatural Acts*. Philadelphia: Temple University Press.

Wineburg, S. S. & Wilson, S. M. (1988). Models of Wisdom in the Teaching of History. *Phi Delta Kappan, 70*, 50–58.

Woestman, K. (2008, August). How TAH Grants Educate Professors: A Report for the Third Annual TAH Symposium. *Organization of American Historians Newsletter*, 36. Accessed online at http://www.oah.org/pubs/nl/2008aug/woestman.html on September 28, 2008.

Yeager, E. & Davis, O. L. (1996). Classroom Teachers' Thinking about Historical Texts: An Exploratory Study. *Theory and Research in Social Education, 24*, 146–166.

Contributor Biographies

Stacie Brensilver Berman teaches eleventh-grade U.S. history. She earned her BA in Diplomatic History from the University of Pennsylvania, her MA in Social Studies Education from New York University, and her MA in History from Hunter College. She has taught at Edward R. Murrow High School in Brooklyn for eight years.

Robert Cohen is a Professor of social studies in the Department of Teaching and Learning and an affiliated professor in the History Department at New York University. He is the author of *When the Old Left Was Young: Student Radicals and America's First Mass Student Movement, 1929–1941* (1993), editor of *Dear Mrs Roosevelt: Letters from Children of the Great Depression* (2002), co-editor of *The Free Speech Movement: Reflections on Berkeley in the 1960s* (2002), and author of *Freedom's Orator: Mario Savio and the Radical Legacy of the 1960s* (2009).

Shari Dickstein is a doctoral candidate in Educational Policy at the Harvard Graduate School of Education. Her research focuses on teacher development and teacher efficacy. She earned her BA in Government from Cornell and her MA in Social Studies Education from New York University. A former New York City high school teacher and adjunct professor at NYU, she is now an independent instructional consultant, has authored articles on pre-service teacher identity and teaching history effectively in urban classroom, and serves as an advisor and advisory curriculum developer for Harvard's Teacher Education Program.

Terrie Epstein is a Professor at Hunter College. She recently published *Interpreting National History: Race, Identity and Pedagogy in Classrooms and Communities* (Routledge, 2009). Her interests include the effects of race, nationality, and other aspects of identity on young people's interpretations of history and society. Currently she is completing a study on the effects of culturally responsive teaching on the historical and contemporary understandings of low-income adolescents of color.

Cara Fenner is in her sixth year of teaching. She currently teaches history at Excel High School in south Boston, where she has enjoyed interacting with and learning from her students for three years.

Dwight Forquignon teaches U.S. history to eleventh- and twelfth-graders. He earned his BA in Social Studies Education from New York University and his MA from City College. He has taught at the High School for Environmental Studies for seven years.

Benjamin Geballe is a middle school teacher at MS 131 in New York's Chinatown. He has taught social studies at the middle and high school levels for the past seven years. A graduate of Yale University, he received his masters degree in education from the University of Minnesota.

Jill Jeffery is a doctoral candidate in New York University's English education program. A 2008–2010 National Academy of Education Adolescent Literacy Predoctoral Fellow, she has written articles and presented conference papers on writing assessment, the transition from secondary to post-secondary writing contexts, and academic language development. These research interests are grounded in her practical experience as a high school English language arts teacher, a literacy consultant to New York City public schools, and an adjunct instructor for NYU's teacher education programs.

Tiffany Lincoln is a literacy coach at a middle school in the Bronx, where she teaches English and social studies. She studied Psychology and American Ethnic Studies at the University of Washington before joining Teach for America. Tiffany received her graduate degree in Education from Pace University.

Terra Lynch currently teaches ninth- and tenth-grade humanities at University Neighborhood High School in New York City. She has also taught Spanish, music appreciation, piano, English, and English as a second language; led professional development sessions; written curriculum; and co-facilitated data inquiry teams. She earned her BA in Ibero-American Studies at the University of Toronto, and her MA in Social Studies Education from New York University. Terra is endorsed by the National School Reform Faculty/New York.

Joan Malczewski is an Assistant Professor of History and Social Studies, and vice-chair of the Department of Teaching and Learning at New York University. Her research is on the relationship between northern philanthropy and southern education, focusing specifically on the development of public education for rural blacks in the early part of the twentieth century. She has served as assistant dean at Teachers College from 1995 to 2001 and at the Steinhardt School of Education from 2003 to 2006.

Rachel Mattson is an Assistant Professor at SUNY New Paltz. She earned a PhD in U.S. History from New York University in 2004, and then served for several years as the Historian-in-Residence in NYU's Department of Teaching and Learning. Her work has appeared, among other places, in the *Radical History Review, Notable American Women,* the *Village Voice,* and *WNYC,* as well as in a forthcoming issue of *Rethinking History.* She is co-author of *History as Art, Art as History: Contemporary Art and Social Studies Education* (Routledge, 2009). An active public historian, Mattson has been involved a range of New York City-based arts and activist organizations for over fourteen years, and currently sits on the advisory board for the group Circus Amok. You can read her blog at http://www.howhistoryfeels.blogspot.com/.

Ashley Merriman earned her BA in History at Sonoma State University, and her MA in Social Studies Education at New York University. She currently teaches seventh-grade Humanities at Isaac Newton Middle School for Math and Science in New York City.

Ryan Mills teaches eleventh-grade U.S. history, participation in government, advanced placement U.S. government and politics, and the Civil Rights movement. He earned his BA from The George Washington University and his MA from New York University. He has taught at Edward R. Murrow High School for eight years.

David Montgomery is a visiting Assistant Professor in the Program in Educational Theatre at New York University. David was a K–12 drama specialist for many years in Queens, New York, and a middle school teacher in Brooklyn, New York. His study "Living an Arts Partnership: The Experience of Three Middle School Classroom Teachers in a Drama Residency" won the NYU Steinhardt Outstanding Dissertation Award in 2007, as well as the Distinguished Dissertation Honorable Mention Award from the American Alliance for Theatre Education (AATE) in 2008.

John Palella has taught high school history for the past seven years and currently teaches U.S. history at Shaker High School in Latham, New York. He earned his BA in History from Ithaca College and his MA in Social Studies Education from New York University. He is currently working toward his PhD in American gender history, with a minor field in transnational constructions of race, at the University at Albany.

Sarah Reiley teaches tenth-grade Global Studies, eleventh-grade U.S. History and twelfth-grade Human Rights Studies. She earned her BA in International Relations from Boston College and her MA in Social Studies Education from New York University. She has been teaching at the NYC Lab School for Collaborative Studies for three years.

Michael Stoll is a doctoral candidate in the Teaching and Learning Department at New York University. He previously taught high school social studies at Hinsdale South High School in Darien, Illinois, and has earned masters degrees in Liberal Studies and Education from Northwestern University. His current research interests include social studies curriculum and assessment development, student self-assessment and goal-setting, and literacy skills development in the content areas.

Diana Turk is an Associate Professor of Social Studies Education in the Department of Teaching and Learning at New York University. She brings to her work in teacher education a passion for civic engagement and a commitment to teaching history for democratic change. She is the author of *Bound by a Mighty Vow: Sisterhood and Women's Fraternities, 1870–1920* (New York University Press, 2004) and of several articles on innovative and interdisciplinary approaches to teaching history and social studies. She is a member of the National Assessment of Educational Progress (NAEP) U.S. History Standing Committee.

Candace Villecco received her MA in Social Studies Education at NYU and is currently pursuing a PhD in formative assessment practices at the Institute of Education in London. She has worked as both a humanities and a special education teacher for the last seven years.

Index